PENGUIN C[...]

ON SPART[...]

PLUTARCH (*c.* 50–*c.* 120 AD) was a writer and thinker born into a wealthy, established family of Chaeronea in central Greece. He received the best possible education in rhetoric and philosophy, and travelled to Asia Minor and Egypt. Later, a series of visits to Rome and Italy contributed to his fame, and it was said that he had received official recognition by the emperors Trajan and Hadrian. Plutarch rendered conscientious service to his province and city (where he continued to live), as well as holding a priesthood at nearby Delphi. His voluminous surviving writings are broadly divided into the 'moral' works and the *Lives* of outstanding Greek and Roman leaders. The former (*Moralia*) are a mixture of rhetorical and antiquarian pieces, together with technical and moral philosophy (sometimes in dialogue form). The *Lives* have been influential from the Renaissance onwards.

RICHARD TALBERT was born in England in 1947. He is a Cambridge Classics graduate and specialized in Greek history for his doctorate, which led to his first book *Timoleon and the Revival of Greek Sicily*. While teaching at Queen's University, Belfast, he turned to Roman history and wrote *The Senate of Imperial Rome*, which won the Goodwin Award of Merit. After three years as Professor of History at McMaster University, Hamilton, Ontario, Canada, in 1988 he moved to the University of North Carolina, Chapel Hill, as William Rand Kenan, Jr., Professor. He has since served as President of the Association of Ancient Historians, and has been awarded Cambridge's Doctor of Letters degree. Recent works edited or co-authored by him include *Barrington Atlas of the Greek and Roman World* (2000), *The Romans from Village to Empire* (2004) and *Space in the Roman World: its Perception and Presentation* (2004). With the support of Chapel Hill's Ancient World Mapping Center, he is currently preparing a major new edition of Peutinger's Roman map.

IAN SCOTT-KILVERT was Director of English Literature at the British Council and Editor of *Writers and their Works*. He translated many of Plutarch's and Cassius Dio's *The Roman History* for Penguin Classics. He died in 1989.

CHRISTOPHER PELLING is Regius Professor of Greek at Oxford University. He published a commentary on Plutarch's *Life of Antony* in 1988 (Cambridge University Press) and an English version of his 1997 Italian commentary on the Lives of Philopoemen and Flamininus (Rizzoli) is to be published by the Classical Press of Wales. Most of his articles on Plutarch were collected in his *Plutarch and History* (Classical Press of Wales and Duckworth, 2002).

PLUTARCH

On Sparta

Revised Edition

Translated with Introduction and Notes by
RICHARD J. A. TALBERT
With Life of Agesilaus *translated by*
IAN SCOTT-KILVERT
and revised by
RICHARD J. A. TALBERT

With Series Preface by CHRISTOPHER PELLING

PENGUIN BOOKS

PENGUIN BOOKS

Published by the Penguin Group
Penguin Books Ltd, 80 Strand, London WC2R 0RL, England
Penguin Group (USA) Inc., 375 Hudson Street, New York, New York 10014, USA
Penguin Group (Canada), 10 Alcorn Avenue, Toronto, Ontario, Canada M4V 3B2
(a division of Pearson Penguin Canada Inc.)
Penguin Ireland, 25 St Stephen's Green, Dublin 2, Ireland
(a division of Penguin Books Ltd)
Penguin Group (Australia), 250 Camberwell Road, Camberwell, Victoria 3124, Australia
(a division of Pearson Australia Group Pty Ltd)
Penguin Books India Pvt Ltd, 11 Community Centre, Panchsheel Park, New Delhi – 110 017, India
Penguin Group (NZ), cnr Airborne and Rosedale Roads, Albany, Auckland 1310, New Zealand
(a division of Pearson New Zealand Ltd)
Penguin Books (South Africa) (Pty) Ltd, 24 Sturdee Avenue, Rosebank 2196, South Africa

Penguin Books Ltd, Registered Offices: 80 Strand, London WC2R 0RL, England

www.penguin.com

This translation first published 1988
Revised edition with *Life of Agesilaus* first published 2005

034

Set in 10.25/12.25 pt PostScript Adobe Sabon
Typeset by Rowland Phototypesetting Ltd, Bury St Edmunds, Suffolk

Printed and bound in Great Britain by Clays Ltd, Elcograf S.p.A.

ISBN-13: 978–0–140–44943–3

www.greenpenguin.co.uk

Contents

Penguin Plutarch

The first Penguin translation of Plutarch appeared in 1958, with Rex Warner's version of six Roman Lives appearing as *Fall of the Roman Republic*. Other volumes followed steadily, three of them by Ian Scott-Kilvert (*The Rise and Fall of Athens* in 1960, *Makers of Rome* in 1965 and *The Age of Alexander* in 1973), and then Richard Talbert's *Plutarch on Sparta* in 1988. Several of the moral essays were also translated by Robin Waterfield in 1992. Now only fourteen of the forty-eight Lives remain. It is planned to include these remaining Lives in a new edition, along with revised versions of those already published.

This is also an opportunity to divide up the Lives in a different way, although it is not straightforward to decide what that different way should be. Nearly all Plutarch's surviving biographies were written in pairs as *Parallel Lives*: thus a 'book' for Plutarch was not just *Theseus* or *Caesar* but *Theseus and Romulus* or *Alexander and Caesar*. Most, but not all, of those pairs have a brief epilogue at the end of the second Life comparing the two heroes, just as many have a prologue before the first Life giving some initial grounds for the comparison. Not much attention was paid to this comparative technique at the time when the Penguin series started to appear, and it seemed natural then to separate each Life from its pair and organize the volumes by period and city. The comparative epilogues were not included in the translations at all.

That now looks very unsatisfactory. The comparative technique has come to be seen as basic to Plutarch's strategy, underlying not only those brief epilogues but also the entire pairings. (It is true, though, that in the last few years scholars have become increasingly alert to the way that *all* the Lives, not just the pairs, are crafted to complement one another.) It is very tempting to keep the pairings in this new series in a way that would respect Plutarch's own authorial intentions.

After some agonizing, we have decided nevertheless to keep to something like the original strategy of the series, though with some refinement. The reason is a practical one. Many, perhaps most, readers of Plutarch will be reading him to see what he has to say about a particular period, and will wish to compare his treatment of the major players to see how the different parts of his historical jigsaw fit together. If one kept the pairings, that would inevitably mean buying several different volumes of the series; and if, say, one organized those volumes by the Greek partner (so that, for instance, *Pericles–Fabius*, *Nicias–Crassus* and *Coriolanus–Alcibiades* made one volume), anyone primarily interested in the Roman Lives of the late Republic would probably need to buy the whole set. That is no way to guarantee these finely crafted works of art the wide reading that they deserve. Keeping the organization by period also allows some other works of Plutarch to be included along with the Lives themselves, for instance the fascinating essay *On the Malice of Herodotus* along with the Lives of Themistocles and Aristides, and (as before) several Spartan essays along with the Spartan Lives.

Of course, the comparative epilogues must now be included, and they will now be translated and printed along with the second Life of each pair, just as the prologues are conventionally printed before the first Life. Each volume will now also usually include more extended introductions to each Life, which will draw attention to the importance of the comparison as well as other features of Plutarch's technique. This is a compromise, and an uncomfortable one; but it still seems the better way.

The volumes will, however, sort the Lives into more logical groups. The early Roman figures will now be grouped together in a single volume entitled *The Rise of Rome*; the Life of Agesilaus will migrate from the *The Age of Alexander* to join the rest of the Spartan Lives, and the Life of Artaxerxes will join the *The Age of Alexander* collection; the rest of the new translations of Roman Lives will join those of the Gracchi, Brutus and Antony in a new *Rome in Crisis* volume. The introductions and notes will be revised where necessary. In due course we hope to include the *Moral Essays* in the project as well.

In a recent bibliometric study (*Ancient Society*, 28 (1997), 265–89) Walter Scheidel observed that the proportion of scholarly articles devoted to most classical authors had remained more or less constant since the 1920s. The one author to stand out for an exceptional rise was Plutarch. That professional pattern has been matched by a similar surge in the interest in Plutarch shown by the general reading public. The Penguin translations have played a large part in fostering that interest, and this new, more comprehensive project will surely play a similar role in the future.

Christopher Pelling
2004

Acknowledgements

The debts incurred in the original preparation of this volume are many. As an undergraduate I had the privilege of tutorials on Sparta with A. G. Woodhead, as well as hearing the lectures of A. H. M. Jones and engaging in discussion with M. I. Finley. However, it was only over a decade later, when I offered some lectures on Sparta myself, that the need for a new translation of certain of the principal texts by Plutarch became clear. Betty Radice immediately supported the proposal to include it in the Penguin Classics: her experience and insight helped to establish the scope and format of the volume. After her death Paul Keegan showed sympathy for the delays caused by other obligations and by my removal to Canada. Here I had the good fortune to find the most dependable of typists in Jacquie Collin. The Arts Research Board of McMaster University assisted an extremely instructive visit to Laconia and Messenia. Most important of all, Ronald Shepherd of University College, Toronto, undertook to check the accuracy and style of my versions. His penetrating, sensitive appreciation of the Greek, and the friendly welcome which he so generously offered a newcomer, prompt my lasting gratitude and admiration. The same tribute is merited by Paul Cartledge, whose trenchant and painstaking comments on a complete draft went far beyond what even an old friend might hope for. The errors and limitations which remain are, naturally, my own responsibility.

In revising and expanding the volume, I have benefited once again from the perceptive advice of old friends and new: in particular, Paul Cartledge as ever, Michael Flower and Stephen Hodkinson. My greatest debt, however, is to my friend and colleague Philip Stadter, who not only commented upon the revisions made for the *Life of Agesilaus*, but was also generous enough to share with me in advance of publication his opinions about the role which Plutarch himself may have played in the compilation of the *Sayings of Spartans* collection; these opinions are gratefully reflected below (p. 137).

Preface to the Original Edition

'A militaristic and totalitarian state, holding down an enslaved population, the helots, by terror and violence, educating its young by a system incorporating all the worst features of the traditional English public school, and deliberately turning its back on the intellectual and artistic life of the rest of Greece.'[1] There could be no better summary of the general modern impression of ancient Sparta. From the Renaissance onwards Plutarch is the classical author who has had the greatest influence in moulding successive generations' estimates of this extraordinary society. Except perhaps for Athens, there is no other ancient Greek city-state which has exerted such a powerful fascination over later students – whether they have chosen to admire (as Machiavelli, Rousseau and Hitler all did in their different ways), or to feel repelled.

Two of the five surviving Lives which Plutarch wrote of Spartans are already available in the Penguin Classics series, *Lysander* in *The Rise and Fall of Athens* and *Agesilaus* in *The Age of Alexander*. Yet it could well be argued that the other three Lives – *Lycurgus, Agis* and *Cleomenes* – have even greater value for an understanding of Spartan society and institutions. A clear, accurate translation of these important texts into modern English is long overdue. The most recent one published – in the Loeb Classical Library – was made in the early years of this century and is now inevitably antiquated in a variety of ways. This volume aims to meet the need. It offers further a translation

1. E. Rawson, *The Spartan Tradition in European Thought* (Oxford University Press, 1969, p. 1).

of *Sayings of Spartans* (with some omissions explained on page 137) and *Sayings of Spartan Women*. Though probably not compiled by Plutarch in fact, these collections of sayings are preserved among his works and incorporate much material to be found in his Lives, especially *Lysander* and *Agesilaus* as it happens – which can go some way to make up for their unavoidable exclusion from this volume. Moreover both collections reflect an admiring, idealistic view of classical Sparta and the sterling qualities of her citizens which Plutarch unquestionably shared. The contents of the volume thus afford the opportunity to gain an all-round impression of his vision of Sparta. As will emerge, how far it was an accurate vision is quite another matter!

For his *Lycurgus* in particular, Plutarch read widely among the many special studies of Sparta produced by Greek authors from the end of the fifth century onwards. The only such work to survive complete – *Spartan Society*, attributed to the Athenian Xenophon – is one of the earliest, and was definitely drawn upon by Plutarch. It is therefore included in an Appendix.

Throughout, my notes aim to do no more than elucidate principal points of historical interest for the general reader. I am well aware, of course, that much more could be said. There is plenty of literary, philosophical and religious interest in Plutarch, for example, while the stream of modern books about different aspects of ancient Sparta shows no sign of letting up. But in this volume it seems most appropriate to let the texts speak for themselves as far as possible. Suggestions for further reading are made at the end.

Richard Talbert
Hamilton
December 1986

Preface to the Expanded Edition

When Laura Barber offered me the opportunity to revise and expand this volume as part of a wider revision and reorganization of Plutarch's *Lives* in the Penguin Classics series, I was delighted to respond. The *Life of Agesilaus*, which is now added, along with a further map, was perhaps the single most regrettable omission from the original edition. In transferring it from Ian Scott-Kilvert's *The Age of Alexander*, I have adhered where possible to his translation, while adjusting for accuracy and striving to ensure that his usage for proper names and technical terms is rendered consistent with my own. Many passages in *Sayings of Spartans* that are also to be found in the *Life of Agesilaus* are now dropped from the selection of *Sayings* presented. The arrangement of the two final paragraphs of Xenophon, *Spartan Society*, is reversed (for discussion, see p. 192), and the recommendations for Further Reading are extensively revised in the light of almost twenty further years' intense scholarly preoccupation with everything Spartan. The many other changes throughout are matters of detail, clarification and re-arrangement.

Richard Talbert
Chapel Hill, North Carolina
March 2004

Introduction

PLUTARCH AND SPARTA

Four volumes of Lives by Plutarch are already available in Penguin Classics, so that by now he needs little introduction to readers of the series.[1] He was a Greek from Chaeronea in Boeotia (part of the Roman province of Achaea), who lived between approximately AD 50 and 120. While he did play a role in the affairs of his city and province, as well as visiting both Egypt and Italy, he was content to live quietly at home for most of his life, and was proud of his long tenure of a priesthood at the shrine of Delphi nearby. At home he pursued his extremely wide intellectual interests, reading and writing with unflagging enthusiasm, especially in the general area of philosophy. Many of his varied philosophical works have survived under the general heading of *Moralia*.[2] In later life an interest in character, among other motives, led him to write Lives which could demonstrate the merit of his subjects and inspire imitation of them. The main series of Lives gradually expanded. A distinctive element was the pairing and formal comparison of a Greek and a Roman – hence the title *Parallel Lives*. This was primarily an artistic feature, but one which also served his moral purpose as well as permitting him to underline the contemporary partnership of the two peoples in the government of a common empire. Thus, for example, the Spartan lawgiver Lycurgus was matched with the second king of Rome, Numa, who was likewise famous for his reforms.

It is essential always to bear in mind that Plutarch came to write Lives through his study of philosophy rather than history.

The Lives are biography (a long-established Greek literary form), not standard history. They have consistently found readers, for two main reasons. First, they display a flair for portraying the personalities and achievements of noted historical figures in a wonderfully humane and engaging way. Second, with the loss of numerous other ancient authors (many of whom Plutarch had read), they offer an immense amount of information no longer obtainable elsewhere. Without Plutarch's Life, for example, our knowledge of the career of King Agis IV of Sparta would remain almost a blank.

The fame and importance of Sparta in the affairs of classical Greece make Plutarch's interest in her society and her great men readily understandable. Moreover the city itself in his day was enjoying an elaborate and highly successful cultural revival. Traditional practices were restored, and tourists (Plutarch among them) flocked to see ceremonies like the whipping of youths at the altar of Artemis Orthia.[3] Plutarch wrote Lives of at least five Spartans – the early lawgiver Lycurgus; the great leaders of the late fifth and early fourth centuries (when Sparta's power was at its height), Lysander and King Agesilaus II; and the reformer kings of the third century, Agis IV and Cleomenes III. In addition he makes a promise to write a Life of the Agiad king Leonidas who died fighting the Persians at the battle of Thermopylae in 480, though he may not have fulfilled it since no such Life appears in the ancient catalogue of his works. However, that catalogue does contain a further work which it is relevant to mention in this context – a Life, now lost, of the Messenian Aristomenes, hero of the great rebellion against Spartan rule in the mid seventh century. Even beyond these there are few of Plutarch's Greek Lives which do not make more or less extensive allusion to Sparta's involvement in the affairs of Greece. It is particularly regrettable that the Life of Plutarch's fellow Boeotian Epaminondas is lost, so that we have no opportunity to see how he handled the achievements of the man who between 371 and 362 played such a decisive role in ending for ever Sparta's dominant position among the Greek states.

LYCURGUS

Historical Introduction

When Plutarch came to write a Life of the early Spartan lawgiver Lycurgus, he was well aware of the controversies surrounding every aspect of his identity and date. Partly for this reason he devotes much of the Life to an explanation and description of the laws and institutions attributed to him, and the resulting sketch of 'Lycurgan' Sparta has always been the main focus of interest for most readers.[4]

Today the same degree of controversy still surrounds Lycurgus' identity and date. He is awkward to fit into what little is generally agreed about the development of early Sparta. The settlement itself was never consolidated as a city, but was just a collection of four scattered villages, which remoteness allowed to remain without an encircling wall until the second century BC. It lies in the northern part of the River Eurotas valley in the region of the south-east Peloponnese called Laconia or Lacedaemon. The valley is fertile, but relatively narrow, enclosed by the steep mountain barriers of Parnon to the east and Taygetus to the west.[5] The first settlers on the site seem to have been Dorian Greeks during the tenth century. The course of their remarkable early expansion is beyond recovery in detail, but it is at least possible to appreciate what they had gained by early in the seventh century. All Laconia had first been secured, as well as the Parnon range to the east and the territory south of it down to Cape Malea. Amyclae, about eight kilometres south of Sparta, was even incorporated as part of the state at an early stage, perhaps during the eighth century. In addition, the Spartans had taken the area named Thyreatis to the north-east of Parnon, and the island of Cythera below Cape Malea. Westwards they had crossed the Taygetus mountains and probably in the late eighth century, after a tremendous struggle, they had at least doubled their territory by the conquest of Messenia, much of it outstandingly fertile land.

In terms of territory and manpower this conquest made Sparta one of the strongest Greek states. But it also created problems.

Jealousy and hostility on the part of neighbouring states increased – especially from Argos to the north-east – resulting in fierce clashes. Worse, the Messenians refused to accept subjugation: probably in the mid seventh century they raised a great rebellion, which Sparta eventually overcame, though only with the utmost difficulty. But at least thereafter Messenia did continue in subjection for over two centuries more, until liberated by the Thebans, following their defeat of Sparta at the battle of Leuctra in 371.

However, the urgent need for the Spartans to prevent any recurrence of Messenian rebellion must have been one main reason why during the sixth century their state ceased to resemble other Greek communities in its cultural development (which both literary and material evidence proves to have been very lively up to that date), and instead took on the austere, military character with which it has been associated ever since. Archaeological investigation has shown that the process was still a gradual one, but nonetheless the sixth century was a period of marked change at Sparta.

In view of this fact it is tempting to link reforms made then with Lycurgus. This is what seems to be done at one point by the earliest surviving author to give an account of him – the fifth-century historian Herodotus.[6] But Herodotus is equally aware of a tradition that places Lycurgus much earlier (by perhaps as much as three centuries), and later ancient authors are similarly in favour of an early date – though just how early remained a matter of unresolved dispute. By placing him in the early eighth century according to our reckoning, Plutarch follows what seems to have been the majority opinion. Even so, we must acknowledge that Lycurgus is thereby pushed back to a time for which lack of evidence renders an accurate historical account impossible. While it is conceivable that one individual named Lycurgus was responsible for a set of early reforms, we are in no position to be more specific than that. The record of the only constitutional changes which we can securely identify – the 'Great Rhetra' and its supplement[7] – contains no reference to Lycurgus, nor is there any allusion to him in surviving fragments of the seventh-century Spartan poet Tyrtaeus. Archaic

Greek communities certainly did appoint individual lawgivers at times of crisis, and Lycurgus could have been one such at Sparta. What certainly remains fantastic, however, as in the case of other lawgivers elsewhere, is the attribution of almost all the city's laws and institutions to him alone. At Sparta that applies on the one hand to the social and educational practices of the state, which must rather be the result of development and modification over a very long period, and on the other to certain measures which are completely anachronistic in an archaic context – like the ban on coinage at a time when no such thing even existed. Finally in the case of Lycurgus it is also necessary to take into account the tradition (which we can again trace as far back as Herodotus) that saw him as divine, not human at all. Altogether he cannot be securely placed in a historical context. It is conceivable that Lycurgus was responsible for certain reforms at some stage: no more definite claim can be made, and the question is of no particular importance for our understanding of Sparta.

Plutarch's Sources

In his treatment of Lycurgus and the society created by his laws, Plutarch described Sparta as he believed it to have been before a variety of major pressures brought sweeping change from the early fourth century onwards. The nature of that Lycurgan Sparta, which had disappeared five hundred years or so before Plutarch's own day, was hard to discover. Its origins and development stretched back long before historical writing began among Greeks around 500. Moreover, even later no contemporary Spartan ever produced a treatment of the subject. Plutarch did study archaic Spartan poetry and he even attempted some exploration of the public archives at Sparta.[8] Naturally, too, from his wide reading he took into account what the great fifth-century historians, Herodotus and Thucydides, had to say, though in neither case was the character of Sparta a topic of more than passing concern to them. Herodotus, it is true, found much at Sparta to fascinate him,[9] and the accounts he gathered from his informants already show signs of a self-conscious desire on the part of Spartans to foster certain images of their society and attitudes. Thucydides, by contrast, came to be frustrated by the Spartans' secretiveness concerning their state affairs.[10]

All later sources were the work of writers who inevitably could have had no first-hand acquaintance with Sparta before it succumbed to major change. The truth was made no easier to discover by further idealization and distortion on the part of a whole range of admirers – among them aristocrats, philosophers, politicians and military thinkers – who found in Lycurgan Sparta models and examples to suit their own ideas. Thus there developed what a French scholar of the 1930s appropriately termed a 'Spartan mirage'. From 369, after the liberation of Messenia, confusion came to be caused by the creation of a 'national' history (vehemently anti-Spartan by definition) for the new state.[11] Further distortion then occurred in the third century when Kings Agis and Cleomenes successively proclaimed themselves restorers of Lycurgan Sparta. Even Plutarch's own approach is by no means altogether objective. He is particularly concerned to demonstrate Lycurgus' devotion to peace and his creation of a constitution and society outstanding both for their balance and their practicality.

For his achievement of this end Plutarch exhibits a characteristically impressive range of reading, which includes many authors now lost. No doubt his main reliance was placed on the group of works devoted to the type of explanation and description of the Spartan constitution that he incorporated in his own *Lycurgus*. He seems to have followed above all the lost *Constitution of the Spartans* prepared in the latter part of the fourth century by Aristotle or his assistants as part of their investigation into the workings of states. In addition he was aware of Aristotle's highly critical appraisal of contemporary Sparta in *The Politics*,[12] and of the investigations in the same general area made by Aristotle's pupil and successor Theophrastus. But he also knew of two of the earliest such 'Spartan Constitutions' – one (lost) by the Athenian oligarch Critias who was killed in 403, the other attributed to Xenophon. This latter is in fact the only one to survive complete and appears here in an Appendix.[13] Later 'Constitutions' which he consulted include those by Dioscorides (of whom little is known, though he cannot have written earlier than the third century) and by the philosopher Sphaerus. The latter was a pupil first of Zeno, then later of Cleanthes, and he personally assisted King Cleomenes III in his reform programme. So it is only to be expected that Sphaerus' two works entitled *On the Spartan Constitution* and *On Lycurgus and Socrates* had a strongly contemporary slant.

Theopompus (fourth century) and Timaeus (late fourth/early third centuries) are standard historians – nearly all of whose work is lost – studied by Plutarch in addition to Herodotus and Thucydides. He has also consulted the important chronographers Eratosthenes and Apollodorus, of the third and second centuries respectively. A number of antiquarians are cited. They certainly include Philostephanus of Cyrene (third century) and two Spartans – Sosibius, who probably lived in the late third and early second centuries, and is the first Spartan known to have written about his own country; and Aristocrates, who belongs to the second century or later. Two even more shadowy figures cited, who were also antiquarians in all probability, are Dieutychidas of Megara and Apollothemis.

Among philosophers, the earliest cited is the fifth-century sophist (or teacher) Hippias of Elis. But Plutarch displays acquaintance above all with Aristotle's master Plato, who shared aristocratic Athenians' admiration for Sparta and was strongly influenced by Spartan practices, especially in *The Laws*.[14] In addition he cites three Peripatetics, Aristoxenus of Tarentum (fourth century), Demetrius of Phalerum (fourth century), who wrote a work *On Peace*, and Hermippus of Smyrna (third century). The latter is known to have composed a huge and sensational biographical work, which included a section on lawgivers.

Despite this weight of learning, Plutarch retains an independence and a freshness that serve to give the Life tremendous appeal. For all the idealism of the moralist and philosopher which it displays, it comes down to us as the latest and fullest account of how Sparta's admirers believed her to have been in the days of her greatness. As such it is an important and compelling document.

Non-Lycurgan Institutions

Plutarch attributes to Lycurgus, and thus describes in the Life, most of the distinctive features of the Spartan state in the classical period, with three notable exceptions.

The first is the dual kingship. He takes this to be already in existence by Lycurgus' time and does not seek to explain its origin. In fact there is reason to conjecture that the first joint kings were Archelaus and Charilaus early in the eighth century, and that the dual kingship reflects some amalgamation of communities in circumstances wholly obscure to us. The existence of kingship as such at a very primitive period is no surprise. What is remarkable and unique, however, is that Sparta maintained two distinct royal lines as far down as the late third century, and that her kings' role never became an altogether formal one. To command the army on campaign was always an exclusive royal prerogative; in practice kings could exercise a decisive influence in other spheres too.

Besides the dual kingship Plutarch takes it for granted that the class and status divisions of Spartiates (full citizens), *perioeci* and helots were already established by Lycurgus' time. The *perioeci* (literally, 'the dwellers round about') we know to have been a substantial group of mixed origin who achieved their status in a number of different ways. In the classical period they occupied land in Laconia and Messenia assigned to them by Sparta in return for supplying military contingents when required. They enjoyed free status and managed the internal affairs of their own communities (none of which has been excavated unfortunately, though perioecic sanctuaries have been dug). Once few, if any, Spartiates practised a manual craft, the commercial and economic role of the *perioeci* must have become a very important one.

The term 'helot' derives either from Helos, a town in the most fertile area of Laconia, said to have been conquered and destroyed by the Spartans at an early date, or (more plausibly) just from the Greek root 'hel-', meaning 'capture'. Helots were, in short, local inhabitants of Laconia and Messenia owned by the Spartan state and placed in total subjection to work for its citizens – an arrangement by no means unique in the Greek world. They are to be distinguished from slaves in that they continued to live in their own country, to have some family and community life (of which we know nothing), and to enjoy certain property rights. Unlike slaves, they could hardly hope ever to improve their status; although some were freed on occasion for military service, this was for a long time exceptional. Otherwise, it was their labour which permitted the Spartiate class to devote itself exclusively to non-productive pursuits.

The third feature of the Spartan state which Plutarch, in contrast to certain other ancient authors,[15] does not attribute to Lycurgus is the *ephorate* or chief magistracy. Rather, he follows Aristotle[16] in making it a reform by King Theopompus. It is impossible to be sure whether this powerful board of five *ephors* elected annually by the assembly from among all Spartiates (with no re-election possible) really was created – or alternatively perhaps gained importance – only after the other main elements in the constitution were functioning. But at least the case put into the mouth of King Cleomenes III by Plutarch[17] – that the ephors were originally no more than assistants of the kings, who little by little transferred authority to themselves – can be seen as consistent with the absence of any mention of them in the one genuinely archaic document about constitutional change which survives.[18] All the same, the claim by Agis' supporters in the mid third century[19] that a pair of kings in agreement always retained the power to override ephors who opposed them, is not heard of as such earlier and gives every impression of having been fabricated for the occasion.

AGESILAUS

Historical Introduction

It must have been with mixed emotions that Plutarch composed his Life of Agesilaus II, the Eurypontid king whose forty-year reign (400–360 BC) was to witness a dramatic decline in Sparta's position, much of it arguably attributable to him. Perhaps it should seem no surprise that the *Life of Pompey* – the great

Roman leader of the Late Republic, with whom Plutarch paired Agesilaus – is nearly twice as long.

When Agesilaus succeeded to the kingship at the beginning of the fourth century, Sparta's influence was at its height. Recent victory over Athens in the long Peloponnesian War (431–404) now enabled her to dominate the Greek world. Agesilaus gloried in that role, but ruthless aggressiveness on his part and that of many other leading Spartans only fuelled the resentment already felt not just by the state's defeated enemies but also by her allies – especially Thebes, the dominant city of Boeotia. Moreover, the Greeks' neighbour to the east, the immense Persian empire, whose resources had been the decisive element in Sparta's victory over Athens, remained willing to intervene in the rivalries of the Greek states. Meanwhile, Sparta provocatively took up the cause of 'liberating' the Greek cities on the eastern seaboard of Asia Minor from Persian overlordship. This was the first major military command that Agesilaus received as king. Officially, he undertook it as a 'panhellenic' initiative – on behalf of all Greeks against their common foe, the Persians – although with what degree of sincerity he and other Spartans ever supported the ideals of Panhellenism is far from clear. Even as he set out in 396 BC, the Thebans lost no time in articulating their objection to his promotion of the expedition as a panhellenic one (Ch. 6). The hostility which they thereby aroused in Agesilaus was only deepened two years later when he found himself recalled prematurely to confront a powerful new anti-Spartan coalition formed by Corinth, Argos, Boeotia and Athens.

Although Agesilaus won the narrowest of victories against Theban-led forces at Coronea in Boeotia, this did nothing to reduce his implacable hatred. How justified he was in regarding Thebes as a menace to the long-term balance of power in Greece is in turn a matter for debate. However, the agreement supported by Persia in 386 (the 'King's Peace') – whereby, in order to eliminate rivalry, each mainland Greek state should remain 'free' and 'autonomous' – pleased him in so far as it gave Sparta the pretext, though not the authority, to enforce these terms. Two successive Spartan commanders, on their own initiative, were sufficiently reckless to make pre-emptive strikes against

Thebes (in 382) and then Athens (in 378) – the former a success, the latter a failure. Agesilaus condoned both, and relished the ensuing clashes with Thebes which continued throughout the 370s. During the peace negotiations in 371, however, he met his match in the Theban commander Epaminondas. Agesilaus asked him whether the principles of the King's Peace did not require the Boeotian confederacy (dominated by Thebes) to be broken up. In response, Epaminondas had the temerity to enquire whether by the same token Sparta's domination of, and reliance upon, the perioecic communities of Laconia should not be brought to an end.

Agesilaus' enraged refusal to continue any negotiations with Thebes at this point led to a pitched battle only twenty days later, at Leuctra in Boeotia, which was a crushing defeat for Sparta. The myth of the army's invincibility was irretrievably shattered here. Even worse blows were to follow during the next decade. Sparta's allies in the Peloponnese and beyond dropped away. Theban forces penetrated not just Laconia, but even (twice) the city of Sparta itself, whose lack of a protective wall had always been a source of pride. Epaminondas removed the entire territory of Messenia from Spartan control, and made it into an independent state with a newly founded capital at Messene; Messenians who had taken refuge abroad now flocked back. In consequence the Spartan state, confined to Laconia, was approximately halved in size and population, as well as being deprived of much fertile land (not to mention the helots who had worked it). Thereafter, not only did a hostile neighbour lie to the west, but northwards, in Arcadia, the new city of Megalopolis was also founded, with the same deliberate aim of thwarting Sparta.

At home, several interrelated problems were sharply exposed. For the most part these were not novel but had developed gradually over a long period, although without doubt their impact was accelerated by Sparta's exceptionally active involvement in the affairs of Greece during the previous half-century. In particular, the number of Spartiates fell to no more than about 1,000, while the distribution of land ownership became extremely unequal. Altogether, Sparta on the model supposedly created by Lycurgus (and portrayed so idealistically by Plutarch in that Life) was brought to an end at long last by Epaminondas and his fellow Boeotian leader Pelopidas. It is true that Thebes' ambitions in turn did not outlast Epaminondas' death in battle at Mantinea in 362 (Pelopidas had met the same fate two years earlier). Sparta, however, never regained Messenia, and never again established herself as a power of more than local significance, despite remarkable efforts much later in the mid third century, recounted by Plutarch in *Agis and Cleomenes* below. In the short term, the state was in such dire need of funds that Agesilaus (aged over eighty) undertook humiliating service as a mercenary commander for profit.

Plutarch's Sources

The early fourth century in Greece was a well-documented period, and there can be no question that Plutarch was familiar with many of the accounts of it; he sometimes explicitly compares them. In this connection we should bear in mind that he also wrote Lives of four other figures whose careers intersect with that of Agesilaus – his fellow Spartan and lover, Lysander; the two Boeotian leaders Epaminondas and Pelopidas; and the Persian Great King from 405/4 to 359/8, Artaxerxes II. In consequence, predictably enough, the length at which he relates an episode, or the perspective which his account adopts, is prone to vary from one Life to another (his *Epaminondas* does not survive, a serious loss). A further influence is Plutarch's own Boeotian background. Much as he may have admired certain aspects of Agesilaus' character and his professed unflinching devotion to traditional Spartan values, at the same time it would only be natural for him to take pride in the leadership of the king's detested foes, Epaminondas and Pelopidas.

Plutarch was furnished with an unapologetically pro-Spartan record by the Athenian Xenophon, Agesilaus' contemporary and friend, who is introduced more fully below in the context of the work *Spartan Society* attributed to him. Xenophon wrote not only *A History of My Times*, in which Agesilaus features prominently and the Thebans' achievements are flagrantly downplayed, but he also composed an encomium specifically of Agesilaus, praising and illustrating his piety, justice, self-control, courage and wisdom. Plutarch likewise, in accordance with his commitment to composing biography rather than history, is concerned above all to record and discuss Agesilaus' personal qualities and behaviour (as king; his life to that point receives only the briefest notice), with the accent on their strengths, although certain limitations are by no means ignored. The campaigns in Asia Minor and Boeotia during the 390s aside, Plutarch's references to the highpoints of Greek history during the following three decades are kept to a minimum.[20] Equally, it is not part of his purpose to offer insight into the opposition to Agesilaus' attitudes and actions which clearly was voiced by fellow Spartiates.

This is not to suggest that Plutarch lacked a full awareness of the history of the period; rather, it is we who lack it. In fact, all the sources about to be mentioned are now lost except for fragments. Plutarch refers elsewhere (though not in this Life) to the standard account written by Ephorus as a contemporary. However, in *Agesilaus* he does refer four times to another standard history, also by a contemporary, Theopompus. A history by Callisthenes that covered the thirty years following the King's Peace is cited once (its author became better known for his first-hand account of Alexander the Great's exploits). Dicaearchus, also cited once, was a prolific author of the late fourth century and contemporary of Theophrastus (cited here twice);[21] both were pupils of Aristotle. Like Theophrastus, Dioscorides (cited here once) wrote specifically about Sparta.[22] Last, but not least, we should note how Plutarch shares findings from his own travels to Sparta and research in the archives there.

AGIS AND CLEOMENES

Historical Introduction

In the absence of reform it is no surprise that Sparta remained weak after the terrible defeat at Leuctra in 371 BC. Though we lack the material to write any connected account of her history for the next century and more, it is at least clear that she did display unflinching hostility to Macedonian domination of Greece, which persisted from the 330s onwards. For the most part the opposition of a state by now so insignificant made little impact. But in 331 King Agis III led a short-lived rising of many Peloponnesian states which ended in crushing defeat and his own death. Early in the third century King Areus I broke with tradition by adopting an ostentatious style of monarchy similar to that of other kings in the eastern Mediterranean world (even issuing Spartan silver coinage for the first time, with his own head on it), and nursed grandiose ambitions of reviving Spartan leadership of the Peloponnese. To this end Macedonian domination had to be shaken off. The first attempt which he organized, in 280, quickly proved abortive. But the second, co-ordinated with Athens in the early 260s, was more serious, though in the end Areus met his death during his third season of campaigning, having failed to break the Macedonians' grip on Corinth and the Isthmus.

Areus received some subsidies from the king of Egypt, Ptolemy II: the interest which he and his successors showed in Greek affairs (and the cash they provided) were to continue making a significant impact. Within Greece the aggressive Aetolian League – a federal state in the north-west, founded around 400 – was to gain increasing prestige and strength during the third century. A second, more ancient, federal state, the Achaean League in the north-west Peloponnese, was revived from 280 onwards, and began to assume considerable importance once Aratus took the leading role in its affairs. He was a dynamic figure who at the age of twenty in 251 seized control of his native Sicyon and at once joined it to the League, thereby taking the first step in what was to become the expansion of a local federation into a much larger, more powerful body. The military operations of the League were conducted by a general (*strategus*) whom the assembly elected to hold office from May each year; no one could be general for more than one year at a time. Aratus first held this office in 245/4 and usually in alternate years thereafter.

In all likelihood the Spartan state had lost many of its traditional distinctive features by the mid third century. The figures given by Plutarch show that the decline in Spartiate numbers and the inequality of landholdings had both become even more serious. The latter trend may have been exacerbated by large land purchases on the part of those Spartiates who resorted to the common expedient of undertaking mercenary service abroad (as Agesilaus had done), and were successful enough to make their fortunes. Taenarum, at the bleak south-western tip of Laconia, had even become the main centre where Greek mercenaries generally were hired.

Plutarch's favourable account of Agis makes clear the need for reform, but leaves much obscure concerning precisely why he undertook it and why he failed to carry it through. Sweeping social reconstruction initiated spontaneously from the top is a rarity in any community at any time. We may wonder whether Agis' programme and the personal sacrifices which he offered to make were not motivated mainly by fear that events might otherwise overtake him: the mass of discontented would rise to deprive him (and other property-owners) of not just wealth, but also position. On the other hand it may be that he was really seeking personal glory and military strength for Sparta by enabling her to raise a large army again. Yet in that case it is remarkable how little he did to take the offensive even in the short time at his disposal. His one expedition was undertaken at the request of the Achaeans; in the course of it Aratus' decision not to let the Spartan troops show their mettle in battle was readily accepted, and no other occasion for action seemed to be sought. Equally unclear is the depth of Agis' devotion to the rule of law and to what he claimed to value as Lycurgan principles. It could be argued that while he was willing (or naive) enough at the outset to have his programme enacted in a constitutional fashion – an attempt which should have succeeded, we may note, if just a single vote had gone the other way in the Gerousia – thereafter he was prepared to abandon all such scruples, first by allowing the deposition of his fellow king and then by removing a hostile board of ephors.

For all Plutarch's scorn, there could have been some justification for the fears expressed by King Leonidas with regard to

Agis' programme: '. . . [he] was pledging the property of the rich to the poor as their payment for making him tyrant, and by his land distributions and cancellations of debts was buying plenty of bodyguards for himself, rather than citizens for Sparta' (*Agis*, Ch. 7). Beyond question, the programme could be represented as merely a variation on the standard form of appeal made by aspiring tyrants to the lower classes in Greek cities. Personal considerations apart, Leonidas was right to be apprehensive, and in fact elements in the narrative show how Sparta was more deeply split over the programme than Plutarch specifically admits. This is highlighted by the vote in the Gerousia, where nearly all the membership must have been wealthy, yet almost half voted in favour of reform; in contrast the board of ephors elected (by the assembly) subsequent to this vote was opposed to reform, despite Plutarch's claim that citizens in general favoured it.

There remains the puzzle of why Agis accepted his uncle's proposal to postpone redistribution of land. It may be that by then he had come entirely under the latter's influence – despite his denial of this to the end. But naivety and inexperience seem the more likely explanations. They are all the more unexpected given the lessons in hard political reality which Agis had been willing enough to learn after rejection of his programme by the Gerousia. At the same time they do also encourage doubts about just how thoroughly he had considered in advance the aims and consequences of his proposals.

In his similarly favourable treatment of Cleomenes, Plutarch leaves the king's activities and ambitions during the early years of the reign unclear. Whether the murder of Agis' brother Archidamus actually prompted him to devise his coup, or instead just influenced the timing of a scheme already planned, we cannot say. At least its execution proved that Cleomenes had learned from Agis' difficulties and hesitation. There was no attempt to act constitutionally. Instead the ephors were violently eliminated, their office abolished, and the entire reform programme imposed at a single stroke. Cleomenes had no compunction about paying mere lip-service to Lycurgan principles, and he made it abundantly clear that his aims were personal glory together with revived military strength for Sparta.

The narrative shows how it was the very success of his reforms which led to his downfall. His leadership of the enlarged and re-equipped Spartan army was brilliant enough to threaten the Achaean League with disintegration, while his social measures at Sparta attracted supporters elsewhere who hoped that he might benefit their cities likewise. It was the strange fact that he did not do so, at Argos above all, which proved a decisive element in his loss of power. At the end of a year and more of submission to him the Argives were still hoping for reform, and the failure to offer it seems baffling. It could be claimed that Cleomenes feared a loss of support among the rich, but he had not been especially concerned to protect their interests at Sparta, and in 224 if he had seen the alternatives before him as either reform and the retention of Argos, or no reform and its loss (with all the consequences for him which were sure to follow), then in self-interest alone the former choice should have appeared obvious. It may possibly be that Cleomenes was apprehensive of Sparta's ability to control a reformed Argos in the long term, though that hardly seems an overwhelming consideration in the crisis. The real stumbling-block may rather have been a failure of imagination. Cleomenes had been committed to sweeping domestic reform of a uniquely Spartan character,[23] but could not conceive that this, or a version of it, was appropriate elsewhere. It is significant that a third Spartan reformer – the tyrant Nabis (207–192) – was to suffer from no such limitation. The success of his programme (at Sparta and Argos) eventually attracted Roman suspicion.[24]

Plutarch's Sources

Since the fullest ancient account of the reigns of Agis and Cleomenes is now lost, their Lives by Plutarch are of immense importance. In fact almost no other material about Agis survives, or about internal affairs at Sparta during the reign of Cleomenes. The fullest account was offered by Phylarchus, a contemporary who came either from Naucratis in Egypt or from Athens (or perhaps moved from the former to the latter). He wrote a history of Greece in twenty-eight books from the death of Pyrrhus in 272 to that of Cleomenes in 219, in which the view of both Agis and Cleomenes is known to have been exceptionally favourable. Plutarch's four citations show that he had read Phylarchus' work, and in all likelihood he actually based his account of the two kings on it.

But at least two hostile views of Cleomenes were also known to him. The first appeared in the extensive *Memoirs* of the Achaeans' leader, Aratus of Sicyon, another contemporary source, also now lost, which Plutarch drew upon primarily in the Life he wrote of Aratus.[25] These *Memoirs* were written as a careful justification of Aratus' career, intended not least to defend his highly controversial appeal for Macedonian help against Cleomenes. The second hostile view of Cleomenes appeared in the *Histories* of Polybius of Megalopolis, which were written in the mid second century and still survive.[26] Though Polybius' main narrative does not begin till 220, he was concerned to explain various background developments in some detail, among them the rise of the Achaean League, in whose affairs he came to take a prominent part himself. Naturally, therefore, he deals with what he calls the 'Cleomenean War' (229/8–222)[27] and later narrates Cleomenes' exile and death in Egypt.[28] Polybius mainly followed Aratus' *Memoirs*, but he did also consult Phylarchus among others, even though he was exasperated by his admiration for Cleomenes and criticized him vehemently for his highly coloured, emotional style of writing. Similarly Plutarch, while sharing Phylarchus' assessment of the two kings, was well aware of his bias, and in his *Aratus*, Ch. 38 even goes so far as to state:

> Phylarchus has in fact given a similar account of these events [just described]. In the absence of testimony by Polybius he does not merit any credence at all since whenever he touches on Cleomenes he is carried away by his partiality for him, and persistently turns his history into a court case in which he opposes Aratus and pleads for Cleomenes.

This is a valuable statement of caution. But the loss of Phylarchus still denies us any chance of assessing in detail the extent to which Plutarch exercised a control on his testimony.

Though Plutarch never refers to it in these Lives, he must presumably have been familiar with Polybius' biography of the Achaean leader Philopoemen, who took part in negotiations with Cleomenes after the fall of Megalopolis and fought at the battle of Sellasia.[29] Plutarch certainly used this biography (now lost) for his own *Life of Philopoemen*. No doubt he consulted works by others, too, relating to Agis and Cleomenes, but none can be identified beyond that of Baton of Sinope.

NOTES

1. For further information on every aspect of what follows see, for example, P. A. Stadter's General Introduction to *Plutarch: Greek Lives* in Oxford's World Classics series (1998).
2. See the selection in Plutarch, *Essays* (Penguin, 1992).
3. See *Lycurgus*, Ch. 18.
4. See in particular E. Rawson, *The Spartan Tradition in European Thought* (Oxford University Press, 1969).
5. See Maps, pp. 215, 217.
6. *The Histories*, 1. 65–6 (Penguin, 2003).
7. Plutarch, *Lycurgus*, Ch. 6.
8. See *Lycurgus*, Ch. 21, and *Agesilaus*, Ch. 19.
9. See under 'Lacedaemonia' and 'Sparta' in the index of the Penguin edition of *The Histories*.
10. *The Peloponnesian War*, 5.68.
11. Known to us best through Pausanias, who wrote an extensive *Guide to Greece* in the latter part of the second century AD: see especially Book 4 (in the second volume of the Penguin edition).
12. 1269a29–1271b19 (rev. edn, Penguin, 1984).
13. See p. 194 below.
14. Penguin, 2004.
15. Among them Xenophon, *Spartan Society*, Ch. 8.
16. *The Politics*, 1313a26 (rev. edn, Penguin, 1992).
17. *Cleomenes*, Ch. 10.
18. See *Lycurgus*, Ch. 6.
19. *Agis*, Ch. 12.

20. As it happens, Agesilaus did not himself participate in either of the key battles at Leuctra and Mantinea.
21. See 'Lycurgus: Plutarch's Sources'.
22. See 'Lycurgus: Plutarch's Sources'.
23. Note that neither king was so radical as to propose a change in the status of the helots. Only in the final crisis did Cleomenes offer them freedom in exchange for military service, and even then at a high price.
24. See Livy, *Rome and the Mediterranean* (Penguin, 1976) under 'Nabis of Sparta' in the index. He is as hostile to Nabis as Plutarch is favourable to Agis and Cleomenes.
25. To appear in *The Rise of Rome* (rev. edn, Penguin, forthcoming).
26. *The Rise of the Roman Empire* (Penguin, 1979).
27. 2.46–71.
28. 5.34–9.
29. See *Cleomenes*, Ch. 24 and note 63.

Further Reading

Scholars will consult, for example, among recent monographs, N. M. Kennell, *The Gymnasium of Virtue: Education and Culture in Ancient Sparta* (University of North Carolina Press, 1995), and S. Hodkinson, *Property and Wealth in Classical Sparta* (Classical Press of Wales, 2000). Among collections of essays, the three co-edited by A. Powell and S. Hodkinson, *The Shadow of Sparta* (Routledge, 1993), *Sparta: New Perspectives* (Classical Press of Wales, 1999) and *Sparta Beyond the Mirage* (Classical Press of Wales, 2002), as well as *Spartan Reflections* by P. Cartledge (Duckworth, 2001). For reference, the two prosopographies by A. S. Bradford, from earliest times to 323 BC (revision of P. Poralla), and from 323 BC to AD 396 (published by Ares, 1985 and Beck, 1977 respectively). In addition, the extensive commentary on Plutarch, *Agesilaus* by D. R. Shipley (Oxford University Press, 1997).

The following brief selection of books in English is intended for the non-expert reader.

Ancient Sources

1. With the focus primarily on society and institutions:

Herodotus, *The Histories* (rev. edn, Penguin, 2003) under 'Lacedaemonia' and 'Sparta' in the index.

Xenophon, *Agesilaus*, in *Hiero the Tyrant and Other Treatises* (Penguin, 1997).

Aristotle, *The Politics* (rev. edn, Penguin, 1992), pp. 139–49.

Pausanias, *Guide to Greece*, Books 3 and 4 (on Laconia and Messenia respectively, Penguin, 1984, vol. 2).

A concise commentary on Xenophon, *Spartan Society*, as well as comparative material about other states, may be found in J. M. Moore, *Aristotle and Xenophon on Democracy and Oligarchy* (rev. edn, Chatto & Windus, 1983).

2. With Spartan history and politics as the principal focus:

Thucydides, *The Peloponnesian War* (Penguin, 1972).

Xenophon, *A History of My Times* (Penguin, 1979).

Plutarch, *Lysander* (in *The Rise and Fall of Athens*, rev. edn, Penguin, forthcoming).

Polybius, *The Rise of the Roman Empire* (Penguin, 1979), 2.46–71; 5.34–9; 6.10 and 45–50.

Modern Studies

For the best introduction, read Cartledge's *Epic History*, and then Whitby.

1. With the focus primarily on society and institutions:

P. A. Cartledge, *Sparta and Lakonia: A Regional History c.1300–362 BC* (rev. edn, Routledge, 2002).

S. B. Pomeroy, *Spartan Women* (Oxford University Press, 2002).

N. Sekunda, *The Spartan Army* (Osprey Elite Series, 66, 1998).

M. Whitby (ed.), *Sparta* (Edinburgh University Press, 2001).

2. With Spartan history as the principal focus:

P. A. Cartledge, *The Spartans: An Epic History* (second edn, Pan, 2003).

P. A. Cartledge, *Agesilaos and the Crisis of Sparta* (Johns Hopkins University Press, 1987, reissued Duckworth, 2000).

P. A. Cartledge and A. Spawforth, *Hellenistic and Roman Sparta: A Tale of Two Cities* (rev. edn, Routledge, 2002).

For the fifth century, A. Powell, *Athens and Sparta: Constructing Greek Political and Social History from 478* BC (second edn, Routledge, 2001), especially Chs. 4 and 6, can be highly recommended; likewise, for the succeeding period, the concise treatments of Athens, Sparta, Thebes and Central Greece, and the Eastern Greek World in L. A. Tritle (ed.), *The Greek World in the Fourth Century* (Routledge, 1996).

A Note on the Texts

For the *Lives* and the *Sayings* I have mostly adhered to the texts of the relevant Teubner editions. The Greek text of the *Sayings* presents persistent problems, as does that of Xenophon, *Spartan Society*, for which I have used the edition by F. Ollier (1934).

LIVES

LYCURGUS

1. Generally speaking it is impossible to make any undisputed statement about Lycurgus the lawgiver, since conflicting accounts have been given of his ancestry, his travels, his death, and above all his activity with respect to his laws and government; but there is least agreement about the period in which the man lived. Some claim that he was in his prime at the same time as Iphitus and was his partner in instituting the Olympic truce.[1] Among those who take this view is Aristotle the philosopher,[2] adducing as proof the discus with Lycurgus' name inscribed[3] on it preserved at Olympia. But others like Eratosthenes and Apollodorus, who calculate his period by the succession of kings at Sparta, make the claim that he lived a great many years before the First Olympiad. Timaeus conjectures that there were two Lycurguses at Sparta at different times, and that the achievements of both were attributed to one because of his renown. The older one might have lived close to Homer's time:[4] there are some who think that he even met Homer in person. Xenophon, too, suggests a very early date in the passage where he states that Lycurgus lived in the time of the Heraclids. Now of course the most recent Spartan kings were in fact Heraclids by ancestry, but Xenophon evidently also wanted to call the first kings Heraclids,[5] as being closely connected with Heracles. Nonetheless, even though this is such a muddled historical topic, we shall attempt to present an account of Lycurgus by following those treatments which offer the smallest contradictions or the most distinguished authorities.

The poet Simonides[6] maintains that Lycurgus' father was not Eunomus, but that both Lycurgus and Eunomus were the sons of Prytanis. Nearly all others, however, trace his genealogy differently, as follows: Procles, son of Aristodemus, was the father of Soüs; Eurypon was Soüs' son; Prytanis was Eurypon's son; Eunomus was Prytanis' son; Eunomus had Polydectes by his first wife, and Lycurgus was his younger son by a second wife, Dionassa. This is the account given by Dieutychidas, which puts Lycurgus in the fifth generation after Procles and in the tenth after Heracles.

2. Among his ancestors Soüs was particularly admired: under him the Spartiates both made slaves of the helots[7] and won further extensive Arcadian territory which they annexed. There is a story that when Soüs was being besieged by the Cleitorians in a rugged waterless spot, he agreed to surrender to them the territory which he had gained in the fighting if he and all those with him might drink from the spring nearby. Once the agreement had been confirmed under oath he assembled his men and offered to confer the kingship of the area upon the one who refrained from drinking. Not one, however, possessed such self-restraint, but they all drank. Soüs went down after everyone else, and with the enemy still there just splashed himself. Then he moved off, but retained control of the land because not everybody had drunk.

Yet even though he was admired for such acts, his family were termed the Eurypontids, not after him but after his son, because Eurypon by courting popularity and ingratiating himself with the masses was evidently the first to relax the excessively autocratic character of the kingship. Such relaxation, however, led to a bolder attitude on the part of the people. Among the succeeding kings some were detested for ruling the people by force, while others were merely tolerated because their rule was either partisan or feeble. As a result, for a long period Sparta was gripped by lawlessness and disorder. It was as a consequence of this that Lycurgus' father, too, met his death while king. He died from being struck by a chef's cleaver in the course of putting a stop to some brawl, and left his throne to his elder son Polydectes.

3. When Polydectes also died not long after, everyone reckoned that Lycurgus ought to become king. And king he was, until it became obvious that his brother's widow was pregnant. As soon as he discovered this, he declared that the kingship belonged to the child if it should turn out to be male, while for his own part he would exercise power simply as a guardian: *prodikoi*[8] was the term used by the Spartans for the guardians of kings without fathers. The mother, however, in secret communications explained to him her wish to abort the baby on condition that while remaining king of Sparta he would marry her. Though he loathed her morals, he raised no objection to the actual proposal, but pretended to approve and accept it. He said that there was no need for her to suffer physical harm and to run risks by inducing a miscarriage and taking drugs, since he would ensure that the child should be disposed of as soon as it was born. By this means he continued to mislead the woman right up until the baby was due. Then as soon as he learned that she was in labour, he sent in observers to be there at her delivery, as well as guards under orders, should the baby turn out to be a girl, to hand it over to the women, but if it should be a boy, to bring it to him personally, whatever he might happen to be doing. It so happened that he was having a meal with the magistrates when a boy was born, and the servants appeared bringing him the infant. The story goes that he took him and said to those present: 'Spartiates, a king is born to you.' Then he laid him in the king's place and named him Charilaus ('People's Joy') because everyone, impressed at how high-minded and fair Lycurgus was, felt overjoyed.

He was king, then, for eight months altogether. There were other reasons, too, for the citizens' admiration. In fact those devoted to him and willing to carry out his orders promptly because of his personal excellence outnumbered those obedient to him because he was a king's guardian and had the royal prerogative. Yet there was also some jealousy, as well as an effort to obstruct his upward rise when he was young, in particular by the relations and friends of the king's mother, who felt injured by him. On one occasion her brother Leonidas abused Lycurgus quite offensively and added that he was fully aware of Lycurgus' intention to become king. Leonidas thus roused suspicion and by his slander laid the ground for accusing Lycurgus of a plot, should the king come to any harm. Similar sorts of remarks were put about by the king's mother too. Since these caused him distress and fear about the uncertain future, he decided to avoid suspicion by going abroad and travelling around until his nephew should come of age and have a son to succeed to his throne.

4. So he set out and came first to Crete. Here he studied the forms of government and associated with the men of the highest reputation. Among the laws there were those that he admired and took note of with the intention of bringing them home and putting them to use, but there were others which he thought little of. By the exercise of charm and friendship he prevailed upon one of those regarded there as shrewd and statesmanlike to undertake a mission to Sparta. This man, Thales, had some reputation as a composer of lyric poetry and had made this art his cover, though in fact his activities were precisely those of the most powerful lawgivers. For his songs were arguments to evoke ready obedience and concord. The accompanying music and rhythms had a notably regular and soothing quality, so that those who heard them would unconsciously mellow in character. In place of the mutual ill-will which at the time prevailed there, they would instead become habituated to striving communally for excellence. Thus in a sense Thales paved the way for Lycurgus' instruction of the Spartiates.

From Crete Lycurgus sailed to Asia. We are told that his plan was to compare the frugal, tough way of life in Crete with the extravagance and luxury of Ionia, and to observe the contrast in the ways of life and government – just like a doctor who compares bodies which are festering or diseased with healthy ones. It was apparently in Ionia that he also first encountered the poems of Homer, which Creophylus'[9] descendants were responsible for preserving. And when he observed that besides their tendencies to unrestrained indulgence they contained political and educational elements which were no less worthy of attention, he enthusiastically had them written down and collected them in order to bring them back home. Homer's epics had already gained a certain vague reputation among the Greeks, and a few individuals had acquired certain portions thanks to chance distribution of these works here and there; but in making them known Lycurgus was the first and most successful.

The Egyptians think that Lycurgus reached them too, and that their separation of the warrior class from the others particularly impressed him – the consequence being that he carried it over to Sparta, and by differentiating labourers[10] and craftsmen demonstrated how genuinely refined and pure his constitution was. There are certainly even some Greek historians who endorse these claims by the Egyptians. Yet so far as I am aware nobody except the Spartiate Aristocrates, the son of Hipparchus, has maintained that Lycurgus also visited both Libya and Iberia, and that in his wanderings round India he talked with the Gymnosophists.[11]

5. The Spartans missed Lycurgus throughout his absence and often summoned him back. To them the kings, while accorded a title and an office, were in other ways not superior to the people, whereas in Lycurgus they recognized a natural leader with the ability to attract a following. In fact even the kings were not reluctant to see him back again: their hope was that with his presence they would receive less offence from the people. So when Lycurgus did return to a populace in this kind of mood, his immediate intention was to sweep away the existing order and to make a complete change of constitution, since piecemeal legislation would have no effect or value. It was like the case of someone in bodily distress from a whole range of different disorders, who will begin a different, new life only by dissolving and changing his existing make-up with drugs and purges. Once Lycurgus had formed this intention he travelled first to Delphi. And after sacrificing to the god and consulting him, he returned bringing that famous oracle[12] in which the Pythia called him 'dear to the gods' and 'a god rather than a man': he had asked for Good Order, and she declared that the god granted this and promised that his constitution would be by far the finest of all.

With this encouragement he made approaches to the most distinguished men and invited them to join in the task with him. Initially he conferred with his friends in secret, yet ever so gradually he won over more men and organized them for action. When the moment came, he ordered his thirty foremost men to proceed under arms into the *agora*[13] at dawn, so as to shock and terrify his opponents. Hermippus has recorded the twenty most distinguished among these men. Arthmiadas is generally named as the one who was particularly associated with Lycurgus in all his operations, and who collaborated with him in formulating legislation. When the disturbance began, King Charilaus took fright because he thought that the whole action was being concerted against him, and so sought sanctuary with the goddess in her Bronze House. But once reassured by an oath he emerged, and as a man of mild temperament played a part in Lycurgus' programme. This mildness is reflected in the story of his fellow king Archelaus, who responded to praise of the youngster by saying: 'How could Charilaus be a gentleman, when he isn't hard even on scoundrels?'

First and most significant among Lycurgus' numerous innovations was the institution of the Elders. According to Plato,[14] its combination with the kings' arrogant rule, and the right to an equal vote on the most important matters, produced security and at the same time sound sense. For the state was unstable, at one moment inclining towards the kings and virtual tyranny, at another towards the people and democracy. But now by placing the office of the Elders in the middle as a kind of ballast, and thus striking a balance, it found the safest arrangement and organization, with the twenty-eight Elders always siding with the kings when it was a matter of resisting democracy, yet in turn reinforcing the people against the development of tyranny. According to Aristotle this number of Elders was instituted because two of Lycurgus' thirty leading associates panicked and abandoned the enterprise. But Sphaerus claims that from the outset there were twenty-eight collaborators in the scheme. Possibly the fact that this number is reached through multiplying seven by four also has something to do with it, as well as the point that being equal to the sum of its own divisors it is the next perfect number after six.[15] Yet in my view the main reason for fixing upon this number of Elders was so that the total should be thirty when the two kings were added to the twenty-eight.

6. Lycurgus was so enthusiastic about this council that he brought an oracle about it from Delphi, which they call a *rhetra*.[16] It goes as follows: 'After dedicating a temple to Zeus Scyllanius and Athena Scyllania, forming *phylai* and creating *obai*, and instituting a Gerousia of thirty including the founder-leaders, then from season to season *apellaze* between Babyca and Cnacion so as to propose and withdraw. But to the people should belong the right to respond as well as power.'[17] In this the phrases 'forming *phylai*' and 'creating *obai*' refer to the division and distribution of the people into groups, the former of which he termed *phylai*, the latter *obai*.[18] The 'founder-leaders' means the kings, while 'to *apellaze*' means to summon the assembly, because Lycurgus related the origin and source of his constitution to Pythian Apollo.[19] Their present names for Babyca and Cnacion are . . . [20] and Oinous. Aristotle says that Cnacion is a river, while Babyca is a bridge. It was between these that they used to hold their assemblies: there were no porticoes nor any other edifice. For in his opinion these were in no way conducive to sound deliberations, but instead harmful. They make those who assemble idiotic and give them silly, mindless notions, when at their meetings they can stare at statues and pictures, or the stages of theatres,[21] or the richly decorated roofs of council chambers. When the populace was assembled, Lycurgus permitted no one else except the Elders and kings to make a proposal, although the authority to decide upon what the latter put forward did belong to the people. Later, however, when the people distorted proposals and mauled them by their deletions and additions, the kings Polydorus and Theopompus supplemented the *rhetra* as follows: 'If the people should make a crooked choice, the Elders and the founder-leaders are to set it aside' – that is, not to confirm it, but to withdraw it completely and to dismiss the people because they are altering and reformulating the proposal contrary to what was best. Moreover these kings persuaded the city that the god had ordered this

supplement – as Tyrtaeus seems to be recalling in the following lines:

Having listened to Phoebus they brought home from Pytho
The oracles of the god and his words which were to be fulfilled:
To rule in council is for the kings (who are esteemed by the gods
And whose care is the lovely city of Sparta),
And for the aged Elders; but then it is for the common people
To respond in turn with straight *rhetras*.[22]

7. While Lycurgus had thus incorporated a blend of elements in the constitution, Spartans after his day nonetheless still saw oligarchy as the one that was undiluted and dominant – or 'inflated and fervent'[23] (as Plato puts it) 'so that they imposed upon it the authority of the ephors to act as a curb'. It was apparently about 130 years after Lycurgus' time that the first ephors were appointed, headed by Elatus, during the reign of Theopompus.[24] This is the king about whom they also relate that when his wife criticized him because the kingship he would hand on to his sons would be less than the one he inherited, he replied: 'No, greater – since it will last longer.' In fact by its renunciation of excessive authority and the related resentment, the Spartan kingship escaped the danger of suffering the fate which the Messenians and Argives inflicted upon their kings, who refused to concede anything or yield any of their authority to the popular element. Lycurgus' skill and foresight in this respect are also seen with special clarity in any review of the civil strife and misgovernment among the Spartans' own kinsmen and neighbours, the Messenian and Argive peoples and kings. Initially their circumstances and those of the Spartans had been equal, and in the allocation of land[25] they may even have seemed to gain more than they did. However, they did not prosper for very long, but through the insolence of their kings on one side and the non-cooperation of their masses on the other, they threw their institutions into complete turmoil – thereby demonstrating what a truly divine blessing the Spartiates enjoyed in the man who constructed their constitution and blended it for them. Yet these developments came later.

8. Lycurgus' second, and most revolutionary, reform was his redistribution of the land. For there was dreadful inequality: many destitute people without means were congregating in the city, while wealth had poured completely into just a few hands. In order to expel arrogance, envy, crime, luxury and those yet older and more serious political afflictions, wealth and poverty, Lycurgus persuaded the citizens to pool all the land and then redistribute it afresh. Then they would all live on equal terms with one another, with the same amount of property to support each, and they would seek to be first only in merit. There would be no distinction or inequality between individuals except for what censure of bad conduct and praise of good would determine.

Acting upon his word Lycurgus distributed the rest of Laconia to the *perioeci* in 30,000 lots, and divided the part subject to the city of Sparta into 9,000.[26] This was the number of lots for Spartiates. However, some say that Lycurgus allocated 6,000 such lots and that Polydorus added 3,000 later. Others say that half the 9,000 were allotted by the latter, and half by Lycurgus. Each person's lot was sufficient to provide a rent of 70 *medimni* of barley[27] for a man, and 12 for his wife, along with proportionate quantities of fresh produce. He thought that just this amount of food would suffice for their proper fitness and health, and they would need nothing more. There is a story that at some later date when on return from abroad he was passing through the country just after the reaping, and saw the heaps of grain side by side and all equal in size, he smiled and remarked to the bystanders that the whole of Laconia had the look of a property which many brothers had recently divided between themselves.[28]

9. He attempted to divide up their movable property too, in order to remove inequalities and contrasts altogether. But when he saw their adverse reaction to outright expropriation, he went about this in a different way and devised constitutional measures against their greed. First he declared that all gold and silver coinage was now invalid, and decreed that only iron should be used as currency;[29] and then he assigned a low value to even a great weight and mass of this, so that a sum of ten *minas*

demanded substantial storage space in a house and a waggon to shift it. Once this was made the legal tender, many types of crime disappeared from Sparta. For who would set out to steal, or accept as a bribe, or rob, or plunder something which could not be hidden, excited no envy when possessed, and could not even be profitably chopped up? For the story is that Lycurgus doused the surface of the red-hot iron with vinegar, thus removing whatever other use and strength it might have, and making it fragile and intractable.

After this he effected an expulsion of useless and superfluous alien crafts. Even without anybody banishing them, most would probably have been eliminated by the common currency, since there was no sale for their products. The iron money, after all, could not be exported elsewhere in Greece, and was considered a joke there, not an object of value. Consequently it was impossible to buy any shoddy foreign goods, and no cargo of merchandise would enter the harbours, no teacher of rhetoric trod Laconian soil, no begging seer, no pimp, no maker of gold or silver ornaments – because there was no coined money. Thus gradually cut off from the things that animate and feed it, luxury atrophied[30] of its own accord. And those who had great possessions won no advantage because there was no public outlet for their wealth, but it had to be kept unused in storage at home. As a result their craftsmanship of everyday essential items of furniture like beds and chairs and tables was first-rate, and the Laconian *kothon* or drinking cup, according to Critias, is especially valued for use on campaigns. Visibly off-putting elements in water which had to be drunk were concealed by its colour, while the dirt in the liquid was trapped by the lip, so that what reached the mouth for drinking was cleaner. The lawgiver was responsible for this too, since craftsmen had been released from useless jobs and now displayed the quality of their skill in essential ones.

10. With the aim of stepping up the attack on luxury and removing the passion for wealth, he introduced his third and finest reform, the establishment of common messes. The intention was that they should assemble together and eat the same

specified meat-sauces and cereals. This prevented them from spending the time at home, lying at table on expensive couches, being waited upon by confectioners and chefs, fattened up in the dark like gluttonous animals, and ruining themselves physically as well as morally, and by giving free rein to every craving and excess which demanded lengthy slumbers, warm baths, plenty of rest, and, in a sense, daily nursing.

This, then, was indeed a great achievement, yet as Theophrastus says, it was an even greater one to have made wealth undesirable and to have produced 'non-wealth' by meals taken in common and by the frugality of the diet. When the rich man would go to the same meal as the poor one, he could have no use nor pleasure from lavish table settings, let alone view them or display them. Thus in Sparta alone of all the states under the sun was seen that proverbial blind Plutus[31] lying inanimate and inert, as if in a picture. It was not even possible for the rich to dine at home first and then to proceed to their messes on a full stomach. Rather, the rest were on the look-out for whoever would not drink and eat along with them, and they would abuse him for having no self-discipline and for being too delicate to consume the common fare.

11. We are told that it was this reform above all which roused the fury of the wealthy against Lycurgus, so that they joined together in a body to jeer at him and to express their anger. Eventually, when many of them pelted him, he ran from the *agora* to escape, and did manage to take refuge in a sanctuary ahead of them. But one particular youth, Alcander – who was by no means unintelligent, though he did have a quick, excitable temper – pressed hard in pursuit, and struck him with his stick when he turned round, knocking his eye out. However, Lycurgus did not give in because of this blow, but stood to confront the citizens and show them his bloodstained face and ruined eye. When they saw this they were overcome with such deep shame and sorrow that they handed Alcander over to him and escorted him home as an expression of their joint outrage. Lycurgus then complimented and dismissed them, but Alcander he brought into his own house: he neither said nor did anything hurtful to

him, but got rid of his usual servants and attendants, and ordered him to act as his servant. Alcander, who was by no means ill-bred, did as he was instructed without a word; and by staying in Lycurgus' house and living with him came to recognize his gentleness, his depth of soul, his ascetic lifestyle and his inexhaustible capacity for work. In consequence Alcander became quite remarkably attached to him, and used to say to his comrades and friends that Lycurgus, far from being severe or unfeeling, was uniquely gentle and mild to others. This, then, was how Alcander was punished and the kind of penalty he paid – a criminal, wilful adolescent who became the most civil and responsible man. In memory of his injury Lycurgus dedicated a shrine of Athena – whom he gave the special name Optilletis, because the Dorians there call eyes *optilloi*. Some writers, however (among them Dioscorides, who produced a work on the Spartan constitution), maintain that although Lycurgus was hit in the eye, he was not blinded, but actually dedicated the shrine to the goddess as a thanksgiving for its recovery. At any rate it was after this incident that the Spartiates gave up the habit of carrying sticks when attending the assembly.

12. While Cretans call messes *andreia*[32] Spartans call them *phiditia*, either because they are places of friendship (*philia*) and kindliness – with the 'd' in *phiditia* in place of the 'l' in *philitia* – or because they instil thriftiness and frugality (*pheido*). Yet, as some claim, it is also tenable that the first letter ('ph') may have been added on arbitrarily to *editia*, which would suggest the way of life and eating (*edode*). They would gather in groups of fifteen or thereabouts, more or less. Each member of the mess would contribute every month a *medimnus* of barley-meal, eight *choes* of wine, five *minas* of cheese, five half-*minas* of figs, and in addition just a small sum of money for fish or meat.[33] Besides, anyone who had made an offering of first-fruits or had been hunting sent a share to the mess. For whenever anyone made a sacrifice or was back late from hunting, he was allowed to have dinner at home, but others had to be at the mess. This practice of messing together was for a long time strictly maintained. Certainly when King Agis returned from the campaign in which

he had defeated the Athenians, he wanted to eat at home with his wife and called for his portions; the *polemarchs* would not send them. Next day in his fury he did not carry out the required sacrifice, and they then fined him.[34]

The boys, too, used to frequent the messes: for them it was like being brought to a school for self-discipline, where they both heard political discussion and witnessed the kind of entertainments appropriate for free men. For their own part they would grow used to making fun and joking without becoming indecent, as well as not taking offence when they were the butt of the joke. In fact this ability to take a joke would seem to be very Spartan. If a joke was too much for someone to take, he could plead with the person making it, and the latter left off.

The oldest member indicated the doors to each person entering and said: 'Not a word goes out through these.' By all accounts anyone desiring to join a mess[35] was vetted in the following way. Each member would take a piece of soft bread in his hand and in silence would throw it, like a ballot, into the bowl which a servant carried on his head. Those in favour threw the bread as it was, while those against squeezed it hard with their hand. The effect of a squeezed piece is that of a hollow ballot.[36] And should they find even one of these, they do not admit the would-be entrant because it is their wish that all should be happy in each other's company. They refer to somebody rejected in this way as *kaddished*, since the bowl into which they throw the pieces of bread is called a *kaddichos*.

The food they think most highly of is the black broth.[37] Thus the older men do not even ask for a helping of meat but leave it to the young ones, while they have broth poured out for themselves and make a meal of it. There is a story that one of the kings of Pontus even bought a Laconian cook for the sake of the broth, but after tasting it was not pleased. At this the cook declared: 'This is broth to be savoured, O king, by those who have bathed in the Eurotas.' After moderate drinking they depart without a torch. Neither for this journey nor for any other are they allowed to walk with a light, so that they should grow used to the darkness and to travelling cheerfully and fearlessly by night. This, then, is how the messes are organized.

13. Lycurgus did not put his laws in writing: in fact one of the so-called *rhetras* is a prohibition[38] to this effect. Instead he reckoned that the guiding principles of most importance for the happiness and excellence of a state would remain securely fixed if they were embedded in the citizens' character and training.[39] This approach would forge a stronger commitment to such principles than the sense of compulsion induced in the young by education, when it gives a full picture of the legislator's arrangements for each of them. In his view it was also better that minor financial agreements where needs change from time to time should not be bound by written constraints and fixed conventions, but that additions and deletions to be made as circumstances require should be allowed for, subject to the approval of experts. In fact he made his whole legislative endeavour altogether depend upon education.[40]

Thus, as has been explained, one of the *rhetras* prohibited the use of written laws. Another in turn was directed against extravagance, to the effect that in every house the ceiling should be made with an axe, and the doors only with a saw, not with any other tools. This idea, which Epaminondas is later said to have expressed at his own table – that there was no treason in such a meal[41] – first occurred to Lycurgus, in that there was no place for luxury or extravagance in a house of this type, nor was there anybody so lacking in taste and intelligence as to bring into a plain, common house beds with legs of silver and bedspreads of purple, as well as gold goblets and the extravagance consequent upon them. Instead, of necessity the bed fits the house and matches it, while the same is true of the bedcovers in relation both to the bed and to the rest of the furniture and fittings. It was such conditioning which (according to the story) prompted the elder Leotychidas,[42] when he was dining at Corinth and viewed the lavish, coffered design of the ceiling of the room, to ask his host if timber there grew square.

A third *rhetra* of Lycurgus is recorded, which banned frequent campaigns against the same foes, so that these should not grow used to defending themselves and thus become skilled in warfare. And this complaint was later laid most notably against King Agesilaus, that by his numerous constant forays and expeditions against Boeotia he made the Thebans a match for the Spartans. Thus when Antalcidas saw him wounded,[43] he remarked: 'What a splendid tuition fee you are receiving from the Thebans for having taught them to fight when they had neither the wish nor the knowledge to do so.'

Ordinances such as these, then, Lycurgus called *rhetras*, because they were considered to come from the god and to be oracles.

14. Since he regarded the upbringing of children as the greatest and noblest responsibility of the legislator, at an early stage he took his start from that by first showing concern for matters relating to marriages and births. Aristotle[44] claims wrongly that he tried to discipline the women but gave up when he could not control the considerable degree of licence and power attained by women because of their husbands' frequent campaigning. At these times the men were forced to leave them in full charge, and consequently they used to dance attendance on them to an improper extent and call them their Ladyships. Lycurgus, rather, showed all possible concern for them too. First he toughened the girls physically by making them run and wrestle and throw the discus and javelin. Thereby their children in embryo would make a strong start in strong bodies and would develop better, while the women themselves would also bear their pregnancies with vigour and would meet the challenge of childbirth in a successful, relaxed way. He did away with prudery, sheltered upbringing and effeminacy of any kind.[45] He made young girls no less than young men grow used to walking nude in processions, as well as to dancing and singing at certain festivals with the young men present and looking on. On some occasions the girls would make fun of each of the young men, helpfully criticizing their mistakes. On other occasions they would rehearse in song the praises which they had composed about those meriting them, so that they filled the youngsters with a great sense of ambition and rivalry. For the one who was praised for his manliness and became a celebrated figure to the girls went off priding himself on their compliments; whereas the jibes of their playful humour were no less cutting than warnings of a

serious type, especially as the kings and the Elders attended the spectacle along with the rest of the citizens.

There was nothing disreputable about the girls' nudity. It was altogether modest, and there was no hint of immorality. Instead it encouraged simple habits and an enthusiasm for physical fitness, as well as giving the female sex a taste of masculine gallantry, since it too was granted equal participation in both excellence and ambition. As a result the women came to talk as well as to think in the way that Leonidas' wife Gorgo[46] is said to have done. For when some woman, evidently a foreigner, said to her: 'You Laconian women are the only ones who can rule men,' she replied: 'That is because we are the only ones who give birth to men.'

15. There were then also these inducements to marry. I mean the processions of girls, and the nudity, and the competitions which the young men watched, attracted by a compulsion not of an intellectual type, but (as Plato[47] says) a sexual one. In addition Lycurgus placed a certain civil disability on those who did not marry, for they were excluded from the spectacle of the Gymnopaediae. In winter the magistrates would order them to parade naked in a circle round the *agora*, and as they paraded they sang a special song composed about themselves, which said that their punishment was fair because they were flouting the laws. In addition they were deprived of the respect and deference which young men habitually showed their elders. Thus nobody objected to what was said to Dercyllidas,[48] even though he was a distinguished general. When he approached, one of the younger men did not give up his seat to him, but said: 'You have produced no son who will give his seat to me.'

The custom was to capture women for marriage – not when they were slight or immature, but when they were in their prime and ripe for it. The so-called 'bridesmaid' took charge of the captured girl. She first shaved her head to the scalp, then dressed her in a man's cloak and sandals, and laid her down alone on a mattress in the dark. The bridegroom – who was not drunk and thus not impotent, but was sober as always – first had dinner in the messes, then would slip in, undo her belt, lift her and carry her to the bed. After spending only a short time with her, he would depart discreetly so as to sleep wherever he usually did along with the other young men. And this continued to be his practice thereafter: while spending the days with his contemporaries, and going to sleep with them, he would warily visit his bride in secret, ashamed and apprehensive in case someone in the house might notice him. His bride at the same time devised schemes and helped to plan how they might meet each other unobserved at suitable moments. It was not just for a short period that young men would do this, but for long enough that some might even have children before they saw their own wives in daylight. Such intercourse was not only an exercise in self-control and moderation, but also meant that partners were fertile physically, always fresh for love, and ready for intercourse rather than being sated and pale from unrestricted sexual activity. Moreover some lingering glow of desire and affection was always left in both.

After making marriage as modest and orderly as this, Lycurgus showed equal concern for removing absurd, unmanly jealousy. While excluding from marriage any kind of outrageous and disorderly behaviour, he made it honourable for worthy men to share children and their production, and derided people who hold that there can be no combination or sharing of such things, and who avenge any by assassinations and wars. Thus if an older man with a young wife should take a liking to one of the well-bred young men and approve of him, he might well introduce him to her so as to fill her with noble sperm and then adopt the child as his own. Conversely a respectable man who admired someone else's wife noted for her lovely children and her good sense, might gain the husband's permission to sleep with her – thereby planting in fruitful soil, so to speak, and producing fine children who would be linked to fine ancestors by blood and family.

First and foremost Lycurgus considered children to belong not privately to their fathers, but jointly to the city, so that he wanted citizens produced not from random partners, but from the best. Moreover he observed a good deal of stupidity and humbug in others' rules on these matters. Such people have their bitches and mares mounted by the finest dogs and stallions whose owners they can prevail upon for a favour or fee. But their wives they lock up and guard, claiming the right to produce *their* children exclusively, even though they may be imbeciles, or past their prime, or diseased. They forget that where children are born of poor stock, the first to suffer from their poor condition are those who possess and rear them, while the same applies conversely to the good qualities of those from sound stock. What was thus practised in the interests of breeding and of the state was at that time so far removed from the laxity for which the women later became notorious, that there was absolutely no notion of adultery among them. There is a story recorded about Geradas, a Spartiate of really ancient times, who when asked by a foreigner what their punishment for adulterers was, said: 'There is no adulterer among us, stranger.' When the latter replied: 'But what if there should be one?', Geradas' answer was: 'His fine would be a great bull which bends over Mount Taygetus to drink from the Eurotas.' The foreigner was amazed at this and said: 'But how could there be a bull of such size?' At which Geradas laughed and said: 'But how could there be an adulterer at Sparta?' This, then, concludes my investigation of their marriages.

16. The father of a newborn child was not entitled to make his own decision about whether to rear it, but brought it in his arms to a particular spot termed a *lesche* where the eldest men of his tribe sat. If after examination the baby proved well-built and sturdy they instructed the father to bring it up, and assigned it one of the 9,000 lots of land.[49] But if it was puny and deformed, they dispatched it to what was called 'the place of rejection' ('Apothetae'), a precipitous spot by Mount Taygetus, considering it better both for itself and the state that the child should die if right from its birth it was poorly endowed for health or strength. And that is why women would test their babies' constitutions by washing them in wine instead of water. The effect of the unmixed wine on ailing and epileptic children is said to be that they lose their senses, and their limbs go stiff, whereas healthy ones are toughened by it and acquire a hardier consti-

tution. The children's nurses exercised special care and skill. To allow free development of limbs and physique, they dispensed with swaddling clothes. They trained children to eat up their food and not to be fussy about it, not to be frightened of the dark or of being left alone, and not to be prone to ill-bred fits of temper or crying. This is why some foreigners bought Laconian wet-nurses for their children. Amycla, who breast-fed the Athenian Alcibiades,[50] is said to have been a Spartan girl.[51]

When Alcibiades needed a tutor, however, Plato states that Pericles gave charge of him to one Zopyrus, who was no more than an ordinary slave. But Lycurgus did not put Spartiate children in the care of any tutors who had been bought or hired. Neither was it permissible for each father to bring up and educate his son in the way he chose. Instead, as soon as boys reached the age of seven, Lycurgus took charge of them all himself and distributed them into Troops:[52] here he accustomed them to live together and be brought up together, playing and learning as a group. The captaincy of the Troop was conferred upon the boy who displayed the soundest judgement and the best fighting spirit. The others kept their eyes on him, responded to his instructions, and endured their punishments from him, so that altogether this training served as a practice in learning ready obedience. Moreover as they exercised boys were constantly watched by their elders, who were always spurring them on to fight and contend with one another: in this their chief object was to get to know each boy's character, in particular how bold he was, and how far he was likely to stand his ground in combat.

The boys learned to read and write no more than was necessary. Otherwise their whole education was aimed at developing smart obedience, perseverance under stress, and victory in battle. So as they grew older they intensified their physical training, and got into the habit of cropping their hair, going barefoot, and exercising naked. From the age of twelve they never wore a tunic, and were given only one cloak a year. Their bodies were rough, and knew nothing of baths or oiling: only on a few days in the year did they experience such delights. They slept together by Squadron[53] and Troop on mattresses which they made up for themselves from the tips of reeds growing along the River Eurotas, broken off by hand without the help of any iron blade. During winter they added the so-called thistle-down and mixed it into the mattresses, since it was a substance thought to give out warmth.

17. By this age the boys came to be courted by lovers from among the respectable young men. The older men, too, showed even more interest, visiting the gymnasia frequently and being present when the boys fought and joked with one another. This was not just idle interest: instead there was a sense in which everyone regarded himself as father, tutor and commander of each boy. As a result everywhere, on all occasions, there would be somebody to reprimand and punish the boy who slipped up. In addition a Trainer-in-Chief[54] was appointed from among the men with outstanding qualities; they in turn chose as leader for each Troop the one out of the so-called Eirens who had the most discretion and fighting spirit. Those who have proceeded two years beyond the boys' class[55] are termed Eirens, and the oldest boys Melleirens ('prospective Eirens').

So such an Eiren, twenty years of age, commands those under him in his Troop's fights, while in his quarters he has them serve him his meals like servants. The burlier boys he instructs to bring wood, the slighter ones to collect vegetables. They steal what they fetch, some of them entering gardens, others slipping into the men's messes with a fine mixture of cunning and caution. If a boy is caught, he receives many lashes of the whip for proving to be a clumsy, unskilled thief. The boys also steal whatever provisions they can, thereby learning how to pounce skilfully upon those who are asleep or keeping guard carelessly. A boy is beaten and goes hungry if he is caught. The aim of providing them with only sparse fare is that they should be driven to make up its deficiencies by resort to daring and villainy. While this is the main purpose of their scanty diet, a subsidiary one is claimed to be the development of their physique, helping them in particular to grow tall. When people over-eat, their breathing is laboured, thus producing a broad, squat frame. In contrast if breath suffers from only slight delay and difficulty and has an easy ascent, the body is enabled to develop freely and comfortably. Good looks are produced in the same way. For where lean, spare features respond to articulation, the sheer weight of obese, over-fed ones makes them resist it. In the same way perhaps, women who take a purge during pregnancy bear babies which are small, but nonetheless have a good, neat shape, since their matter is more amenable to moulding because of its lightness. All the same, why this should be so is an open question still to be investigated.

18. The care which the boys take over their stealing is illustrated by the story of the one who had stolen a fox cub and had it concealed inside his cloak: in order to escape detection he was prepared to have his insides clawed and bitten out by the animal, and even to die. This tale is certainly not incredible, judging from Spartan ephebes[56] today. I have witnessed many of them dying under the lashes they received at the altar of Artemis Orthia.[57]

As he reclined after his meal the Eiren would tell one boy to sing, while to another he would pose a question which called for a considered reply, like 'Who among the men is the best?', or 'What is your opinion of so-and-so's action?' Thereby boys grew accustomed to judging excellence and to making a critical appraisal of the citizens right from the start. When asked which citizen was good, or whose reputation was low, the boy who proved to be at a loss for an answer was regarded as a sluggard whose mind showed no sign of any ambition to excel. Answers had to be reasoned, supported by argument, and at the same time expressed with brevity and conciseness. A bite on the thumb by the Eiren was the punishment for a boy who gave a wrong answer. The Eiren often used to chastise boys in the presence of elders and magistrates, thus offering a demonstration that his punishments were reasonable and necessary. He was permitted to administer punishment without interference, but once the boys had been dismissed he had to give an explanation if his punishments were harsher than necessary or, in contrast, if they were considered inappropriately light.

Whether a boy's standing was good or bad, his lover shared it. There is a story that once when a boy had let slip a despicable cry in the course of a fight, it was his lover whom the magistrates fined. Sexual relationships of this type were so highly valued that respectable women would in fact have love affairs with unmarried girls. Yet there was no rivalry; instead, if individual males found that their affections had the same object, they made this the foundation for mutual friendship, and eagerly pursued joint efforts to perfect their loved one's character.

19. Boys were further taught to express themselves in a style which was at once sharp, yet at the same time attractive and suited to concise exposition of a variety of points. While in the case of his iron money, as I have explained, Lycurgus arranged for heavy weight to be matched by low value, he did the opposite for the currency of speech. Here he developed the technique of expressing a wide range of ideas in just a few, spare words. In his scheme boys, by staying silent most of the time, were led to give pithy, well-trained answers. By contrast the talk of the person who babbles constantly turns out vapid and mindless, just as excessive sexual activity for the most part leads to barrenness and sterility. Indeed when some Athenian made a joke about how short Laconian swords were, and spoke of the ease with which theatrical conjurors swallow them, King Agis retorted: 'All the same, we certainly reach the enemy with our daggers.'[58] While the Laconian style of speech may seem brief, in my view it certainly does penetrate to the heart of a matter, and makes a forcible impression upon its hearers' minds.

Judging by his recorded remarks, Lycurgus himself in fact seems to have been a man of just a few, well-chosen words. Take, for instance, what he said about government to the person who advocated making the city a democracy: 'Make your own household a democracy first.' And his remark about sacrifices to the person who inquired why the ones he arranged were so small and economical: 'So that we may never cease to honour the gods.' Moreover, when it came to athletics, he would permit citizens to take part only in those games where a hand is not raised.[59] There are accounts of similar replies which he made to the citizens by letter. Asked: 'How should we repel an enemy attack?' he replied: 'If you stay poverty-stricken and each man among you has no passion to be greater than another.' And again with reference to walls he said: 'A city cannot be unfortified if it is ringed with brave men and not bricks.' It is difficult to say, however, just how much credence should be attached to these letters and others like them.

20. Spartans' distaste for prolixity can be demonstrated from their pointed remarks. For instance, when somebody engaged Leonidas at an inappropriate moment about business which was by no means trivial, the king said: 'Friend, the question you raise is a good one, but your timing is not good.' When Charilaus, Lycurgus' nephew, was asked why his uncle had made so few laws, his reply was that men of few words need few laws. There was criticism of the sophist Hecataeus in some quarters because he had been invited to the mess, and would then say nothing; Archidamidas'[60] response was that: 'An expert at speaking also knows when to do so.'

Here are some cxamples of those remarks which I mentioned earlier as being sharp, yet attractive. A wretched character bombarded Demaratus[61] with inopportune questions, and in particular the persistent query: 'Who is the best of the Spartiates?' Demaratus' answer was: 'The one least like you.' When approval was being expressed of the Eleans' expert and fair management of the Olympic Games, Agis[62] inquired: 'What is so remarkable about fair conduct by the Eleans on one day every four years?' When some foreigner was expressing his goodwill towards Sparta and claiming that in his own city he was called a friend of Sparta, Theopompus said: 'Stranger, it would be more honourable for you to be called a friend of your own city.' The reaction of Pausanias' son, Pleistoanax,[63] to an Athenian politician's disparagement of Spartans as uneducated, was to say: 'Your point is correct, since we are the only Greeks who have learned nothing wicked from you Athenians.' Archidamidas' answer to a man who inquired how many Spartiates there were was: 'Enough, my friend, to keep out undesirables.'

The Spartans' character may equally be illustrated from their humorous remarks. It was their habit never to waste words and to articulate nothing which did not in some way or other contain an idea meriting serious consideration. One Spartan[64] on being invited to listen to a man imitating the nightingale replied: 'I've heard the nightingale herself.' Another on reading this epitaph:

> These men were once cut down by brazen Ares[65] as they were
> Extinguishing tyranny: they died around the gates of Selinus,

remarked: 'Those men deserved to die because they should have let tyranny burn out totally.' When someone promised to give a young man cockerels that would die in combat, the latter retorted: 'Don't give me those, but let me have ones that kill in combat.' Another Spartan, when he saw men sitting on stools in a lavatory, declared: 'May I never sit where it is impossible for me to get up and offer my seat to an older man.' This, then, was the character of their sayings, and it justifies some people's claim that devotion to the intellect is more characteristic of Spartans than love of physical exercise.

21. They were no less enthusiastic about training in lyric poetry and singing than they were about good style and purity in speech. Moreover their songs offered stimulus to rouse the spirit and encouragement for energetic, effective action; in style they were plain and unpretentious, while their subject-matter was serious and calculated to mould character. For the most part they were praises applauding the good fortune of those who had died for Sparta; condemnations of cowards (*tresantes*)[66] whose lives were filled with grief and misery; and promises to be brave, or boasts about their bravery, depending upon the singers' ages. There is value in citing by way of illustration one example of the last type. At festivals three choirs would be formed corresponding to the three age groups. The choir of old men would sing first:

> 'We were once valiant young men.'

Next the choir of men in their prime would respond with the words:

> 'But we are the valiant ones now; put us to the test, if you wish.'

Then the third choir, that of the boys, would sing:

> 'But we shall be far mightier.'

Altogether anyone who has studied Spartan poetry (some specimens of which have survived even to the present day), and has examined the marching rhythms which they used to an accompaniment of pipes when advancing upon the enemy, would not think both Terpander and Pindar[67] wrong to connect bravery and music. The former wrote as follows about the Spartans:

> Young men's warlike spirit flourishes there, along with
> The clear-sounding Muse and Justice in the wide streets.

Pindar says:

> The councils of old men
> Are pre-eminent there, and the spears of young men,
> And choirs and the Muse and Festivity.

Thus the two poets portray the Spartans as being at one and the same time the most musical and the most warlike of people: 'Fine lyre-playing matches iron weaponry,' as the Spartan poet[68] has put it. In fact at time of battle the king would first sacrifice to the Muses, thereby apparently reminding his men of their training and their trials, so that they should be ready to face the dangers ahead, and should perform memorable feats in the fighting.

22. It was in wartime that they relaxed the harshest elements of the young men's training: they did not stop them grooming their hair and decorating their weapons and clothes, but were pleased at the sight of them like horses prancing and neighing before a contest. So they wore their hair long as soon as they had passed the age of ephebes; they took particular care over it in the face

of danger, making it look sleek and combing it. They bore in mind one of Lycurgus' statements about long hair, that it renders handsome men better looking, and ugly ones more frightening. On campaign also their physical exercises were less demanding and they permitted the young men a lifestyle which was generally less subject to punishment and scrutiny, with the result that for them uniquely among mankind war represented a respite from their military training. Once their phalanx[69] was marshalled together in sight of the enemy, the king sacrificed the customary she-goat, instructed everyone to put on garlands, and ordered the pipers to play Castor's Air.[70] At the same time he began the marching paean, so that it was a sight at once solemn and terrifying to see them marching in step to the pipes, creating no gap in the phalanx nor suffering any disturbance of spirit, but approaching the confrontation calmly and happily in time to the music. In all likelihood men in this frame of mind feel neither fear nor exceptional anger, but with hope and courage they steadily maintain their purpose, believing heaven to be with them.

The king advanced against the enemy with an escort of those who had won a contest for which the prize was a crown. The story is told of one man at the Olympic Games who, when offered an immense sum of money, refused it and with a great struggle beat his opponent in wrestling. When he was asked: 'What have you gained by your victory, Spartan?', he replied with a smile: 'In battle against the enemy my place will be in front of the king.' After they had beaten the enemy and made them flee, they gave chase only far enough to confirm the victory by their opponents' flight, and then at once pulled back, because in their view it was neither noble nor Hellenic to butcher and slaughter men who had given up and yielded their ground. This practice was not only splendid and magnanimous, it also paid dividends: it was known that Spartans would kill those who stood in their way, but would spare those who surrendered, so that adversaries saw it as more advantageous to flee than to stand their ground.

23. Hippias the sophist states that Lycurgus personally enjoyed making war and took part in many campaigns, while according

to Philostephanus he was even responsible for forming the cavalry into *oulami*. Under his arrangements an *oulamus* was a body of fifty cavalrymen marshalled in a square formation. Demetrius of Phalerum, however, says that he had no involvement in military actions and established his constitution in peacetime. Certainly his scheme for the Olympic truce does seem to bear the stamp of a mild man of peaceful disposition. And yet, as Hermippus mentions, some say that Lycurgus was initially neither interested in Iphitus' group, nor associated with them, but just happened to be at Olympia for other reasons as a spectator. In this version he heard behind him what sounded like a man's voice criticizing him and expressing surprise at his failure to urge citizens to take part in the festival. But when he turned round, the person who had spoken was nowhere to be seen, so he considered the voice to be divine, joined Iphitus, and was his partner in putting the festival on a more illustrious and secure footing.

24. Spartiates' training extended into adulthood, for no one was permitted to live as he pleased. Instead, just as in a camp, so in the city, they followed a prescribed lifestyle and devoted themselves to communal concerns. They viewed themselves absolutely as part of their country, rather than as individuals, and so unless assigned a particular job they would always be observing the boys and giving them some useful piece of instruction, or learning themselves from their elders. Abundant leisure was unquestionably among the wonderful benefits which Lycurgus had conferred upon his fellow citizens. While he totally banned their involvement in any manual craft, there was equally no need for them to amass wealth (with all the work and concentration which that entails), since riches were emphatically neither envied nor esteemed. The helots worked the land for them and paid over the amount mentioned earlier.[71] There was a Spartiate who happened to be in Athens when the courts were sitting, and he learned that a man who had incurred some penalty for refusal to work[72] was going home depressed, escorted by sympathetic friends who shared his mood. The Spartiate requested those who were there with him to point out

this man who had been penalized for his freedom. This illustrates how they thought of a preoccupation with working at a craft and with moneymaking as only fit for slaves! As might be expected, legal disputes disappeared along with coinage, since there was no longer greed nor want among them, but instead equal enjoyment of plenty and the sense of ease which comes from simple living. Except when they went on campaign, all their time was taken up by choral dances, festivals, feasts, hunting expeditions, physical exercise and conversation.

25. Those under the age of thirty generally would not do their own shopping, but would have their domestic needs met by relatives and lovers. It was equally frowned upon for older men to be seen constantly taking time over these matters rather than spending most of the day around the gymnasia and the so-called *leschae*. By meeting in these they would make suitable use of their leisure together. No remarks would be passed about anything relating to moneymaking or commercial dealings. Instead the main function of the time spent thus would be to bestow some praise on good conduct or criticism on bad – in a light-hearted, humorous way which made warning and correction easy to accept. In fact Lycurgus himself was not uncompromisingly austere. But rather, according to Sosibius, it was he who dedicated the little statue of Laughter[73] with the idea of suitably introducing humour to their drinking-parties and such diversions, so as to sweeten their rigorous lifestyle.

Altogether he accustomed citizens to have no desire for a private life, nor knowledge of one, but rather to be like bees, always attached to the community, swarming together around their leader, and almost ecstatic with fervent ambition to devote themselves entirely to their country. This attitude can also be detected in some of their remarks. When Pedaritus[74] was not selected as one of the Three Hundred, he withdrew looking very cheerful, thus expressing his happiness that the city possessed 300 men better than he was. Polystratidas, as one of a group of envoys to the Great King's generals, was asked by them whether they were taking a private initiative, or had been sent by the state. His reply was: 'If we succeed, the latter; if we fail, the former.' When some Amphipolitans came to Sparta and visited Brasidas'[75] mother, Argileonis, she asked them if his death had been a noble one, worthy of Sparta. As they were heaping praise on him and claiming that there was no one in Sparta to match him, she declared: 'Don't say that, strangers. Noble and brave Brasidas was, but Sparta has many better men than he.'

26. As already mentioned, Lycurgus himself appointed Elders initially from among those who had been associated with his plan. But later he arranged that whenever an Elder died his place should be taken by the man over sixty whose merits were regarded as most outstanding. And this contest seemed to be the greatest in the world and the one most worth competing for. In it a man was to be chosen not as the swiftest of swift men nor the strongest of strong ones, but as the best and wisest of the good and wise, who as a lifelong reward for his merits would have in effect sweeping authority in the state, with control over death and loss of citizen rights and the most important matters generally. The selection was made in the following way. The assembly gathered, and picked men were shut up in a nearby building where they could neither see out nor be seen, but could only hear the shouts of those in the assembly. For in this instance, as in others, it was by shouting that they decided between the competitors. These were brought in, not all together, but one by one in an order determined by lot, and each walked through the assembly in silence. The men who had been shut up had writing-tablets, and so in each case they noted the volume of shouting without knowing the identity of the competitor, except that he was the first brought in, or the second, or the third, and so on. Whoever was met with the most shouting, and the loudest, was the man declared elected. Then, wearing a crown, he made a round of the sanctuaries of the gods. He was followed by many young men full of admiration and praise for him, and by many women who sang in celebration of his excellence and proclaimed his good fortune in life. Everyone close to him would serve him a meal, with a declaration that the dinner was a sign of the city's respect. After making his round he went off to his mess. Here everything was as usual for him except that he was

served a second portion, which he took and kept by him. After the meal, when his female relatives gathered at the entrance to the mess, he would call forward the one for whom he had the highest esteem, and present the portion, saying that he was giving to her this mark of distinction which he had received. Consequently she too was congratulated and escorted by the other women.

27. Furthermore Lycurgus made excellent arrangements for their funerals. First he removed all superstition by not placing any ban on burial of the dead within the city or on siting tombs close to temples. Thus through their upbringing young people came to regard such sights as familiar and normal; they were not disturbed by them, nor did they fear death as liable to pollute anyone who touched a corpse or walked between gravestones. Secondly Lycurgus did not allow anything to be buried with the dead: instead they would lay out the body wrapped just in a red cloak[76] and olive leaves. Those who buried a dead person were not permitted to inscribe the name on a grave except in the cases of a man who had died on campaign or a woman who had died in labour.[77] He prescribed only a brief period of mourning – eleven days. On the twelfth day mourners were to sacrifice to Demeter and abandon their grief.[78] In truth Lycurgus left nothing undone or neglected, but incorporated into each essential function some stimulus to good conduct or disparagement of bad. Indeed he completely filled the city with a quantity of models which would necessarily be encountered all the time by those aiming for excellence, and become familiar to them, so that they would be guided and influenced in this way.

Consequently he did not grant Spartiates permission to be away from the city and to travel freely, acquiring foreign habits and copying lifestyles based upon no training as well as types of government different from that of Sparta. In fact he even expelled those people who were pouring into the city and congregating there for no useful purpose. He was not afraid (as Thucydides[79] claims) that they might imitate the form of government or might gain some knowledge to enhance their personal qualities: his fear was rather that they might develop into teachers of evil practices. By definition foreigners must bring in foreign ideas with them, and novel ideas lead to novel attitudes. Hence inevitably many emotions and preferences emerge which – if the existing government be likened to a piece of music – are out of tune with it. Thus it was the need to protect the city from being invaded by harmful practices which concerned him more than any physical infection by unhealthy immigrants.

28. In all this there is no trace of the inequity or arrogance with which Lycurgus' laws are charged by some people: in their view the laws are well designed to develop valour, but fail to foster the practice of justice. It may be that Plato[80] was likewise led to this opinion of Lycurgus and his constitution because of the Spartiates' so-called *krypteia* – assuming this really was one of Lycurgus' institutions, as Aristotle has maintained. Its character was as follows.[81]

Periodically the overseers of the young men would dispatch into the countryside in different directions the ones who appeared to be particularly intelligent; they were equipped with daggers and basic rations, but nothing else. By day they would disperse to obscure spots in order to hide and rest. At night they made their way to roads and murdered any helot whom they caught. Frequently, too, they made their way through the fields, killing the helots who stood out for their physique and strength. Similarly in his *History of the Peloponnesian War*[82] Thucydides tells how those helots who had been singled out by the Spartiates for their bravery were first crowned as if they had been granted their freedom, and made a round of the sanctuaries of the gods; but then a little later they all vanished – over 2,000 of them – and nobody either at the time itself or later was able to explain how they had been eliminated. Aristotle makes the further notable point that immediately upon taking up office the ephors would declare war on the helots, so that they could be killed without pollution.

In other ways, too, Spartiates' treatment of helots was callous and brutal. They would force them, for instance, to drink quantities of unmixed wine[83] and then they would bring them into messes to show the young men what drunkenness was like. They would also order them to perform songs and dances which were vulgar and ludicrous, while excluding them from ones fit for free men. So later, according to reports, when Theban forces penetrated Laconia[84] and told the helots they captured to sing the works of Terpander and Alcman and Spendon the Spartan,[85] the latter declined to, claiming that their masters did not approve. The class distinction is reflected fully in the statement that there is nothing to match either the freedom of the free man at Sparta or the slavery of the slave.[86] In my view such ill-treatment on the part of the Spartiates only developed later – especially after the Great Earthquake, when the helots are said to have taken the offensive with the Messenians, to have done the country tremendous damage and to have posed a dire threat to the city.[87] Personally I would not attribute such a foul exercise as the *krypteia* to Lycurgus: in my estimation his disposition was otherwise mild and fair, a view which the god[88] showed that he shared too.

29. Once he saw that his most vital measures had gained firm acceptance, and the form of government fostered by him was acquiring enough strength to support and protect itself unaided, then, like the god in Plato's description[89] who was delighted at his universe coming into being and making its first movement, Lycurgus was deeply moved and well pleased by the beauty and extent of his legislation now that it was in action and proceeding on its way. In so far as human foresight could achieve this, he longed to leave it immortal and immutable in the future. So he summoned everyone to an assembly and declared that while what had already been established was sufficient and appropriate to secure the happiness and excellence of the state, there remained the greatest, most essential measure, which would not be disclosed to them before he had consulted the oracle. Consequently they must abide by the laws laid down without dropping or changing any until he should return in person from Delphi. On his return he would do whatever the god recommended. When they unanimously agreed to this and urged him to proceed, Lycurgus made first the kings and Elders, and

then the other citizens, swear that they would abide by the established constitution, and continue to use it until he should return. Then he set out for Delphi.

Once he had reached the oracle and sacrificed to the god, he inquired if the laws which he had laid down were of sufficient quality to secure the happiness and excellence of the state. The god replied that the quality of the laws was high and that by adhering to Lycurgus' constitution the city would enjoy the most brilliant reputation. Lycurgus had this oracle written down and sent it to Sparta. He then made a second, personal sacrifice to the god, embraced his friends and his son, and determined never to release the citizens from their oath, but to commit voluntary suicide on the spot. He had reached an age when a choice can properly be made of whether or not to go on living, and when those close to him seemed comfortably enough settled. So he starved himself to death. In his opinion it was wrong for a statesman's death to be of no benefit to his city or for the ending of his life to be valueless; instead there should be an element of distinction and effectiveness about it. In his own case, after his wonderful achievements, his end really would serve to crown his good fortune. As to the citizens, he would leave them his death as guarantor of the excellent benefits which he had provided for them during his lifetime, since they had sworn to observe his constitution until he should return. And he was not mistaken in his reckoning, since Sparta occupied the front rank in Greece for Good Order and reputation for some 500 years thanks to her use of the laws of Lycurgus, which were not altered by any of the fourteen kings after him down to Agis the son of Archidamus.[90] For the institution of ephors served to reinforce the constitution rather than weaken it, and even though it appeared to be to the people's advantage, in fact it strengthened the aristocracy.

30. But during Agis' reign money first poured into Sparta, and with money there developed greed and a passion for riches. Lysander[91] was responsible, because even though incorruptible himself, he filled his country with a passion for wealth and luxury through bringing back gold and silver from the war, and

thereby undermining the laws[92] of Lycurgus. Previously, while these prevailed, it was not so much the constitution of a state which Sparta followed as the lifestyle of a trained, intelligent individual. To put it differently, just as poets tell stories of Heracles roaming the world with his lion-skin and his club, punishing lawless and bestial despots, so this city used to control a willingly compliant Greece with just a *skytale* and cloak. She would disband unjust juntas and tyrannies in the states, as well as arbitrating in wars and quelling civil strife, frequently without having raised a single shield, but merely with the dispatch of one envoy, to whose instructions everyone would instantly respond, like bees which on the appearance of their leader cluster together and range themselves in order. This demonstrates how outstanding was Sparta's Good Order and justice!

Personally I am surprised by the claim that while the Spartans knew how to obey, they had no idea of how to command. Those who make this claim endorse the remark of King Theopompus, who when somebody said that Sparta was preserved by her kings' talent for command, replied: 'No, by her citizens' readiness to obey.' Men do not submit to orders from those with no ability for leadership, but such obedience is in fact a lesson taught by the commander. (It is the good leader who produces good followers. Just as the object of schooling a horse is to produce one that is docile and responsive, so the science of kingship has the function of instilling prompt obedience in men.) What the Spartans instilled in others was not just prompt obedience but a positive desire to come under their command and submit to them. It was not ships or money or hoplites that these other Greeks would ask Sparta to send them, but just a single Spartiate commander. Once they obtained him they would treat him with respect and awe, as the Sicilians and Chalcidians treated Gylippus and Brasidas[93] respectively, and all the Greeks living in Asia treated Lysander, Callicratidas and Agesilaus.[94] These men they termed *harmosts* and discipliners of peoples and rulers everywhere, while the Spartiates' entire city they viewed as a tutor or instructor in decent living and orderly government. It was this view which Stratonicus[95] seems to have been mocking when for a joke he proposed a law which required Athenians to supervise Mysteries and processions, and the Eleans to organize Games (because this is what they did most splendidly), while Spartans were to be whipped for any mistakes these others might make. This was proposed merely to raise a laugh. But Antisthenes the Socratic was more serious when he witnessed the Thebans' conceit after the battle of Leuctra and remarked that they were like youngsters made cocky because they had given their tutor a beating.

31. All the same it was not Lycurgus' main aim at the time to leave his city as the leader of so many other cities. Instead his view was that happiness in the life of a whole city, as in that of one individual, derives from its own merits and from its internal concord: it was to this end that all his arrangements and his structures were combined, so that Spartans should be free and self-sufficient, and should have the good sense to continue thus for a very long time. This theory of government was adopted by Plato, Diogenes, Zeno[96] and all those who are praised for their attempts to make some statement about these matters, even though they left only paper theories. Lycurgus on the other hand brought into the light of day, not paper theories, but a functioning constitution which is quite unmatched. To those who suspect that it is impracticable for a theoretical structure to be centred upon a Sage, he has exhibited his whole city practising philosophy, and has deservedly won greater renown than all those who have ever governed so far among the Greeks. It is for this reason that Aristotle claims the honours granted him at Sparta to be slighter than he merits, even though they are the highest ones. For he has a temple, and sacrifices are made to him every year as if to a god. Moreover it is said that when his remains had been brought home, lightning struck his tomb. This is something which has occurred in the case of hardly any other famous later person except Euripides,[97] who died and was buried near Arethusa in Macedonia. Consequently the fact that what happened to him after his death had occurred previously only in the case of a man who was outstandingly devout and dear to the gods is for admirers of Euripides a strong argument and piece of evidence in his favour.

Some say that Lycurgus died in Cirrha; Apollothemis says that he had been conveyed to Elis; Timaeus and Aristoxenus say that he ended his life in Crete, and Aristoxenus claims that Cretans point out his tomb at Pergamia by the 'Strangers' road. It is said further that he left an only son, Antiorus,[98] and when he died childless the family was extinct. But his comrades and relatives set up a kind of successor group which continued in existence a long time; and the days on which they used to meet they called 'Lycurgid'. Aristocrates the son of Hipparchus says that after Lycurgus' death in Crete his hosts burnt the body and scattered the ashes in the sea. They did this in accordance with his own request, for he wished to prevent his remains ever being brought back to Sparta, since such a return might cause the cancellation of his oath, followed by changes to the constitution. This concludes my treatment of Lycurgus.

AGESILAUS

1. Archidamus, the son of Zeuxidamus, proved himself to be an illustrious king of Sparta. When he died, he left a son Agis by Lampido, a woman of noble birth, and a much younger son, Agesilaus,[1] whose mother was Eupolia, the daughter of Melesippidas. Since Agis was the legitimate heir to the throne, it was expected that Agesilaus would spend his life as a private citizen, and he was therefore brought up according to what Spartans term the *agoge*,[2] an austere lifestyle, full of hardships, but also one designed to train young men to obey orders. It was for this reason, we are told, that Simonides[3] applied to Sparta the epithet 'man-taming', because the effect of her customs was above all to make her citizens obedient and submissive to the laws, like horses which are broken in as young as possible. The law exempts any heir-apparent to the throne from the necessity of undergoing this upbringing, and so Agesilaus was exceptional in this respect, namely that by the time he came to rule he did not lack training in obeying rules. The result was that he was on much more harmonious terms with his subjects than any of the other kings, because he possessed commanding and regal qualities by nature, and from the *agoge* acquired kindliness as well as a regard for people.

2. When he was a member of the so-called Troops[4] of boys brought up together, he had as his lover Lysander,[5] who was especially struck by his disciplined nature. Agesilaus was the most aggressive and competitive of the youngsters; he longed to be first in all things, and he had in him a vehemence and an impetuosity which defied all defeat or submission. Yet at the

same time he was so gentle and ready to obey authority that he did whatever was demanded of him. He acted in this way from a sense of honour, not of fear, and what upset him was any reprimand, rather than the imposition of hardships. As for the deformity in his lame leg, the beauty of his physique in the prime of his youth made it pass almost unnoticed, and the ease and light-heartedness with which he endured it went far to compensate for the disability, since he was the first to joke and make fun of himself on this subject. In fact his lameness served to reveal his ambition even more clearly, since he never allowed himself to abandon any struggle or venture on its account. No likeness of his appearance has come down to us, because he personally forbade any; he even declared on his deathbed that there was to be no statue or painting made of him. He is described as having been a small man with a rather insignificant presence. On the other hand, thanks to his cheerfulness and positive attitude in all circumstances, as well as his sense of humour (which lacked all trace of harshness or animosity in word or look), he inspired more affection even in old age than young, handsome men. But it is worth noting that Archidamus was fined[6] by the ephors, according to Theophrastus, for having married a small woman. They declared, 'She will bear us kinglets instead of kings.'

3. It was during Agis' reign that Alcibiades[7] reached Sparta from Sicily as a fugitive, and he had not been long in the city before he was accused of committing adultery with Timaea, King Agis' wife. When she bore a child, Agis refused to acknowledge it as his own, and declared that Alcibiades was the father. Duris[8] tells us that Timaea was not at all put out by this, and that when she was at home, in the presence of her helot maids, she would under her breath call the child Alcibiades instead of Leotychidas. Also according to Duris, Alcibiades himself said that he had seduced Timaea not out of mere passion, but because he cherished the ambition that his descendants should reign over the Spartiates. It was for this reason, namely fear of Agis, that Alcibiades decamped from Sparta. As for the child [Leotychidas], he was always regarded with suspicion by Agis, and

was never given the honours that a legitimate son would have received. However, when Agis fell ill, Leotychidas, on his knees, tearfully prevailed upon Agis to acknowledge him as his son in the presence of many witnesses. Even so, after Agis' death, Lysander – who, as a result of his naval victory over the Athenians,[9] had gained the greatest influence at Sparta – tried to promote Agesilaus' claim to the throne on the grounds that illegitimacy disqualified Leotychidas.[10] Many other citizens welcomed this initiative and gave their enthusiastic support because of Agesilaus' personal qualities, and because they had shared the same upbringing in the *agoge*. But there was a diviner in Sparta named Diopeithes, who had an extraordinary knowledge of ancient prophecies and enjoyed a great reputation for his skill in interpreting religious matters. He declared that it was contrary to the will of heaven for a lame man to become king of Sparta, and when the matter came before a court, he cited the following oracle:

> 'Though *you* are sound of limb, proud Sparta, beware
> That from your stock there stems no lame kingship.
> For then unlooked-for ordeals shall oppress you for ages,
> And the man-killing, rolling waves of war.'

Lysander's reply to this was that if the Spartiates were really disturbed by the oracle, it was against Leotychidas that they should be on their guard. It did not matter to the god that a man who was literally lame should become king; the danger was that he might not be legitimate nor even a descendant of Heracles,[11] and this is what 'lame kingship' referred to. For his part Agesilaus declared that Poseidon had testified to Leotychidas' illegitimacy, because an earthquake[12] of his had driven Agis from his bedroom, and after this more than ten months had elapsed before Leotychidas was born.

4. These were the circumstances in which Agesilaus ascended the throne. He at once proceeded to banish Leotychidas because of his illegitimacy, and to take possession of Agis' property. But observing that his relatives on his mother's side, although

respectable enough, were extremely poor, he distributed half of the property among them, and in this way made sure that his inheritance should bring him credit and goodwill instead of envy and hostility. As for Xenophon's assertion that, by obeying his countrymen's will in everything, Agesilaus gained so much power that he could do what he liked, the facts are as follows. At that time the supreme power in the state was exercised by the ephors and the Elders. Ephors hold office for only a year, while Elders enjoy their distinction for life – the role of both being to curb the exercise of absolute power by the kings, as I have explained in my *Lycurgus*.[13] This was why a state of perpetual feud and hostility had grown up from the very earliest times between the kings and these officeholders. Agesilaus, however, was determined to break with this tradition. Instead of opposing and clashing with these men, he cultivated them. He took no initiative without involving them, and if summoned, he hurried to the meeting at more than walking-pace. If ever the ephors appeared when he was seated on the throne and transacting business, he would rise, and on the induction of every new Elder he would send him a cloak and an ox as a mark of recognition. Thus all the time that he appeared to be honouring and exalting the dignity of their office, he was unobtrusively increasing his own authority and strengthening the power of the kingship through the goodwill which he attracted to himself.

5. In his dealings with the rest of the citizens he behaved with more principle towards his enemies than towards his friends. By this I mean that he would never act towards the former without just cause, but would sometimes associate himself with injustices committed by the latter. In the same way he was too generous not to give credit to his enemies if they were in the right, but he could not bring himself to condemn his friends if they were in the wrong, indeed he was even proud to aid and abet their offences. In short he considered that nothing done to help a friend was dishonourable. On the other hand, if any of his adversaries fell into misfortune, he would be the first to sympathize and show himself ready to help if they wished it,

and in this way he won the hearts and engaged the loyalty of his whole people. So when the ephors saw this they began to be afraid of his power, and fined him[14] on the ground that he was making the state's citizens into a personal following.

Now natural philosophers believe that if the forces of conflict and discord were to be eliminated from the universe, the heavenly bodies would stand still, and in the resulting complete harmony the process of motion and generation would be brought to a dead stop.[15] In the same way Sparta's lawgiver[16] seems to have introduced the spirit of ambition and contention into the constitution as an incitement to virtue. He wanted there always to be some point of difference between good men, and thus an element of rivalry among them. He believed that the kind of acquiescence which feebly gives way without contesting the intentions of the other side, and avoids any exertion or struggle, does not deserve the name of harmony. Some people believe that Homer, too, definitely thought the same, and that he would not have made Agamemnon rejoice on the occasion when Odysseus and Achilles are sufficiently carried away to abuse each other 'with fearsome words',[17] unless he thought that this rivalry and quarrelling between the chieftains would produce some large general benefit. However, it would be wrong to accept this notion unreservedly, since dissensions of this kind, if they are pushed to extremes, are harmful to states and carry great dangers with them.

6. Soon after Agesilaus had been raised to the throne, reports arrived from Asia that the Persian king was assembling a great fleet with which he intended to sweep the Spartans from the sea. Now Lysander was keen to be sent to Asia again in order to help his friends there; these were men whom he had left behind as governors and administrators of the cities, but who, because of their unjust and violent rule, were being driven out by the citizens and put to death. So he persuaded Agesilaus to undertake a campaign – to be fought on behalf of Greece, but very far from the mainland – which would cross the sea and strike first to anticipate the Persians' preparations. At the same time Lysander wrote to his friends in Asia urging them to contact

Sparta calling for Agesilaus to be their general. Accordingly Agesilaus appeared before the assembly and agreed to undertake the campaign if they would give him thirty Spartiates to act as commanders and advisers, a picked body of 2,000 *neodamodeis*, and a force of 6,000 allied troops. Thanks to Lysander's support, the assembly readily approved all this, and dispatched Agesilaus[18] at once with the thirty Spartiates. Lysander assumed the leadership of these advisers, not only because of his prestige and influence, but also because of his friendship with Agesilaus; the latter considered that in securing him this command Lysander had done him an even greater service than in raising him to the throne.

While this expedition was assembling at Geraestus, Agesilaus himself travelled with friends to Aulis, where he spent the night. As he slept, he dreamed that he heard a voice which said to him: 'King of the Spartans, you should be aware that no man has ever been chosen as the commander of all Greece except Agamemnon in time past, and now yourself. Since you command the same people, are making war against the same enemy, and setting out from the same place, it is right that you should offer to the goddess the same sacrifice as he did here before he set sail.' Agesilaus at once remembered how Agamemnon had sacrificed his own daughter in obedience to the soothsayers.[19] However, he did not allow himself to be disturbed by the dream, but as soon as he rose he told his friends about it, and said that he intended to honour the goddess with a sacrifice which she should find appropriately pleasing, but that he would not imitate the callous insensibility of his predecessor Agamemnon. He then had a hind crowned with garlands and gave orders for the sacrifice to be performed by his own diviner, instead of the one customarily appointed for the purpose by the Boeotians. So when the Boeotarchs[20] heard of this, they were very angry and sent their assistants to forbid Agesilaus to offer a sacrifice in a manner contrary to the laws and customs of the Boeotians. Not content with just delivering this message, these assistants also threw the hind's thighs off the altar. Agesilaus was very disturbed as he sailed away; he was furious with the Thebans, as well as pessimistic about the omen, which could signify that his enterprise would be frustrated and the expedition fail to achieve its purpose.

7. When he arrived at Ephesus, he was immediately irked and annoyed by Lysander's power and high reputation there. There was always a crowd milling round his door, and everyone was following him about and paying court to him, as if Agesilaus were no more than the nominal commander of the expedition and held this position only as a legal fiction, while the real power, supreme authority and overall initiative rested with Lysander. In fact no [Greek] general sent to Asia ever won so much glory or made himself so feared as Lysander, nor did anyone else confer greater rewards on his friends or inflict graver injuries on his enemies. People were still very much aware of all this, and when they observed Agesilaus' simple, plain and unassuming manner, and noted that Lysander's behaviour was as brusque, harsh and overbearing as before, they absolutely grovelled before Lysander and gave him their exclusive attention. As a result, first, the other Spartiates were deeply offended when they found themselves treated as subordinates of Lysander rather than as advisers to the king. Secondly, although Agesilaus was by no means an envious man, nor one who resented honours being paid to others, still he very much cherished ambitions of his own and was determined to assert himself, and he now began to fear that any brilliant success which he might achieve would be credited to Lysander because of his reputation. He therefore proceeded as follows.[21]

First, he opposed Lysander's advice. If there was any course of action which Lysander recommended enthusiastically, he made a point of putting it aside or ignoring it and of taking up another in its place. Next, whenever he believed that someone who approached him with a request had been specifically influenced by Lysander, he sent him away empty-handed. On the same principle, any party to a lawsuit for whom Lysander expressed contempt could be sure of winning his case, while by contrast, those whom Lysander was plainly eager to help would be hard put to avoid being fined. All this was done not casually but deliberately and systematically, and when Lysander understood the reason, he made no attempt to hide it from his friends. He told them that it was on his account they were being slighted, and he urged them to go and ingratiate themselves with the king and with those who possessed more influence than himself.

8. As even these remarks and actions of Lysander's appeared to have been designed to arouse ill-feeling against the king, Agesilaus determined to assail him still further. He appointed him to be his meat-carver, and (we are told) remarked in front of a large company, 'Now let all these petitioners go and pay court to my meat-carver.' Lysander, upset at this, said to him, 'I see, Agesilaus, that you know very well how to humiliate your friends.' 'Yes, I do,' the king retorted, 'or at any rate those who want to be more powerful than myself.' Lysander continued, 'Well, perhaps what you have said is wiser than what I have done. In that case, find me some post or some place where I can be useful to you without causing offence.'

After this, Lysander was sent to the Hellespont, and there he brought over to Agesilaus' side a Persian named Spithridates, who lived in Pharnabazus'[22] territory and had ample resources at his disposal, as well as 200 horsemen. But his anger never abated; for ever afterwards he continued to nurse his resentment, and plotted to deprive the two royal families of the crown and throw open the succession to all Spartiates alike. He might even have brought about a great upheaval in consequence of this quarrel, if he had not been forestalled by death on campaign[23] in Boeotia. We may note that ambitious spirits do far more harm than good in a state, unless they can keep their aspirations within proper limits. Yet even though Lysander behaved with an insufferable arrogance, as he undoubtedly did in pursuing his ambitions without any restraint, Agesilaus could surely have devised some less objectionable way of correcting the faults of a man of his distinction and ambitious temperament. As it was, they both seem to have suffered from a similar obsession, so that the one would not acknowledge the authority of his superior, while the other could not bear being ignored by his associate.

9. At first Tissaphernes[24] was afraid of Agesilaus and concluded a treaty with him by which he would release the Greek cities to him and free them from the Persian king's control. But later, when he believed he had gathered a strong enough force, he declared war, and Agesilaus gladly took up the challenge. He had high hopes for the campaign, and thought it would be dreadful if Xenophon and his Ten Thousand could reach the sea and defeat the Persian king in battle[25] as often as they chose, while he, the leader of the Spartans, who were supreme by land and sea, could achieve no success for the Greeks to remember. So he repaid Tissaphernes' treachery with a justifiable deception of his own, and indicated that he intended to march to Caria; but once his barbarian opponent had gathered forces there, he set off to raid Phrygia.[26] Here he captured many cities and seized a huge quantity of loot. In this way he demonstrated to his friends that to break a solemn agreement shows contempt for the gods, whereas to outwit one's enemy at once satisfies justice, earns great glory, and combines pleasure with profit.

However, since he was short of cavalry, and his sacrificial victims proved to lack lobes,[27] he fell back to Ephesus. Here he began to recruit a force of cavalry, and gave the well-to-do the alternative of furnishing a horse and rider if they did not wish to serve themselves. Many opted for this alternative, and so Agesilaus soon turned out to have a large force of aggressive horsemen instead of cowardly hoplites. In his view, Agamemnon had definitely shown great sense in accepting a good mare from a worthless rich man and then exempting him from military service.[28] Once, on Agesilaus' orders, the men responsible for selling off booty stripped the prisoners before offering them to buyers. As a result, the clothes found plenty of buyers, but the naked bodies – all white and tender because they had not been exposed to the sun – were derided as useless and worthless. Agesilaus, who was standing nearby, remarked, 'These are the men you fight, and these are the things you're fighting for.'

10. At the next season for invading enemy territory,[29] Agesilaus let it be known that he would march into Lydia, and on this occasion he had no intention of misleading Tissaphernes.

However, the latter managed to deceive himself, for he distrusted Agesilaus on account of the trick he had played before. He concluded that this time Agesilaus really would invade Caria, because its landscape is ill-suited for cavalry operations and he was still outmatched in cavalry. But Agesilaus did exactly what he had said and marched into the plain of Sardis. Tissaphernes was obliged to return there again from Caria without delay and come to the rescue. As he advanced with his cavalry, he killed many of the Greeks who were plundering the plain in a disordered way. Agesilaus observed that the enemy's infantry had not yet arrived, while he had his whole army at hand, and so he made haste to attack. He combined his *peltasts* and his cavalry, and ordered them to advance at full speed and charge the enemy, while he immediately led forward the hoplites himself. The barbarians were routed, and the Greeks in hot pursuit captured their camp with great slaughter. This battle not only left the Greeks free to plunder the Great King's[30] territory unmolested, but it also allowed them to see Tissaphernes receive the punishment he deserved as a detestable man who was utterly hated by everyone Greek. The Great King immediately sent Tithraustes to arrest him. Tithraustes had him beheaded, and then appealed to Agesilaus to make terms and sail back to Greece, and offered him money to do this. Agesilaus replied that it was only his city that had the authority to make peace, that he took more pleasure in enriching his soldiers than himself, and that Greeks, moreover, only consider it honourable to take spoils from their enemies, not gifts. However, as he wished to oblige Tithraustes for having punished Tissaphernes, that common enemy of the Greeks, he withdrew his army into Phrygia, after accepting thirty *talents* from him for the expenses of the march.

While he was on his way, he received a dispatch[31] from the authorities at home appointing him to the command of the naval forces as well as the land ones – a distinction unique to Agesilaus. He was by general consent at once the most powerful and the most famous man of his time, as even Theopompus has said somewhere, but he took more pride in his personal merits than in his command. Yet he is considered to have made a mistake at this point in delegating the command of the fleet to

Peisander, when there were older and more experienced men available. In assigning this naval command Agesilaus' real purpose was to please his wife, who was Peisander's sister; hence he was acting out of family loyalty rather than in the interests of his country.

11. Agesilaus now stationed his army in the territory governed by Pharnabazus, where not only was food altogether plentiful, but he also collected a large amount of money. He advanced as far as Paphlagonia and entered into an alliance with Paphlagonia's king Cotys; Agesilaus' distinction and integrity made Cotys want to be his friend. Agesilaus was accompanied on all his journeys and campaigns by Spithridates, who had previously defected from Pharnabazus and joined him. Spithridates had a very handsome young son, Megabates, with whom Agesilaus was passionately in love, as well as a beautiful daughter of marriageable age, whom Agesilaus persuaded Cotys to marry. Cotys placed 1,000 horsemen and 2,000 peltasts under Agesilaus' command, and with these he returned to Phrygia once more and devastated Pharnabazus' territory. The latter did not dare to meet Agesilaus in the field nor to trust his own fortresses. Instead he kept most of his valuable and cherished possessions with him at all times, constantly retreating and evading and shifting his base from one part of his territory to another. Eventually Spithridates, who had watched him closely, attacked him with the help of the Spartiate Herippidas, captured his camp, and seized all his valuables. On this occasion, however, Herippidas acted severely in supervising the distribution of the spoils. He compelled the barbarians to hand over everything they had taken, then checked and scrutinized each item, and in the end so annoyed Spithridates that he immediately returned to Sardis, taking the Paphlagonians with him.

No incident, we are told, distressed Agesilaus more than this one. He was grieved at losing a gallant soldier in Spithridates, together with his by no means inconsiderable force, and he was ashamed at having incurred the charge of meanness and pennypinching from which he had always taken pride in keeping both himself and his country free. Apart from the public aspect of the affair, he was irritated beyond all measure for a more personal reason, namely his love for young Megabates, which had become deep-rooted, although in Megabates' presence he would summon up all his determination and struggle to master his passion. In fact, on one occasion when Megabates came up as if to embrace and kiss him, Agesilaus turned away.[32] In his embarrassment Megabates did not repeat the attempt, and in future kept his distance when he addressed him. Agesilaus, who in turn became upset and regretted having rebuffed the kiss, pretended to be surprised, and queried what had happened to Megabates and why he no longer greeted him with a kiss. 'It is your fault,' Agesilaus' companions told him. 'Instead of having the courage to stand firm and receive the attractive young man's kiss, you ran away;[33] but even now he could still be persuaded to come close enough to you for a kiss, although this time be sure not to flinch.' Agesilaus thought for a while in silence, and then said, 'No, there's no need for you to persuade him. For my part, I think I would rather fight that battle of the kiss again than have all the gold I've ever seen.' This was how he acted when Megabates was on the spot. But when he was gone, Agesilaus was still so fired with passion that it is hard to say whether he would have had the strength to refuse a kiss from him, had he all of a sudden reappeared.

12. After this Pharnabazus wanted to hold a conference with Agesilaus, and it was arranged by Apollophanes of Cyzicus, who was a guest-friend[34] to them both. Agesilaus arrived at the place first with his friends and, choosing a shady spot where the grass was thick, he threw himself down and awaited Pharnabazus. When the latter arrived, embroidered rugs and soft cushions were spread out for him, but seeing Agesilaus just lying there as he was, he felt embarrassed, and so he, too, simply reclined on the grassy ground, in spite of the marvellously delicate, colourful clothes he was wearing. After they had exchanged civilities, Pharnabazus had a number of just complaints to make. He pointed out that although he had rendered the Spartans many important services in their war against the Athenians,[35] they were now devastating his territory. Agesilaus

saw that the Spartiates with him were sufficiently ashamed to keep their eyes to the ground and were at a loss for what to say, because they realized that Pharnabazus had been badly treated. Agesilaus answered: 'While we were on friendly terms with the [Persian] king in the past, Pharnabazus, we treated all that belongs to him in friendly fashion. Now that we have become enemies, our treatment is hostile. Since we see that you, too, want to be one of the Great King's possessions, naturally we injure him through you. But from the day you consider yourself worthy to be called a friend and ally of the Greeks, instead of a slave to the Great King, you have a right to regard this army, these weapons and ships, and all of us Greeks as the guardians of your possessions and of your liberty, without which nothing in human life is honourable or desirable.' At this Pharnabazus explained his own intentions. 'Should the Great King send out another general in my place, I shall be on your side. But if he gives me the command, I shall gladly fight you on his behalf and do you all the mischief in my power.' This answer delighted Agesilaus, and as the two men rose to their feet, he took Pharnabazus by the hand and said, 'I hope a man like you may become our friend instead of our enemy.'

13. As Pharnabazus and his friends were leaving, his son lagged behind and then ran up to Agesilaus and said with a smile, 'I'd like to make you my guest-friend, Agesilaus', presenting him with a javelin which he was holding in his hand. Agesilaus accepted it, and since he was pleased with the boy's looks and courteous manner, he glanced around among his entourage in case one of them might have something to make a suitable return gift for one so handsome and generous. He spotted a horse belonging to his secretary Idaeus which was wearing ornamental cheek-pieces; these he quickly removed and gave to the youngster. Agesilaus never forgot this connection, and at a later date when this son's brothers deprived him of his home and drove him into exile in the Peloponnese, he showed considerable concern for him and even helped in one of his love affairs. The Persian was in love with an Athenian boy-athlete who, because of his size and toughness, was in danger of being debarred from

competing at Olympia. So he asked Agesilaus to help on the boy's behalf, and the king was willing to oblige him even in this matter, achieving a successful outcome after a good deal of trouble.[36]

For the most part, Agesilaus was a man of strict principles who stood by the letter of the law, but in matters of friendship he considered that to maintain excessive rectitude was merely an excuse for being unhelpful. At any rate it is reported that he wrote a letter to Hidrieus the Carian, which ran as follows: 'As for Nicias,[37] if he is not guilty, acquit him; but even if he is guilty, acquit him for my sake; in any case, acquit him.' This was how Agesilaus acted in most instances where the interests of his friends were concerned, but there were times when he exploited a situation to suit himself. One example was when he had to break camp in some confusion and left behind his boy-friend who was sick. The latter begged him and called after him as he was leaving, whereupon Agesilaus turned and remarked that it was difficult to be compassionate and prudent at the same time. Hieronymus the philosopher[38] recorded this story.

14. Agesilaus was now nearing the end of the second year of his command.[39] By this time his fame had spread within the Persian empire, and he had gained an almost legendary reputation for self-discipline, moderation, and the simplicity of his way of life. Whenever he travelled, he made a point of taking up his quarters in the most sacred precincts by himself,[40] and so made the gods observe and witness that side of our life which few fellow humans see. Among those thousands of soldiers in Agesilaus' army, it would have been difficult to find one with a bed inferior to his, and in his resistance to the variations of heat and cold he seemed to be constituted as though nature had given him alone the power to endure consistently whatever seasons or weather heaven might send. In particular it delighted the Greek inhabitants of Asia to see their former governors and generals – who had long been intolerably harsh and had revelled in wealth and luxury – now bowing and trembling before a man who walked about in a coarse cloak, and changing their whole bearing and appearance in response to a single, curt and 'laconic' statement

from him. Timotheus'[41] line was on many men's lips: 'Ares is lord: Greece has no fear of gold.'

15. By this time Asia was in a state of ferment, and many regions were ripe for revolt. Agesilaus re-established order among the cities there, and restored to them their proper constitutional forms of government without resorting to any executions or banishments. Next he determined to advance further and to transfer the war from the Greek seaboard, making its focus the person of the Great King and the wealth of Ecbatana and Susa,[42] and above all depriving the King of the leisure that allowed him to sit there and arbitrate between the Greek states in their wars and to corrupt their popular leaders. But just at this moment the Spartiate Epicydidas arrived to inform Agesilaus that Sparta had become embroiled in a great war in Greece,[43] and that the ephors were summoning him with orders to give assistance at home.

> Such talented Greeks, to match barbarians in cruelty![44]

How else can one describe that spirit of envy which now diverted the attention of the Greeks to forming alliances and conspiracies against one another, which laid hands on fortune as it was rising, and which turned against themselves again both the weapons being aimed at barbarians and the warfare only recently banished from Greece? I certainly cannot agree with Demaratus the Corinthian,[45] who said that those Greeks who did not live to see Alexander seated on the throne of Darius had been deprived of a great pleasure. On the contrary, I believe that they would have been more likely to weep when they remembered that this achievement was left for Alexander and the Macedonians by those who previously squandered the lives of Greek generals on the battlefields of Leuctra, Coronea, Corinth and Arcadia.[46]

At any rate nothing Agesilaus ever did was greater or nobler than his return home on this occasion, nor can a finer example be found of just obedience to higher authority. Hannibal was already in grave difficulties and on the point of being driven out of Italy, yet it was only with the greatest reluctance that he obeyed the order to return to the war at home;[47] and Alexander, when he heard of Antipater's battle[48] with Agis, merely joked about it and remarked, 'Gentlemen, it seems that while we have been conquering Darius here, there has been some battle of mice over there in Arcadia.' How fortunate it was for Sparta, then, that Agesilaus so honoured her and had such respect for her laws. The moment the message (*skytale*) was delivered to him, although he was then at the height of his power and good fortune, he abandoned these, gave up the great hopes which beckoned him on, and immediately sailed away 'leaving his task unfulfilled'.[49]

He left many regrets behind him among his allies in Asia, and emphatically gave the lie to that saying of Erasistratus,[50] the son of Phaeax, who remarked that Spartans are better men in public life, but Athenians in private. Agesilaus demonstrated what an excellent king and general he was, but he proved himself an even better, dearer friend and companion to those who knew him privately.

Persian coinage carried the design of an archer, and as he departed Agesilaus declared that the Great King was driving him out of Asia with 30,000 archers. This was the sum of money which had been sent to Athens and Thebes and distributed to their popular leaders, and it was their people who were at war with the Spartiates.

16. Agesilaus now proceeded to cross the Hellespont and march through Thrace. On his way he made no demands upon any of the barbarians, but merely sent envoys to each people, asking whether he should treat them as friends or as enemies as he passed through their territory. All received him in friendly fashion and did what they could to help him on his way. The one exception was the so-called Trochalians. Even Xerxes,[51] so tradition has it, gave them presents, and they now demanded of Agesilaus a hundred *talents* of silver and the same number of women as their price for his passage through their territory. He answered them with contempt, however. 'Why don't they just come and take it all straight away?' he said, and continued on.

When they formed up in battle array, he attacked and routed them with great slaughter.

He also put the same question as he had done elsewhere to the king of Macedonia, who replied that he would consider the matter. 'Let him consider it then,' said Agesilaus, 'while we just march on.' The king was both amazed and alarmed by his audacity, and gave orders to let him pass as a friend. Since the Thessalians were in alliance with Sparta's enemies, Agesilaus proceeded to ravage the country, but he sent Xenocles and Scythes to Larissa in the hope of establishing friendly relations. The two men were arrested and imprisoned, however. Agesilaus' entourage was greatly offended at this, and thought that he ought to pitch camp before Larissa and lay siege to it. But he declared that it mattered more to him to lose either of these men than to conquer the whole of Thessaly, and so he made terms to recover them. We should not be surprised by this behaviour on Agesilaus' part. When the news reached him that a great battle had been fought near Corinth, and that the loss of Spartiates had only been slight, but those of the enemy very heavy, he showed no sign of pleasure or pride, but sighed deeply and said, 'Alas for Greece, how many men have you killed with your own hands. Were they alive, they could beat absolutely all the barbarians in battle.'

However, when the Pharsalians dogged him and harassed his army with 500 horsemen, he ordered his men to attack, routed the enemy, and set up a trophy at the foot of Mount Narthacium. He was especially pleased with this victory, because with no more than a cavalry force which was entirely of his own making he defeated the proudest of horsemen.

17. At this point Diphridas, one of the ephors from Sparta, met him and gave him orders to invade Boeotia immediately. His own plan had been to do this later, after gathering reinforcements, but he saw no cause to disobey the magistrates, and remarked to those with him that the day for which they had returned from Asia was now close at hand; he also sent for two *moras*[52] of the army stationed near Corinth. Meanwhile the Spartans at home, as a mark of honour to him, issued a

proclamation that any young man might enlist to assist the king. When they all enlisted eagerly, the magistrates selected the fifty of finest physique and most active, and dispatched them.

Agesilaus marched through the pass of Thermopylae, crossed the territory of Phocis, which was friendly to him, and then on entering Boeotia pitched camp near Chaeronea. He observed a partial eclipse of the sun, and at the very same time learned of the death of Peisander, who had been defeated in a sea-battle off Cnidus by Pharnabazus and Conon.[53] He was naturally very distressed at the news, for both Peisander's sake and that of the state. However, to avoid spreading alarm or despondency among his troops as they went into battle, he ordered the naval messengers to state the opposite result and report a victory in the sea-battle. He himself appeared wearing a garland, offered up sacrifice for good news, and distributed portions of the victims to his friends.

18. When his advance had taken him as far as Coronea, he and the enemy came within sight of one another. He then drew up his troops in battle order, placing the Orchomenians on the left wing, while he led the right in person. In the opposing army the Thebans held the right wing themselves, and the Argives the left. Xenophon says that there was no other battle to match this one during his time. He was present himself fighting on Agesilaus' side, after the march from Asia with him. When the two lines first met, the shock was not very violent, nor was the fighting heavy. The Thebans quickly routed the Orchomenians, and Agesilaus made short work of the Argives. But both sets of victors turned back when they learned that their respective left wings had been broken and were in retreat. At this point Agesilaus might easily have won a victory if he had resisted the impulse to make a frontal attack on the Thebans, and instead had taken them in the rear after they had passed him. As it was, his natural ardour and fighting spirit prompted him to attack head on, with the intention of driving the men back by sheer force. But the Thebans resisted just as staunchly, and a fierce action developed all along the line, although it was fiercest where the king himself was stationed with the fifty volunteers.

It was evidently their determination on the king's behalf that served to save his life. Although they fought furiously and recklessly, they could not prevent him from being wounded by many thrusts from swords and spears which pierced his armour and entered his body; but they did succeed, with great difficulty, in dragging him away alive. They formed a tight line in front of him and killed great numbers of the enemy, but suffered great numbers of casualties themselves. Since eventually it proved too difficult to break the Thebans head on, they were compelled to adopt the manoeuvre which they rejected at the beginning. They parted their ranks and allowed the enemy to pass through, and then, when the Thebans had moved beyond them and were in looser formation, the Spartans followed at the double and attacked them on both sides. But they failed to put them to rout. The Thebans withdrew to Mount Helicon, proud of their achievement in keeping their own contingent undefeated in this battle.

19. Agesilaus was suffering great pain from his many wounds, but he refused to retire to his tent until he had first been taken on a stretcher to the battle-front and seen all the dead brought within the Spartan lines. Besides this he gave orders that all those of the enemy who had taken refuge in the sanctuary should be allowed to depart. This is the nearby temple of Athena Itonia, in front of which stood a trophy erected long ago[54] by the Boeotians, after their army under Sparton defeated the Athenians and killed Tolmides there.

Early the next morning Agesilaus wanted to determine whether the Thebans would resume the fighting, so he gave orders for the soldiers to wear garlands, for the pipers to play, and for a trophy to be set up and decorated to signify a Spartan victory. When the enemy requested permission to collect their dead, he granted them a truce, and having in this way established that he had won,[55] he proceeded to Delphi where the Pythian Games were being held. Here he took part in the procession in honour of the god,[56] and dedicated a tenth of his spoils from Asia, an offering of a hundred *talents*.

When he returned home, his behaviour and lifestyle immediately earned him the citizens' affection and admiration. Unlike most commanders, he came back from abroad the same man as he had gone out. He had not become enchanted with foreign customs, nor was he restive and dissatisfied with things at home, but had just as much respect and regard for them as did men who had yet to cross the Eurotas for the first time. He made no change to his dining or bathing habits, to his care for his wife, to the style of his armour, or the furnishings of his house. In fact he even kept the doors of the house just as they were, although they were so ancient that they might appear to be the original ones put there by Aristodemus.[57]

Xenophon also tells us that his daughter's *cannathron* was no more elaborate than any other girl's: *cannathron* is their term for wooden carriages carved in the shape of a griffin or goat-stag, in which girls are carried in processions. Xenophon, it is true, did not record the name of Agesilaus' daughter, and Dicaearchus remarks with some indignation that we do not know the name either of Agesilaus' daughter or of Epaminondas'[58] mother. However, I have discovered in the Spartan records that Agesilaus' wife was named Cleora, and his daughters Eupolia and Hippolyta. His spear, too, has been preserved in Sparta; it can still be seen at the present day, but is no different from other men's.

20. However, Agesilaus had noticed that some citizens took pride in breeding racehorses and gave themselves great airs in consequence, and so he persuaded his sister Cynisca to enter a chariot-team at the Olympic Games:[59] he wanted to prove to the Greeks that to win there in this event was no proof of personal excellence, but merely the result of having money and spending it. At this time Xenophon the philosopher was a valued member of his circle, and he pressed him to send for his sons and bring them up in Sparta,[60] so that they should learn the finest of all lessons, how to take orders and to give them.

After Lysander's death Agesilaus discovered that a substantial group in opposition to himself was still in existence, formed by Lysander immediately on returning from Asia. So he set out to expose what kind of citizen Lysander had been during his lifetime. He found a speech, all about revolution and altering the constitution, left behind in a document. Cleon of Halicarnassus was the author, but Lysander was planning to take it and read it at an assembly.[61] Agesilaus wanted to make the speech public, but one of the Elders who had read it and was fearful of its cunning urged him not to disinter Lysander, but rather to inter the speech with him; Agesilaus was convinced, and kept quiet. As for his opponents, he did them no open injury, but arranged that some of them should routinely be sent away as commanders and governors. By this means he exposed them if they proved unscrupulous or grasping in the exercise of their authority. Then, when they were put on trial, he would help them again and support them, and thus win them over to become friends rather than enemies, until there would be nobody to oppose him.

The other king, Agesipolis, was barely an adult. His father had been banished,[62] and since he himself was of a mild and modest disposition, he played little part in public life; even so, Agesilaus succeeded in bringing him too under his influence. Whenever the kings are at Sparta, they go and eat together at the same mess. Now Agesilaus knew that Agesipolis, like himself, was prone to fall in love with boys, and so he consistently turned the conversation to the subject of attractive boys, and encouraged the young king to develop the same enthusiasms and passions and to pursue relationships together. There is nothing disgraceful about these Spartan love affairs; they are highly honourable, and inspire ambition and the desire to excel, as I have described in my *Lycurgus*.[63]

21. Agesilaus had now become the most powerful man in Sparta. Hence he arranged for Teleutias, his half-brother on his mother's side, to be given command of the fleet, and made an expedition against Corinth in which he captured the Long Walls[64] with his land forces, while Teleutias and the fleet [seized the enemy's ships and dockyards]. At the time Corinth was held by the Argives. At the moment when Agesilaus appeared,[65] they were celebrating the Isthmian Games; he drove them out just after they had made a sacrifice to the god, and they left behind all their equipment. Then a number of Corinthian exiles who

happened to be on the spot begged Agesilaus to take charge of the games, but he refused to do so, although he did remain there and provide security while they took charge and celebrated the festival. Later, after his departure, the Isthmian Games were celebrated again by the Argives, with the result that some of the competitors gained victories for the second time, while others were recorded as having been victorious on the first occasion but defeated on the second. Agesilaus remarked that the Argives had proved themselves by this action to be great cowards, since they regarded it as a significant honour to hold the games, yet had not shown the courage to fight for it.

For his part he thought it right to show only a moderate interest in all such celebrations. He saw to it that Sparta's choric and athletic festivals were carried out with due ceremony, he attended them with plenty of enthusiasm and interest, and he never missed a contest in which boys or girls competed.[66] But on some occasions when he saw that other people were impressed, he simply seemed baffled himself. For example, Callippides the tragic actor, who was famous throughout the Greek world and universally idolized, first came up to Agesilaus and addressed him, then made an exhibition of himself by boastfully thrusting into his entourage with the expectation that the king would initiate some cordial exchange, and finally asked, 'Sire, do you not recognize me?' Agesilaus stared at him and said, 'Why, aren't you Callippidas the *deicelictas*?' – using the Spartan term for men who perform mimes. On another occasion, when he was invited to listen to a man who imitated the nightingale's song,[67] he declined and remarked, 'I've heard the actual bird.' The doctor Menecrates, who had been hailed as Zeus because of his success in a number of desperate cases, used this nickname with such vulgarity that he even had the impertinence to begin a letter with 'Menecrates Zeus to King Agesilaus, greetings', to which Agesilaus replied, 'King Agesilaus to Menecrates, sanity'.

22. During his time on Corinthian territory[68] Agesilaus seized the temple of Hera. As he watched his soldiers taking and removing the spoils, envoys arrived from Thebes to negotiate

for peace. He always hated that city, and this now struck him as the perfect opportunity to insult it, so he pretended neither to see nor hear the envoys when they presented themselves. However, this behaviour soon brought its retribution, because before these Thebans left he received news that a *mora* had been cut to pieces by Iphicrates.[69] This was the greatest disaster that the Spartans had suffered for many years, for they lost many brave men – moreover these were hoplites overcome by peltasts, and Spartans by mercenaries.

Agesilaus immediately leapt up to render assistance, but when he learned that the men were already annihilated, he returned to the temple of Hera, and now instructed the Boeotians to reappear for negotiations. This was their chance to insult him in return, so they made no further mention of peace, but merely requested a safe conduct to Corinth. Agesilaus was enraged at this and said, 'If you wish to see your friends exulting over their success, you can do so safely enough tomorrow.' The next day he took the envoys with him, ravaged Corinthian territory, and advanced right up to the city itself. After this demonstration that the Corinthians dared not resist him, he dismissed the delegation. He himself collected the survivors from the *mora*, and led them back to Sparta. On his march he made a point of breaking camp before it was daylight and only pitching camp after dark. His object was to prevent gloating by those Arcadians who hated Sparta and maligned it.

Next,[70] in order to oblige the Achaeans, he joined them in taking an army over to Acarnania, where he secured a great deal of plunder and defeated the Acarnanians in battle. But when the Achaeans asked him to make his winter quarters there so as to prevent the enemy from sowing their fields, he told them that his tactics would be exactly the opposite, for the enemy would be far more afraid of a war if they had their land all sown[71] when summer arrived. This was exactly what happened, for when the Acarnanians heard that they were to be invaded again, they came to terms with the Achaeans.

23. Conon and Pharnabazus, with the Great King's fleet, controlled the seas and were raiding the coast of Laconia; the

city-walls of Athens had also been rebuilt with money provided by Pharnabazus. In these circumstances the Spartans decided to make peace with the Great King. They sent Antalcidas to negotiate with Tiribazus,[72] and in the most shameful and outrageous way they handed over to the King the Greeks living in Asia, on whose behalf Agesilaus had fought his campaign. Consequently Agesilaus had no part in this infamous act, for Antalcidas was his enemy, who sought peace on any terms because in his view war would boost Agesilaus and give him unrivalled power and reputation. Nonetheless when someone said that the Spartans were 'medizing', Agesilaus replied that it was rather a case of the Medes 'laconizing'.[73] What is more, by threatening to make war upon those states which refused to accept the peace, Agesilaus forced all the Greeks to abide by the terms demanded by the Great King. As his actions later made clear, he had the Thebans particularly in mind, since they would be weakened if they had to let Boeotia become independent.[74] So when Phoebidas committed the outrage of seizing the Cadmeia[75] at a time when peace prevailed by treaty, the Greeks were universally indignant, the Spartiates were angry, and Agesilaus' opponents in particular furiously asked Phoebidas on whose authority he had done this. The question was intended to cast suspicion on Agesilaus. But he had no hesitation in supporting Phoebidas and in stating plainly that what had to be considered was whether the action was advantageous or not; if Sparta's interests were served, then it was fine to act independently, even if nobody gave an order.

Now Agesilaus would declare that in principle justice was absolutely the first of the virtues, for courage is of no use unless it is accompanied by justice, and if everyone were to act justly then there would be no need for courage. When people said that the Great King's wish is such-and-such, Agesilaus would ask, 'How can he be greater than I am, unless he is also more just?' Thus his opinion was the right and noble one that justice should be as it were a regal standard, which serves to measure the superiority of one ruler to another. After the peace had been concluded, the Great King sent him a letter proposing that they become personal guest-friends, but he declined the offer and said that the public friendship between their states was sufficient, and that while this held there was no need for a private relationship. In practice, however, Agesilaus did not always observe these principles, but was often carried away by ambition and competitiveness, and above all by his feelings against the Thebans. Thus he not only saved Phoebidas, but also persuaded the state itself to take responsibility for his crime and to make the occupation of the Cadmeia official. He also arranged for Archias and Leontiadas – the men responsible for Phoebidas' entry and capture of the acropolis – to take political and administrative charge of Thebes.

24. This behaviour naturally aroused the suspicion that while Phoebidas had been the instrument, the plan had been conceived by Agesilaus, and his subsequent actions caused this accusation to be generally believed. When the Thebans drove out the garrison and liberated their city,[76] Agesilaus charged them with the murder of Archias and Leontiadas – who were *polemarchs* in name,[77] but tyrants in reality – and made war against them. By this time Agesipolis was dead,[78] and it was his successor as king, Cleombrotus, who was sent into Boeotia in command of an army. Agesilaus declined this appointment, on the grounds that it was forty years since he had reached adulthood and so by law he was now exempt from military service.[79] The real reason, however, was that he had only recently been at war with Phlius[80] to restore its exiles, and was embarrassed to be seen now attacking Thebes on its tyrants' behalf.

Among the group opposed to Agesilaus was a certain Spartan named Sphodrias, who had been appointed *harmost* at Thespiae. He was a man by no means lacking in either courage or ambition, but his actions were constantly influenced by an abundance of hope rather than sound judgement. He longed to create a great name for himself, and reflection on what a renowned celebrity Phoebidas had been made by *his* daring at Thebes convinced him that he could achieve something even finer and more dazzling by seizing the Piraeus[81] on his own initiative; his plan was to make a surprise approach from the landward side, and so deprive the Athenians of their access to the sea. It is said that this scheme was originally devised by the Boeotarchs Pelopidas and Melon. They secretly sent men to Sphodrias, who praised him and flatteringly said that he alone was capable of such a feat, thereby encouraging and inciting him to launch an exploit which was just as immoral and illegal as Phoebidas', although his daring and his good fortune turned out to be lacking too. For Sphodrias had hoped to attack the Piraeus by night, but daylight overtook him when he was still in the Thriasian plain. Then, the story goes, his soldiers took fright and panicked when they saw light coming from some of the sanctuaries at Eleusis, and he himself lost his nerve once the element of surprise was lost. So after ravaging the country for a short while, he ignominiously and ingloriously withdrew back to Thespiae. In consequence the Athenians sent a delegation to Sparta to denounce him, but they found that the magistrates had no need of their accusation to enable them to act, because they had already indicted Sphodrias on a capital charge. He decided not to stand trial, since he dreaded the anger of the citizens, who felt only shame towards the Athenians, and wanted to be regarded as their fellow victims rather than as Sphodrias' fellow criminals.

25. Sphodrias had a handsome son named Cleonymus, still a boy, with whom Archidamus,[82] Agesilaus' son, was in love. Archidamus, as was natural, shared Cleonymus' distress at the danger in which his father stood, but it was impossible for him to take his side openly and help, because Sphodrias was one of Agesilaus' opponents. Cleonymus came to Archidamus and begged him with tears to try and make Agesilaus supportive, since he was the person whom they had most reason to dread. For three or four days, out of fear and respect for his father, Archidamus said nothing as he followed him about. But finally, with the trial imminent, he summoned up courage to mention to Agesilaus that Cleonymus had begged his assistance with his father's case. Agesilaus knew that Archidamus was Cleonymus' lover, but had not put a stop to the relationship, since right from boyhood he had shown promise of becoming as fine a man as any. But for the moment Agesilaus held out no hope that his

son's plea would produce any tangible result or concession. All he said as he went away was that he would consider what was the most honourable and appropriate course. Archidamus was embarrassed at this and stayed away from Cleonymus' company, although before he had been accustomed to see him many times daily. So Sphodrias' circle became even more despondent about his case, until in a conversation Etymocles, one of Agesilaus' friends, revealed Agesilaus' attitude to them. This was that, while he utterly condemned what Sphodrias had done, he still considered him to be a man of worth and recognized the city's need for soldiers like him. This is what Agesilaus consistently said about the case, and he did so to gratify his son. Cleonymus instantly appreciated Archidamus' efforts, while Sphodrias' friends took heart and rallied to his support. Agesilaus was in fact extremely fond of children, and there is a well-known story about him playing with them: when his children[83] were toddlers he used to play with them at home, riding a stick as a hobby-horse. Seen by one of his friends, Agesilaus asked him to tell nobody until he too became the father of a family.

26. At any rate Sphodrias was acquitted. Once the Athenians heard the news they prepared to go to war, and Agesilaus became very unpopular. It was considered that he had obstructed the course of justice at the trial, implicating the city in major outrages against other Greek states – and merely to indulge a child's absurd impulses. Besides this, when he saw that Cleombrotus had little enthusiasm for making war against the Thebans, Agesilaus now disregarded the law by which he had claimed exemption from service previously, and this time invaded Boeotia himself. He inflicted losses on the Thebans, but also suffered losses in return. This caused Antalcidas to say on one occasion when Agesilaus was wounded, 'How well the Thebans are paying you for teaching them to fight, when they had no desire to do so, and no skill either.' In fact the Thebans, so it is said, surpassed themselves in military actions at this period because of all the training they received from the Spartans' many expeditions against them. This was why, in his three so-called *rhetras*,[84] Lycurgus of old had forbidden frequent

campaigns against the same people, his object being to prevent their learning how to wage war.

Sparta's allies also resented Agesilaus' conduct. In their view he was bent on destroying Thebes not on account of any public quarrel, but from some obsessive urge of his own. Accordingly, they said, they had no wish to be led hither and thither to destruction every year, especially when it was a matter of so many of them all having to follow so few Spartans. It was on this occasion, we are told, that Agesilaus used the following device to demonstrate the unimportance of their mere numbers. He ordered all the allies to sit down together at random, and the Spartans separately on their own. Next he announced that the potters should stand up first, and when they had done so, then the smiths second, then in turn carpenters, builders, and workers in every other craft. In this way almost all the allies stood up, but not one of the Spartans, since they were forbidden to practise or learn a manual craft.[85] So Agesilaus remarked with a laugh, 'You see, my men, how many more soldiers we send out than you.'

27. When he was leading his army back from Thebes[86] and was at Megara, walking up to the city hall on the acropolis, he was seized with cramp and suffered intense pain in his sound leg. Next it swelled up and seemed to become clotted with blood, and there were signs of acute inflammation. A Syracusan doctor opened the vein below the ankle, which relieved the pain and blood poured out; but its flow could not be controlled, so that Agesilaus lost consciousness and his condition became extremely dangerous. However, it was evidently this collapse that checked his haemorrhage, and he was carried to Sparta, where he remained for a long time in a weak condition, unable to go on campaign.

During this period the Spartiates suffered many reverses by both land and sea. The most important of these was at Tegyra, where for the first time they were defeated in a pitched battle by the Thebans. So everyone was in favour of universal peace, and ambassadors from all over Greece assembled in Sparta to negotiate a settlement.[87] One of these was Epaminondas, a man who was already renowned for his culture and learning, but had not yet given any proof of his military ability. Noticing that all the others deferred to Agesilaus, he alone maintained the presence of mind to speak out freely. Accordingly he delivered a speech not on behalf of the Thebans, but of Greece as a whole. In this he demonstrated that war strengthened Sparta at the expense of everyone else's suffering; he urged that peace be secured on the basis of equality and justice, saying that it would only endure if all parties were on an equal footing.

28. Agesilaus noticed that the other Greek delegates listened to Epaminondas with exceptional attentiveness and admiration, and so he asked him if he thought it would be just and equitable for Boeotia to be made independent. Epaminondas promptly and boldly responded with another question – did Agesilaus think it just for Laconia to be made independent?[88] At this Agesilaus grew angry, jumped to his feet and asked him to state unequivocally whether he intended to make Boeotia independent, whereupon Epaminondas merely repeated his question about making Laconia independent. Agesilaus was now so furious that he was delighted to have this pretext of at once erasing the Thebans' name from the peace treaty and declaring war on them. He told the rest of the Greeks to depart now that they had settled most of their differences; peace would take care of those that could be settled, but it would be for war to deal with those that could not, since it had proved impossible to clear up and remove all their differences.

It so happened that at this time Cleombrotus was in Phocis with an army, and the ephors at once dispatched him orders to lead his forces against Thebes. They also sent round messengers to assemble contingents from their allies, who showed no enthusiasm for the campaign and resented it, although they did not yet dare to oppose or disobey the Spartans. Many distressing portents now appeared as I have noted in my *Life of Epaminondas*, and although Prothous the Laconian[89] opposed the campaign, Agesilaus refused to give way. Instead he forced the declaration of war, anticipating that, with all the rest of Greece standing together and the Thebans excluded from the treaty, this was the right moment to take revenge on them. However, the timing of the campaign demonstrates that it was undertaken in a spirit of anger rather than one of reason. The treaty was concluded at Sparta on the fourteenth of Scirophorion, and it was on the fifth of Hecatombeion, twenty days later, that the defeat at Leuctra occurred. A thousand Spartans fell, including King Cleombrotus, and with him the pick of the Spartiates. Among these, we are told, was Cleonymus, the handsome son of Sphodrias, who was struck down three times in front of the king,[90] and each time got to his feet again until he died fighting the Thebans.

29. The Spartans had met with an unexpected reverse here, while for the Thebans, against all probability, it was a success unprecedented in other wars between Greeks. Even so, the courage of the defeated side was as admirable and inspiring as that of the victors. Xenophon[91] rightly says that there is something worth remembering even in the remarks and comments which noble men make when they are drinking or relaxing; but it is even more valuable to mark and observe how they handle misfortune and what they say to maintain their dignity. It so happened that Sparta was celebrating a festival – the Gymnopaediae – and was full of visitors, with choirs competing in the theatre. This was when the messengers arrived from Leuctra with news of the disaster. Despite it being at once clear that this was a fatal blow to Sparta and that her supremacy was lost, the ephors did not allow a single choir to drop out nor would they change the programme for the festival; but they sent out messengers to communicate the names of the dead to their families house by house, while they themselves continued to concentrate on the arrangements for the spectacle and the choral competition. On the following morning, when everyone was aware of who was dead and who had survived, the fathers, relatives and friends of the dead went down into the *agora* and greeted one another, full of pride and joy, their faces radiant. Male relatives of survivors, on the other hand, stayed at home with the females, as if in mourning; any who had to go out reflected dejection and humiliation in his appearance, voice and

expression. There was an even more striking contrast visible among the women. Any who had learned that her son was alive and was expecting him back from the battle remained dispirited and silent, whereas mothers of men reported killed at once made the round of the sanctuaries and visited one another in a proud, cheerful mood.[92]

30. However, when their allies deserted them and it was expected that the victorious Epaminondas would triumphantly invade the Peloponnese, many Spartans remembered the oracles concerning the lameness of Agesilaus. They were filled with dismay and were fearful of the gods, imagining that the city's misfortunes stemmed from their banishment of the sound-footed king and preference for a lame disabled one – the very choice which the god had instructed them to weigh carefully and beware of. Yet in other respects Agesilaus had such power, courage and prestige that they continued to employ him not only as their king and commander in war, but also as their physician and arbiter in civil dilemmas. Among the latter was the problem of those who had shown cowardice in the battle, men termed *tresantes*[93] by Spartans. There was reluctance to enforce the loss of rights prescribed for them by law, since they were a large, powerful group who (it was feared) might stir up a revolution. Not only are *tresantes* disqualified from holding any office, but it is also a disgrace for a woman to be given to one in marriage or for a man to pick one of their female relatives as a bride. Anybody who meets them can feel free to strike them. They have to suffer going around unwashed and shabby, wearing cloaks patched with rags of different colours, and shaving one half of their moustaches but letting the other half grow. To keep an eye on a large number of such *tresantes* in the city was taxing when so few soldiers were available, so Agesilaus was elected as lawgiver. He neither added nor removed nor changed a word in any law, but came into the Spartan assembly and said that the laws must be allowed to sleep on that day, although from the next day onwards they would resume their force. By this means he ensured that the city kept its laws and its men their status. Then, as he was anxious to dispel the

prevailing despair and despondency among the young men, he invaded Arcadia.[94] He was very careful to avoid fighting a battle with the enemy, but he did capture a small town belonging to the Mantineans and overran the territory there. In this way he made the Spartans more optimistic, and raised the happier prospect that all was not lost.

31. After this Epaminondas arrived in Laconia with his allies, a force of no less than 40,000 hoplites. Many lightly armed troops and unarmed marauders accompanied them too, so that the horde sweeping in and descending on Laconia amounted in all to 70,000. It was at least 600 years since Dorians had settled in Sparta, and throughout that time this was the first enemy force ever seen in the country; before this nobody dared to invade. Now they burst into an unravaged and inviolate territory, and burned and plundered up to the River Eurotas and the city. Not a man came out to oppose them because Agesilaus would not let the Spartans resist 'such a surging torrent of war', to borrow Theopompus' phrase. Instead Agesilaus clustered his hoplites in the city's central and most vital sectors, and patiently endured the threats and boasts of the Thebans, who called on him by name and challenged him to fight for his country, since he had been the cause of its misfortunes by igniting this war.

But this was not the greatest of Agesilaus' trials. He was equally distracted by the commotion within the city, with people shrieking and rushing to and fro. The older men were enraged at what was happening, and the women could not keep quiet, but went berserk when they heard the enemy's shouts and saw their campfires. He was also tormented by the thought of his own reputation. He had begun his reign when Sparta was at the height of her power; now he saw her prestige humbled, and the lie had been given to the boast (one which he had often uttered himself) that no Spartan woman had ever seen the smoke of an enemy's fire. There is a story that an Athenian remarked to Antalcidas when they were arguing about bravery, 'At any rate we have often driven you away from the River Cephisus', to which Antalcidas replied, 'Yes, but we have never driven you from the River Eurotas.' This is very like the response which a less well known Spartiate gave to an Argive who had said, 'Many of your men lie buried in the Argolid.' To which the Spartiate replied, 'Yes, but not one of you lies buried in Laconia.'

32. On the present occasion, however, Antalcidas, who was an ephor, is said to have been so alarmed that he sent his children away to Cythera. When the enemy attempted to cross the river and storm the city, Agesilaus drew up his troops in front of the central, raised areas and abandoned the rest. At this time,[95] after snowfall, the volume and height of the Eurotas were at record high levels, and the really tough obstacle for the Thebans proved to be the current rather than the cold or the harsh conditions. As Epaminondas advanced at the head of his phalanx, he was pointed out to Agesilaus, who apparently watched him for a long time, shifting his gaze as Epaminondas moved, and saying nothing more than simply, 'There is a man determined to do great things.' Epaminondas was eager to join battle within the city and set up a trophy there, but when he proved incapable of either dislodging Agesilaus or luring him out, he pulled back and ravaged the countryside.

Meanwhile at Sparta 200 of the men who had long been unreliable and worthless banded together and seized the Issorium, a well-protected and easily defensible position where the temple of Artemis[96] is. The Spartans wanted to expel them at once, but Agesilaus, who feared revolution, told them to stay still. He, on the other hand, protected by no more than a cloak and accompanied by only one servant, went forward himself, shouting out to the mutineers that they had misheard their orders: they had not been told to gather at the Issorium nor all stay together, but some were to take another position over there (to which he pointed), and others to go elsewhere in the city. When the men heard this, they were delighted to think that their disloyalty had gone undetected, and so they dispersed and went off to the places to which Agesilaus had ordered them. He immediately brought up other troops and seized the Issorium; then he had about fifteen of the group arrested and killed during the night. He received information about another, more serious conspiracy, which consisted of a group of Spartiates who met secretly in a house to plot revolution. At a moment of such turmoil there was no possibility of bringing these men to trial, but neither could he overlook their plotting. Accordingly, after consulting the ephors, Agesilaus had these men executed without trial, despite the fact that up to that time no Spartiate had ever been executed without trial. At this moment the Spartans were also greatly disheartened by the fact that large numbers of the *perioeci* and helots who had been conscripted into the army were escaping from the city and going over to the enemy. So Agesilaus instructed his servants to visit these men's quarters every morning, and to collect and hide the arms of those who had left, so that the number of desertions would not be known.

There are differing accounts of why the Thebans withdrew from Laconia. Some say that the winter weather was the cause, and the fact that the Arcadians began to leave, just slipping away at random. Others point out that the Thebans had been in the country for three whole months and had ravaged most of it. Theopompus' version is that after the Boeotarchs had already decided to leave, a Spartiate named Phrixus came to them from Agesilaus bringing ten *talents* to pay for the withdrawal; hence the Thebans merely carried out a longstanding decision, but with the bonus of having their expenses met by the enemy.

33. How Theopompus alone came to discover this story when others are unaware of it, I do not know. But certainly all writers agree that Sparta owed her deliverance at this time to Agesilaus, who laid aside his natural impulse to strive for success and victory, and adopted a cautious policy. This is not to say that after the defeat he was able to restore the state's power and prestige. Sparta was like a human body which is healthy in itself, but has consistently followed too strict and severe a lifestyle: just one error tipped the scales and overturned its entire success. We should not be surprised by this. The Spartans' constitution was perfectly designed to promote virtue and peace and harmony. But they then added empire and sovereignty won by force, elements which in Lycurgus' view were unnecessary for maintaining the happy life of any state;[97] and so they were overthrown.

Agesilaus himself now declined military service because of his age, but his son Archidamus – with the help of a contingent sent from Sicily by the tyrant – defeated the Arcadians in what is known as the 'Tearless Battle',[98] in which he lost none of his own men, but killed large numbers of the enemy. This victory gave clearest proof of Sparta's weakness. In the past they had regarded the defeat of their enemies as such a natural and commonplace event that the only sacrifice in the city to the gods to celebrate a victory was that of a cock; those who had taken part in the fighting did not boast, and those who learned of it showed no special elation. Even after the battle of Mantinea, which Thucydides[99] described, the man who brought the first report of the victory received no reward for the good news beyond a piece of meat, which the magistrates sent from their mess. But now, at the news of this battle and the approach of Archidamus, nobody could restrain their feelings. His father went out first to meet him, weeping for joy, and after him the magistrates; most of the older men and the women went down to the river, raising their hands and giving thanks to the gods, as if Sparta were cleared of all undeserved reproach and once again saw the light shining bright as of old. For before this battle, we are told, the men had felt so ashamed of their defeats that they would not even look their wives in the face.

34. When the city of Messene[100] was being established by Epaminondas' men, and its former citizens were thronging to it from all quarters, the Spartans did not dare to oppose this development, yet neither were they capable of preventing it. It was against Agesilaus that they were filled with bitter anger, because it was during his reign that they lost this territory which had benefited them for so long, one as extensive as Laconia and among the most fertile in Greece. It was for this reason too that Agesilaus refused the peace settlement which the Thebans proposed. He was so combative that, even though the territory was actually under their control, he was unwilling to cede it to them formally; as a result he was outmanoeuvred and not only failed to recover that territory, but also came near to losing Sparta itself. The occasion was when the Mantineans in their

turn rebelled against the Thebans, and called in the Spartans to help.[101] Once Epaminondas learned that Agesilaus had marched out with his forces and was approaching, he broke camp at Tegea during the night (without attracting the Mantineans' attention), headed his army for Sparta, eluded Agesilaus, and very nearly took the city suddenly when it was without defenders. However, Agesilaus was warned by Euthynus of Thespiae, according to Callisthenes (or by a Cretan in Xenophon's version). He quickly dispatched a horseman to take the news to Sparta, and soon afterwards arrived himself. It was not long before the Thebans crossed the River Eurotas and began to attack the city, but Agesilaus defended it staunchly and with an energy far beyond his years.[102] He did not consider, as he had before, that this was the time for a cautious, guarded approach, but rather that the situation demanded desperate courage. He had not trusted to such tactics previously, nor attempted to apply them, but this time it was only by these means that he averted the danger. He snatched the city from Epaminondas' grasp, set up a trophy, and showed Sparta's women and children that their men were repaying their country in the noblest possible fashion for the upbringing it had given them. Archidamus was in the forefront of these defenders, conspicuous both for the depth of his courage and for the speed of his movements; he ran through the narrow streets to give support wherever the defence was hard pressed, and everywhere with a handful of others stood firm against the enemy. But it was Phoebidas' son Isadas who I think made a magnificent spectacle, admired not only by his own fellow citizens, but also by the enemy. Handsome in appearance and tall in stature, he was at the age when the human physique reaches perfection as boyhood merges into manhood. He had just anointed his body with oil and dashed out of the house naked, holding a spear in one hand and a sword in the other, but wearing neither clothes nor protective armour. Then forcing his way through the midst of the combatants, he threw himself at the ranks of the enemy, striking and laying low all who opposed him. Nobody wounded him, either because a god protected him for his valour, or because his opponents regarded him as something of superhuman size and strength. It is said that the ephors first crowned him for this feat, and then fined him 1,000 *drachmas* because he had dared to risk fighting without armour.

35. A few days afterwards the two sides fought a battle near Mantinea. Epaminondas had already routed the Spartans' front ranks, and was eagerly pressing forward in pursuit, when a Spartan named Anticrates faced him and struck him down. Dioscorides' story is that he used a spear, but the Spartans to this day refer to Anticrates' descendants as *Machairiones* because he struck the blow with a sword (*machaira*). Epaminondas had inspired such dread in the Spartans while he was alive that they felt an extraordinary admiration and affection for his killer; they voted honours and rewards for Anticrates himself, as well as exemption from taxes for his descendants, a privilege still being enjoyed today by one of them, a man named Callicrates.

After the battle and the death of Epaminondas the Greeks concluded a peace with one another. Agesilaus and his associates tried to exclude the Messenians from the oath on the grounds that they had no state. Then, after all the other Greeks admitted the Messenians and accepted their oaths, the Spartans withdrew and alone remained in a state of war with them in the hope of recovering Messenia. Agesilaus thus appeared harsh, implacable and insatiably fond of war, because he did everything in his power to undermine and assail a general settlement. Worse still, lack of funds forced him to burden his friends at Sparta with requests for loans and contributions. Rather, having reached this point, he should have been taking the chance to end the state's troubles. After letting go of a great empire in its entirety, with its cities and its sway over land and sea, he should not have become so frantic about possessions and revenues in Messenia.

36. He diminished his reputation still further by offering to serve as a commander for the Egyptian Tachos.[103] It was considered unworthy for a man who had once been regarded as the noblest in Greece, with a worldwide reputation,[104] to put himself at the disposal of a foreigner rebelling against the Great King, and to hire out his name and distinction to serve for money acting as a

mercenary commander. And in fact, now that he had passed the age of eighty and his whole body was scarred from wounds, even supposing that he had resumed the leadership of the noble undertaking to restore the freedom of the Greeks,[105] his ambition would still not have been regarded as entirely blameless. Every honourable action has its proper time and season, and really it is altogether a sense of proper proportion that distinguishes good behaviour from bad. Agesilaus, however, ignored these considerations, and did not regard any public service as beneath his dignity; instead it would be unworthy of him, in his view, to live a life of inaction in Sparta sitting and waiting for death. So he used money sent him by Tachos to recruit mercenaries, embarked them on ships and set sail. As once before, he took thirty Spartiates with him as advisers.

When he reached Egypt, the king's top generals and officials at once came on board to pay their respects. Agesilaus' name and fame had aroused great interest and high expectations among Egyptians generally, and everyone thronged to catch a glimpse of him. When the sight proved to be nothing brilliant or elaborate, but a pathetic old man of slight build, wrapped in a coarse, shabby cloak, and lying on a patch of grass by the sea, they began to laugh and make fun of him, remarking that here was the perfect illustration of the saying about the mountain being in labour and then giving birth to a mouse.

When gifts of welcome were fetched and presented to him, the Egyptians were still more surprised at his unconventional behaviour because he accepted the flour, calves and geese, but declined the dried fruits, pastries and perfumes. When pressed insistently to accept these, he gave orders for them to be taken and given to his helots. However, according to Theophrastus, he did like the papyrus[106] used for making garlands, because the results were so neat and simple, and when he left Egypt he made the king a request to take some of it.

37. However, when Agesilaus joined Tachos who was then making preparations for his campaign, he was not offered the leadership of the entire force, but only the command of the mercenaries. An Athenian, Chabrias, was in charge of the fleet,

while Tachos reserved overall command for himself. This was Agesilaus' first cause for annoyance. Then he also found himself obliged to endure Tachos' arrogant pretentiousness, which was intensely provoking. He sailed with him on an expedition against the Phoenicians, and setting aside his own dignity and natural feelings he did behave with tolerance and deference towards him, until he found the right opportunity. This came when Tachos' cousin Nectanebis, who commanded part of the forces, raised a revolt against him. Nectanebis was proclaimed king by the Egyptians, and then approached Agesilaus for help; he appealed to Chabrias, too, and offered both men great rewards. When Tachos learned of this, and begged both men to stand by him, Chabrias tried gentle persuasion to keep Agesilaus on good terms with Tachos. But Agesilaus answered, 'You, Chabrias, came here on your own account, and so you are free to act as you choose, but I was given to the Egyptians as a commander by my country. It would be dishonourable for me to fight against those to whom I was sent as an ally, unless my country should instruct me otherwise.' After making this declaration, he sent messengers to Sparta whom he told to denounce Tachos and support Nectanebis. Both Egyptians also sent envoys of their own to appeal to the Spartans for help, Tachos stressing that he had long been their friend and ally, and Nectanebis claiming that he would prove an even better, more active friend to them. Having heard all this, the Spartans' public response to the Egyptians was that these were matters for Agesilaus to determine; at the same time they instructed him by letter to see that he act in Sparta's interests. Consequently Agesilaus took his mercenaries and changed sides from Tachos to Nectanebis. He made his country's interests the screen for his strange and unnatural decision, one which – if this pretext be removed – is most fairly described as treachery. Whenever any question of honour arises, it is characteristic of Spartans to give priority to their country's interests; justice, as they see it and understand it, is only whatever they believe will advance Sparta.[107]

38. When Tachos found himself deserted by his mercenaries, he fled, but then another claimant challenged Nectanebis. This

man, from Mendes, was proclaimed king and advanced with the force of 100,000 that he had gathered. Nectanebis sought to reassure Agesilaus by telling him that although the enemy were strong in numbers, they were a rabble of artisans whose lack of campaign experience made them worthless. 'It's not their numbers that make me anxious,' Agesilaus told him, 'it is exactly this ignorance and inexperience, which may make it difficult to outwit them. If part of your enemy's defence strategy is to suspect or anticipate what you are going to do, then they may be deceived by an unexpected trick. But an enemy that fails to suspect or anticipate allows you no scope for deception. It's the same in wrestling, where if your opponent stands still, there is no chance to throw him.' Later the claimant from Mendes also made overtures to Agesilaus and tried to win him over. When Nectanebis took fright at this, Agesilaus urged him to engage the enemy as soon as possible rather than to attempt a long drawn out campaign against men who lacked battle experience, but still possessed the numerical superiority to encircle him, surround him with trenches, forestall him in various ways, and seize the initiative. This advice only confirmed Nectanebis in his fears and suspicions, and he withdrew to a well-defended city with a high circuit wall. Such lack of trust angered and irked Agesilaus, but he was ashamed to change sides yet again and return home without having achieved anything, so he stayed with Nectanebis and joined him within the walls.

39. When the enemy came up and began to surround the city with a trench, Nectanebis became alarmed at the prospect of a siege, and so now returned to the plan of risking a battle, with the Greeks all very much in favour, since the place lacked provisions. Agesilaus, however, would not agree to the plan, but blocked it. As a result, the Egyptians abused him even more insultingly than before and called him a traitor to their king. By this time he was able to bear their slanders more patiently, and he waited for the right moment to put his plan into effect.

This was as follows. The enemy were digging a deep trench outside the city wall, so that those within would be completely enclosed. So when the digging was almost finished, and the two ends of the trench were about to meet and encircle the city, Agesilaus waited for the evening and ordered the Greeks to take up their arms. Then he went to Nectanebis and said, 'This is the moment when we can save ourselves, young man. I did not speak of it until the time came, for fear of spoiling our opportunity. The enemy themselves, with their own hands, have given us security. They have dug their trench so far that the finished part prevents them deploying their full strength, while the gap remaining gives us the chance of fighting them on fair and equal terms. So be eager now to prove yourself a man of courage, follow us as we charge, and save yourself and your army. Those of the enemy that we ram head on will not be able to withstand us, while the trench will prevent the rest from harming us.' Nectanebis was filled with admiration at Agesilaus' astuteness, placed himself in the middle of the Greek ranks, attacked with them, and easily routed his opponents. Once Agesilaus had gained Nectanebis' trust, he proceeded to repeat the same tactics against the enemy, like a feint in wrestling. By variously pulling back, coming forward and swinging round, he manoeuvred the whole body of the enemy into a place with a deep canal flowing either side. He then blocked off this space in between by deploying the front of his phalanx there, and thus matched the number of men that the enemy could use against him, since it was impossible for them to outflank or surround him. Consequently, after a short resistance they were routed. Many were killed, while fugitives were dispersed and melted away.

40. After this, Nectanebis' affairs prospered and his position was definitely secure. He showed his regard and affection for Agesilaus by pressing him to stay and spend the winter with him. However, Agesilaus wanted to set off for the war at home,[108] because he knew that Sparta was short of money and was employing mercenaries. So Nectanebis not only arranged a magnificent, dignified leave-taking, but also among other gifts and honours presented him with 230 *talents*[109] of silver for the war. Since it was by now winter, Agesilaus kept his ships close in to shore, and it was when they reached a deserted spot in Libya known as Menelaus' Harbour that he died, aged

eighty-four.[110] He had been king of Sparta for forty-one years. For more than thirty of these his strength and authority were unequalled, and he was regarded as king and leader of almost the whole of Greece, until the battle of Leuctra.

When other Spartans died in a foreign country, the custom was to leave their bodies there after burial, but kings' bodies were brought home.[111] So the Spartiates here embalmed the body in wax (since they could not obtain honey) and conveyed it back to Sparta. The succession passed to his son, Archidamus, and remained in the family down to Agis, who was executed by Leonidas, because he tried to restore the ancient constitution. This Agis was the fifth in descent from Agesilaus.[112]

AGIS AND CLEOMENES

AGIS

1. It is not a strange nor thoughtless supposition on the part of some that the myth about Ixion was composed for seekers of glory: I mean the one where he raped Nephele instead of Hera, which led to the birth of the Centaurs. In fact the glory to which such persons attach themselves is a kind of illusion of true distinction, so that they achieve nothing pure or generally acknowledged, but much that is spurious and of mongrel character. They are drawn in different directions at different times as they follow their ambitions and emotions. For example, Sophocles'[1] herdsmen say of their flocks:

> 'Whilst masters of these we are enslaved to them,
> And must listen to them even though they are dumb.'

This really is the predicament of men in public life who respond to the caprices and impulses of mobs: they make themselves slaves and followers so that they may be called leaders of the people and rulers. For in just the same way as the forward look-outs spot what lies ahead before the helmsmen do, yet respect them and carry out their instructions, so those politicians, too, whose sights are set on glory, are servants of the crowd even though they are called rulers.

2. The man who is flawless and perfectly good would have no need at all of glory except in so far as it offers an avenue of achievement, since he comes to be trusted as a result of gaining

it. By contrast a man who is still young and ambitious may be permitted both to feel a certain pride and to boast of the glory gained from his fine exploits. For the qualities budding and growing in men of that age (as Theophrastus says) will be confirmed by praise of their successes, and will develop thereafter under the stimulus of pride. To push too far is risky in all circumstances, but when political ambitions are involved it is fatal. In the case of those who have gained high authority, it drives them to madness and plain insanity once they no longer accept that what is honourable is in fact glorious, but believe that what is glorious is also good. When Phocion was asked by Antipater[2] to do something which was not at all honourable, he said to him: 'You cannot have Phocion both as a friend *and* as a toady.' It is this, then, or something like it, which needs to be said to the crowd: 'The same man cannot be your ruler *and* your servant.' When this actually does occur, his situation is like that of the snake in the fable. Its tail rebelled against its head and demanded to take a turn at leading rather than continually following the head. So it took the lead and got into difficulties itself by going off the road as well as bruising the head, which was forced quite unnaturally to follow a part of the snake that was blind and stupid. We observe this to have been the predicament of many of those whose sole concern in politics is to win popularity. After making themselves dependent upon capriciously shifting mobs, they have later been unable either to reassert themselves or to control the disorder.

I was prompted to make these points about glory derived from the populace after reflecting upon the tremendous impact it made upon the fortunes of Tiberius and Gaius Gracchus.[3] Their own birth, their upbringing and their political principles were all uniformly outstanding; yet they were destroyed not so much by a limitless passion for glory as by a fear of losing the glory they had. The reason for this was by no means discreditable, because they had enjoyed the great goodwill of the citizens and were ashamed at not repaying it – as if it were a debt. They always strove to outdo the honours conferred on them by adopting beneficial policies, and then because these were appreciated they were honoured more. Thus they became fired personally with as much ambition for the people as were the people for them. In consequence they unwittingly came to adopt policies with which it was no longer proper to remain associated, but which by that stage it would be dishonourable for them to abandon.

At any rate this will be for you to decide upon from my account. With the Gracchi we shall compare a pair of popular leaders at Sparta, the kings Agis and Cleomenes. Like the Gracchi, these two exalted the people and restored a fine, just constitution which had been in abeyance for a long period. But they, too, were hated by powerful citizens who refused to abandon their characteristic greed. While the Spartans were not actually brothers, they did adopt related policies, very much akin to one another. This is how they got their start.

3. A lust for silver and gold wormed its way into the city, and while the acquisition of wealth was first accompanied by greed and meanness, its use and enjoyment later led to luxury, pampering and extravagance. As soon as this happened, Sparta largely lost her honourable character and behaved in a shabby fashion unworthy of her, until the period in which Agis and Leonidas were the kings. Agis was a Eurypontid, son of Eudamidas, and sixth in line from the Agesilaus who crossed over to Asia and won more power than any other Greek. Now Agesilaus had a son Archidamus, who was killed by the Messapii near Mandorium in Italy. Archidamus' elder son was Agis, and his younger one Eudamidas. After Agis had been killed by Antipater near Megalopolis[4] leaving no child, Eudamidas became king. He was succeeded by Archidamus; then another Eudamidas succeeded Archidamus; then Eudamidas was followed by the Agis[5] who is our present subject.

Leonidas the son of Cleonymus, on the other hand, was an Agiad belonging to the other royal house, eighth in line from the Pausanias who defeated Mardonius in battle at Plataea. Now Pausanias had a son, Pleistoanax; Pleistoanax in turn had a son, Pausanias, who when he went into exile from Sparta at Tegea[6] was replaced as king first by his elder son Agesipolis, and then when he died childless, by his younger son Cleombrotus.

Cleombrotus in turn had two sons, another Agesipolis and Cleomenes. Of these, Agesipolis neither reigned for a long period nor had children; Cleomenes, by contrast, who became king after Agesipolis, lost the elder of his sons, Acrotatus, during his lifetime, but did leave a younger one, Cleonymus. Cleonymus did not become king, but Cleomenes' grandson Areus, the son of Acrotatus, did. After Areus met his death near Corinth, his son Acrotatus became king. He, too, was defeated in battle near Megalopolis by the tyrant Aristodemus, but his wife was pregnant at the time of his death.[7] The child born was a boy and Leonidas the son of Cleonymus acted as guardian. But then before he grew up the child died, and the kingship came to Leonidas, who by no means saw eye to eye with the citizens. For although with the ruin of the constitution there had already been a general decline all round, Leonidas' behaviour did make a marked contrast with traditional standards since he had spent a long time dancing attendance at satraps' courts and in the service of Seleucus,[8] and then quite unsuitably introduced the pomp found there into the Greek world with its traditions of government.

4. Agis, by contrast, was both morally and intellectually superior not just to Leonidas, but to almost all the kings since the great Agesilaus' day. Even though he had been brought up by women – his mother Agesistrata and his grandmother Archidamia, the richest of all the Spartans – amidst wealth and high living, before he was twenty he had become firmly opposed to all self-indulgence. He abandoned finery of any kind, especially anything which might serve to enhance personal appearance, and having once renounced all extravagance he steered clear of it thereafter. Instead he took pride in wearing the traditional cloak and in conforming to Spartan diet, baths and lifestyle. He professed that he was interested in becoming king only if he could thereby restore the ancestral laws and system of education.

5. The Spartans' slide towards weakness and collapse began almost as soon as they had put an end to the Athenian hegemony,[9] and the state became flooded with gold and silver.

All the same, where succession to property was concerned the number of households laid down by Lycurgus did continue to be maintained, and every father still bequeathed his lot of land to his son.[10] As a result, the maintenance of equality under these arrangements at least saved the city from many other errors. But this was to change when a man named Epitadeus became ephor, a powerful, self-willed character, with a harsh temper. Since he was at odds with his son, he proposed a *rhetra* which made it possible for a man to dispose of his property and lot to anyone of his choice, either by gift during his lifetime, or by will. The introduction of this law thus satisfied Epitadeus' own private purpose; but others, too, welcomed it out of greed, and by approving it wrecked what had been an excellent system. For now influential people could acquire unlimited property. Relatives' claims to inheritances were thrust aside, so that wealth was soon concentrated in just a few hands, and the city generally was impoverished. In consequence people had no time for any honourable activities: they became subservient, as well as envious and hostile towards those who did own property. Thus there were no more than 700 Spartiates left, of whom perhaps 100 owned land in addition to their lot. Though they lacked rights or resources, the remaining mass of the population continued to squat in the city. They became dilatory and unenthusiastic in repelling external attacks, and all the time they kept looking for some opportunity to revolt and change their present condition.

6. In view of this Agis rightly considered that it would be a splendid achievement to restore a full body of equal citizens, and he began to sound out public opinion. The younger men responded quickly, and more eagerly than he had expected: as a group they stripped to show their mettle, as if their clothes represented a way of life which they were all discarding in the cause of liberty. The older men by contrast were more deeply tainted by corruption: most of them, like slaves being returned to a master from whom they had fled, shook with fear at the name of Lycurgus, and criticized Agis for deploring the present condition of the state and for being so eager to restore Sparta's

ancient renown. Yet Agis' ambitions were publicized by Lysander the son of Libys, Mandrocleidas the son of Ecphanes, and Agesilaus, all of whom urged him on. Lysander was a citizen of the highest standing, while Mandrocleidas' combination of intelligence, cunning and audacity had won him the foremost reputation as a schemer throughout Greece. Agesilaus, the king's uncle on his mother's side, was a forceful speaker, but in other respects a weak, money-grubbing character who was openly encouraged and spurred on by his son Hippomedon; the latter's part in many campaigns had won him considerable prestige, and through the good opinion of the younger men he had become influential. But the decisive factor which swayed Agesilaus to support Agis' programme was his heavy burden of debts, which he hoped would be removed by revolution. So as soon as he had Agesilaus on his side, Agis enlisted his support to bring over his own mother: she took a prominent part in public life, and with so many dependants, friends and debtors was a figure of great influence.

7. After listening to the young man she was at first shocked and tried to stop him from proceeding with a scheme that seemed neither feasible nor rewarding. But Agesilaus explained to her how splendidly it would work out and what a valuable service it would perform, and the king personally begged his mother to contribute her wealth for the sake of his glory and aspirations. His argument was that even though he could not be on a par with other kings in material terms (since the servants of satraps and the slaves of Ptolemy's and Seleucus' officials owned more than all the Spartan kings put together), nonetheless, if in self-discipline and high-minded simplicity he could outdo all their affluence and make the citizens equals and partners, then he would truly win the name and glory of a great king. Consequently, inspired by the young man's aspirations, the ladies changed their minds and were filled with such great enthusiasm for his noble purpose that together they urged Agis on and told him to proceed faster. At the same time they called in their male friends, asking them to join and to talk to the other women, since they were aware that Spartan men were always subject to

their wives and allowed them to interfere in affairs of state more than they themselves did in private ones.

Now at that time most of the wealth at Sparta was in the hands of women, and it was this which made Agis' task troublesome and awkward. For the women opposed him, not only because they would lose the luxury which seemed to them with their lack of taste to be true happiness, but also because they saw that they would be deprived of both the respect and the influence which their wealth afforded them. So they approached Leonidas and repeatedly appealed to him, as the older man, to control Agis and block his schemes. Now Leonidas was certainly willing to assist the rich, since he was frightened of the people in their enthusiasm for change. He offered no open opposition, but made constant secret efforts to damage the project and wreck it, slandering Agis in discussions he had with the magistrates. According to him, Agis was pledging the property of the rich to the poor as their payment for making him tyrant, and by his land distributions and cancellations of debts was buying plenty of bodyguards for himself, rather than citizens for Sparta.

8. Agis, however, managed to have Lysander elected an ephor,[11] and through him he at once proposed to the Elders a *rhetra*, the main clauses of which were that debtors should be relieved of their obligations, and that there should be a redistribution of land. The territory between the stream beside Pellene and Taygetus, Malea and Sellasia should comprise 4,500 lots, while that beyond it should comprise 15,000. And this outer territory would be divided among those of the *perioeci* fit to bear arms, while the territory inside it would be for the Spartiates themselves. Their numbers would be restored from those *perioeci* and foreigners who had been brought up as free men and were in other respects physically appealing and at the peak of condition for their age. Spartiates would be organized into fifteen messes of 400 and 200,[12] and they would adopt the same pattern of life as their ancestors.[13]

9. Once the *rhetra* had been proposed and the Elders proved by no means unanimous in their view of it, Lysander called an

assembly and personally discussed the matter with the citizens,[14] while Mandrocleidas and Agesilaus begged them not to ignore Sparta's ruined reputation just because of the handful who lived in luxury. They should rather remember the earlier oracles which instructed them to beware of avarice as fatal to Sparta, as well as the ones brought to them recently from Pasiphaë. Now there was a temple and much respected oracle of Pasiphaë at Thalamae.[15] According to some, she was one of the daughters of Atlas, and Ammon was her child by Zeus. Others, however, maintain that this was where Priam's daughter Cassandra died and that because she disclosed (*phainein*) her oracles to everyone (*pasi*), the place was called Pasiphaë. But Phylarchus claims that she was a daughter of Amyclas called Daphne, and that when she escaped from Apollo, who wanted to have intercourse with her, she changed into the laurel tree (*daphne*), and was then honoured by the god and gained prophetic power. They said, then, that her oracles were instructing the Spartiates all to become equal in accordance with the legislation originally drawn up by Lycurgus. After everyone else, King Agis came forward and in a short statement declared his intention to offer the largest contribution to the state that he was trying to establish. First he was making over his own property to it, consisting of substantial tracts of arable land and pasture, and besides this 600 *talents* in cash. Then his mother and grandmother were doing likewise, along with their friends and relatives, who were the wealthiest of the Spartiates.

10. As a result the people were astounded at the young man's magnanimity and delighted that after some 300 years there had emerged a king worthy of Sparta. But it was from this point especially that Leonidas battled in opposition. For he reckoned that while he would be forced to do the same as Agis, he would not win equal gratitude from the citizens, because once everyone alike had surrendered their possessions, only the originator of the idea would be given credit for so doing.

So he asked Agis if he believed Lycurgus to have been a just and thoughtful person. When Agis replied in the affirmative, Leonidas said: 'How was it then that Lycurgus permitted cancellation of debts or enrolled foreigners in the state, since in his opinion a state which did not expel foreigners was by no means healthy?' Agis replied that he was not surprised if Leonidas, brought up abroad and the father of children by a satrap's daughter, was unaware that Lycurgus banished borrowing and lending from the city along with coinage, while men whose attitudes and lifestyles were incompatible with his own irritated him much more than foreigners in the cities. He certainly did expel the latter – not because he was hostile to their physical presence, but because their behaviour and character worried him as being liable to contaminate the citizens and generate enthusiasm for luxury, effeminacy and greed. Yet Terpander, Thales and Pherecydes,[16] despite being foreigners, were particularly honoured at Sparta because the spirit of their odes and their philosophies was consistently the same as that of Lycurgus. Agis said: 'On the one hand you praise Ecprepes,[17] who as ephor took an adze and cut away two of the nine strings from the musician Phrynis' lyre, as well as those who again did the same to Timotheus.[18] Yet on the other hand you complain about my attempt to rid Sparta of luxury, extravagance and pretentiousness, as if those magistrates too were not determined to prevent affected and extravagant elements in music penetrating here. But now the imbalance and the dissonance which have developed in our lives and our behaviour have rendered the city off pitch and out of harmony with itself.'

11. After this the ordinary people supported Agis, but the rich continued to beg Leonidas not to abandon them; they also pleaded with the Elders – who had authority in the matter of preliminary approval[19] – and were successful in convincing them to the extent that those who voted against the *rhetra* were in a majority of one.[20] But Lysander, who was still in office, quickly initiated a prosecution of Leonidas on the basis of an archaic law which forbade any descendant of Heracles to have children by a foreign woman, and ordered that one who left Sparta to emigrate elsewhere should be executed. After instructing others to bring these charges against Leonidas, he and his fellow magistrates proceeded to look for the sign, which is as follows.

Every nine years the ephors pick a clear, moonless night, and sit in silence gazing up at the sky. Should, then, a star shoot from one sector to another sector, they conclude that the kings have committed some fault relating to religion, and they suspend them from their office until an oracle comes from Delphi or Olympia to support the kings who have been convicted by the omen.[21] It was this sign which Lysander now claimed had appeared to him. He had Leonidas brought to trial and produced witnesses to say that he had had two children by an Asian woman whom he had acquired as a spouse from one of Seleucus' officers; but then, when he found her intolerable and was loathed in return, he came home unexpectedly and occupied the kingship since there was no heir to it. While bringing this case, Lysander also tried to persuade Cleombrotus, Leonidas' son-in-law and of royal birth, to lay claim to the kingship. So Leonidas panicked and became a suppliant of Athena in the Bronze House; his daughter, too, left her husband Cleombrotus and took sanctuary with her father. When he was called to trial and did not emerge, the court deprived him of his kingship and conferred it on Cleombrotus.

12. At this point Lysander went out of office because his term had expired. The newly installed ephors[22] brought Leonidas out of his sanctuary, while prosecuting Lysander and Mandrocleidas on a charge of having illegally voted for cancellation of debts and redistribution of land. So in this hazardous predicament the pair of them persuaded the kings to act jointly and to ignore the ephors' resolutions. Their argument was that this magistracy derived its power from disagreements between the kings by adding its vote to that of the one who expressed the better opinion whenever the other disputed a beneficial policy. But when the pair of them were of the same mind their authority was absolute, and opposition to them was unlawful;[23] it was the ephors' proper function to mediate and arbitrate between them when they were in dispute, but not to interfere when they were in agreement. Thus convinced, the two kings and their friends descended on the *agora*, and first removed the ephors from their chairs, and then appointed others,[24] including Agesilaus, to take

their places. Next, by arming a considerable number of young men and releasing prisoners, they made their opponents afraid that a massacre would occur. But in fact the kings killed no one. Agesilaus did want to murder Leonidas as he stole away to Tegea, and did send men after him along the road; but when Agis discovered this, he despatched another group of trustworthy men, who escorted Leonidas and delivered him safely to Tegea.

13. With the kings' policy thus going forward without anyone opposing or blocking it, one man, Agesilaus, now upset and ruined everything: it was that most infamous affliction – avarice – which prompted him to wreck a most splendid and most Spartan plan. For although he was the owner of notably extensive and fertile land, he had also borrowed very heavily. As a result he could not pay off his debts, nor did he want to surrender his land. So he persuaded Agis that it would be too great a revolution for the city if both steps were taken simultaneously, but that if property-owners were first conciliated by remission of debts, then they would cheerfully and peaceably accept the redistribution of land later. This was the view also taken by Lysander's circle, who were all similarly duped by Agesilaus. So together they brought into the *agora* the debtors' documents (which they call *klaria*), made a single pile of them all, and burnt them. Once the flames rose, the wealthy men and creditors left in deep distress, while by way of mocking them Agesilaus declared that never had he seen a brighter light or a clearer blaze than that.

Then the crowd demanded that the division of land should also be made at once, and the kings gave orders for this to be done. But by constantly alleging pressure of other business and by producing excuses, Agesilaus wasted time until Sparta's allies the Achaeans demanded her help, and the expedition fell to Agis. The reason was that the Aetolians were expected to invade the Peloponnese through the territory of Megara; to prevent this the Achaean general Aratus was assembling a force and wrote to the ephors.[25]

14. They immediately despatched Agis, who felt stirred by the aspirations and enthusiasm of his fellow soldiers, most of whom were poor young men. Now that they had gained remission of their debts and were freed in that respect, their hope was that, should they return from the campaign, the land would be distributed. So they proved themselves admirable in Agis' eyes. And as they marched meekly through the Peloponnese, doing no damage and virtually silent, they presented such a spectacle to the cities that the Greeks were astonished and asked themselves what discipline a Spartan army must have had when led by Agesilaus, or the famous Lysander, or the Leonidas[26] of the distant past, when here there was such respect and fear on the part of the troops towards a lad who was virtually the youngest of them all. Certainly the young man himself took pride in being economical, in displaying a zest for hard work, and in not being dressed or armed any more distinctively than a private: as such he was a sight to be seen and admired by ordinary people. The rich, however, did not approve of his revolution and were frightened that it might serve as a spur and an example to the masses everywhere.

15. When Agis linked up with him near Corinth, Aratus was still debating whether to confront the enemy in a set battle. Agis adopted an attitude which was notably enthusiastic and bold, though not immature or thoughtless. For he said that while he favoured a decisive battle, so as not to abandon the gates of the Peloponnese and let the war spread inside them, nonetheless he would act as Aratus decided: Aratus, after all, was senior to him in age and was the general of the Achaeans – whom he had come to campaign with and to assist, not to order about or command. Baton of Sinope[27] claims that Agis refused to offer battle when Aratus gave the order, but he has not come across what Aratus wrote about this matter: as he explained it, since the farmers by this time had finished harvesting nearly all the crops, he thought it better to let the enemy through rather than to risk everything in a battle. So then, after deciding against a battle, Aratus complimented his allies and released them, and Agis (who had been much admired) dismissed his forces.[28]

By this time there was a great deal of turbulence and upheaval in Sparta's internal affairs. 16. For as an ephor Agesilaus, now freed from his earlier constraints, was leaving no extortionate malpractice unexploited, but contrary to the set arrangement of the calendar inserted a thirteenth month not required at that stage of the cycle, and demanded taxes for it. Because he feared those he was injuring – quite apart from the hatred universally shown him – he began maintaining swordsmen who protected him when he went down to the magistrates' headquarters. And as for the kings, he wanted to convey the impression that while he completely despised one, he did feel a certain respect for Agis, though more because he was his relative than because he was king. He spread the word that he was also going to have a further term as ephor.[29]

So his enemies were quick to run the risk of joining forces and openly bringing Leonidas back from Tegea to resume his rule. Even the ordinary people looked with favour on this, because after being cheated out of the distribution of land they were now furious. Agesilaus was spirited away and thus saved by his son Hippomedon, who pleaded with the citizens and was in any case universally popular because of his manly qualities. Of the kings, Agis took refuge with Athena in the Bronze House, while Cleombrotus went as a suppliant to the shrine of Poseidon.[30] It was certainly towards him that Leonidas' attitude seemed more severe: he left Agis alone, but moved against Cleombrotus with troops. He also angrily accused Cleombrotus of conspiring against his own father-in-law as well as depriving him of his kingship and helping to drive him from his homeland.

17. Cleombrotus had no response to make to this, but sat bewildered and silent. Not so Leonidas' daughter Chilonis, however. Before, when her father had been wronged she had felt wronged too, and when Cleombrotus usurped the kingship she left him and looked after her father in his plight. While he was still in Sparta she was a suppliant with him, and then when he was in exile she mourned for him and continued her resentment against Cleombrotus. Yet now, when their fortunes changed again, she changed sides with them and was seen sitting

as a suppliant beside her husband, with her arms flung around him and her children at her feet, one on either side. Everyone was astonished and moved to tears at the woman's goodness and devotion. Clutching her dishevelled clothes and hair, she spoke out:

'Father, it was not out of pity for Cleombrotus that I adopted this clothing and this appearance; rather, ever since the time of your misfortunes and your exile I have been attended and accompanied constantly by sorrow. When now you enjoy the triumph of again being king in Sparta, must I then accept life in this sad plight, or am I to put on a glittering royal costume after witnessing your slaughter of the husband I married when I was young? If he neither moves you with his pleas nor sways you by the tears of his children and wife, he will suffer a more severe penalty for his bad judgement than you wish him to when he sees me, the person dearest to him, dying before him. For how could I live and converse freely with other women when neither my husband nor my father pitied my pleas? In fact as both wife and daughter it has been my role in life to share the misfortunes and disgrace of those close to me. In my husband's case, even if he did have some proper justification, I deprived him of it when I took your side and testified against the events of his reign. On the other hand you make his offence easy to excuse by clearly showing the kingship to be so mighty and so worth the struggle that sons-in-law may justifiably be murdered for it and children disregarded.'

18. Following this outburst Chilonis laid her face on Cleombrotus' head and turned her gaze towards those present, her eyes blinded and melted by grief. Leonidas, after conferring with his friends, directed Cleombrotus to leave his sanctuary and go into exile, but he begged his daughter to stay behind in Sparta and not to abandon him, since he loved her so much and had freely granted her the deliverance of her husband. All the same she was not persuaded, and when her husband left the sanctuary she prostrated herself before the altar of the goddess and then departed with him, giving him one of their children to carry and taking the other herself. As a result, if Cleombrotus had not been

totally consumed by futile ambition, he would have realized that because of his wife his exile was of greater value to him than the kingship.

After dislodging Cleombrotus, Leonidas removed the existing ephors from office and appointed others; then he at once began to lay plans against Agis. To begin with, he tried to persuade him to leave his sanctuary and take a share in the kingship, on the understanding that the citizens had granted him a pardon because his youth and his ambition had led him to be among those duped by Agesilaus. But Agis felt suspicious and stayed where he was. Leonidas himself then gave up trying to trick and deceive him, but Amphares, Damochares and Arcesilaus made a habit of going up and engaging him in conversation. On one occasion they even formed an escort to take him down to the bath, and then after his bath they brought him back again to the temple. While they were all Agis' close friends, Amphares had in addition recently borrowed some clothing and goblets of very great value from Agesistrata, and thus was scheming against the king and the women so as not to have to return these. Also it was he who is said to have been most responsive to Leonidas and to have whipped up the ephors (of whom he was one himself).

19. Although Agis otherwise spent his time in the temple, it was his habit to go down to the bath now and again: so it was there that they determined to arrest him, when he should be out of sanctuary. After carefully watching for when he had bathed, they came to meet him, greeted him and walked along with him to chat and joke as with any close young friend. But at one point on the way there was a turning which led to the prison, and when they reached there as they walked along, Amphares by virtue of his authority gripped Agis and said: 'I am bringing you before the ephors, Agis, to give an account of your conduct in office.' Damochares, who was strong and tall, threw his cloak over him and pulled it round his neck. As agreed beforehand the others shoved from behind, and since Agis was all on his own with no one to help him, they got him into the prison. Leonidas at once appeared with plenty of mercenaries and

surrounded the outside of the building, while the ephors went in to Agis. They also called inside those Elders who shared their views (as if Agis was to be put on trial),[31] and told him to account for his past actions. When the young man laughed at this hypocrisy of theirs, Amphares told him that he would be sorry for it and would pay a price for his audacity. But another of the ephors, as though making Agis a concession and offering him a means of escaping the charge, inquired if he had acted as he did under compulsion from Lysander and Agesilaus. Agis replied that he had been under no compulsion, but that his wish had been to imitate Lycurgus and so revive his constitution. Again, when the same ephor asked if he regretted what he had done, the young man declared that he felt no regret for a plan that had been most splendidly conceived, despite the realization that he would face the extreme penalty.

So they condemned him to death and instructed their attendants to convey him to what is called the *Dechas*. This is a chamber in the prison where condemned men are executed by throttling. But the attendants did not dare take hold of Agis, and those of the mercenaries standing by similarly turned away and shirked this duty, as it was taboo and illegal to lay hands on the person of a king. When Damochares saw this he threatened them and abused them, and personally hauled Agis into the chamber. For by now it was widely known that the arrest had been made; there was an uproar at the entrance and many people with torches; both Agis' mother and grandmother were there making loud demands that the king of the Spartiates should be allowed to speak and to be tried in front of the citizens. So the ephors pushed ahead even more with his execution, in fear that during the night further people might gather and he might be snatched away.

20. When Agis was on his way to execution by strangling and noticed one of the attendants in tears and distraught, he said to him: 'Man, stop crying for me, since my death contrary to law and justice makes me superior to my murderers.' With these words he readily allowed the noose to be placed around his neck. When Amphares then came forward to the entrance,

Agesistrata went down on her knees to him recalling their closeness and friendship. He brought her to her feet with an assurance that nothing violent or fatal would happen to Agis, and told her to go inside to her son, if she would like to. When she requested that her mother also accompany her, Amphares said that there was no objection. And after letting both women in and giving instructions for the prison doors to be shut again, he handed over Archidamia for execution first: she was by now very elderly, and in her old age enjoyed the highest esteem among Spartiate women. Once she was dead he told Agesistrata to step inside. When she came in and saw her son lying on the ground and her mother's corpse hanging from the noose, she personally helped the attendants take it down, then laid out the body next to that of Agis, arranged it decently and covered it. Next she threw herself upon her son, kissed his face and said: 'Son, it is your abundant discretion, mildness and consideration for others which have ruined you, and us too.' When Amphares glimpsed from the door what was going on and heard what she was saying, he came on in and spoke angrily to Agesistrata. 'If you approved of the same ideas as your son,' he said, 'then you will suffer the same fate too.' And Agesistrata stood up to fit on the noose, with the words: 'May this only be of service to Sparta.'

21. When the tragedy was made known throughout the city and the three bodies were being brought out, the citizens were not sufficiently terrorized to conceal either their grief at these events or their hatred of Leonidas and Amphares: their opinion was that nothing more ghastly or more sacrilegious had been perpetrated at Sparta since the Dorians had settled in the Peloponnese. For it seems that even enemies encountering a Spartan king in battle were reluctant to lay hands on him, but would turn away in fear and respect for his majesty. Thus despite the many clashes between Spartans and other Greeks only one king died a violent death before the time of Philip of Macedon – Cleombrotus from a spear-thrust at Leuctra. The Messenians claim that Theopompus as well was killed by Aristomenes;[32] but this is denied by the Spartans, who say that he was only hit.

While there may be some dispute about that, certainly Agis was the first reigning king at Sparta to be put to death by ephors. The course of action he chose to follow was admirable and worthy of Sparta, even though he was of an age at which men who make mistakes gain pardon for them. His friends had more justification for finding fault with him than his enemies, because among the latter he actually saved Leonidas' life and trusted the others, thanks to his very gentle and mild nature.

CLEOMENES

1. After Agis' death his brother Archidamus at once fled, so that Leonidas was too late to arrest him. But he did forcibly remove Agis' wife (who had a newborn infant)[1] from her home and marry her to his son Cleomenes: he was not quite of a suitable age to marry, but Leonidas did not want the woman to be given to anyone else. For Agiatis was heiress to the substantial property of her father Gylippus, as well as being much more beautiful and lovelier than other Greek women, and of equable temperament. The story is that she therefore pleaded hard against being forced, but that once married to Cleomenes, while continuing to detest Leonidas, she did make the young man a good, loving wife. For his part, as soon as he married her he fell in love with her, and in a sense sympathized with his wife's devotion to Agis and her remembrance of him. Consequently he often asked about what had happened, and paid careful attention when she explained Agis' purpose and policy.

Cleomenes, too, was ambitious and idealistic in addition to being as well endowed as Agis with self-discipline and restraint. But he did not possess Agis' exceptional discretion and mildness. Instead his character contained an active and forceful element, and an extremely strong impulse to aim for any worthwhile goal. He regarded it as excellent to dominate willing followers, yet honourable also to overcome disobedient ones and force them into a better path.

2. He was certainly not satisfied with the state of affairs in the city, where the citizens had been lulled by inactivity and indulgence, and the king let all business slide so long as no one disturbed him in his desire to live a life of leisure and luxury in affluent circumstances. Public affairs were disregarded as everyone amassed profits for themselves privately. As for training, self-discipline on the part of the young, stamina and equality, it was unsafe so much as to mention these now that Agis and his family were dead.

While still a youth Cleomenes is also said to have taken part in philosophical discussions at the time when Sphaerus from Olbia[2] visited Sparta and devoted a good deal of attention to both the young men and the ephebes. Sphaerus had become one of the leading followers of Zeno of Citium, and apparently he was delighted by the manliness of Cleomenes' character and tried to fire his ambition. There is a story that when the Leonidas of ancient times was asked his impression of Tyrtaeus'[3] quality as a poet, he replied: 'A good one for firing the spirits of the young.' For the poems filled them with such excitement that they stopped caring for themselves in battle. But where great and passionate characters are concerned, Stoic doctrine has an element that is unstable and hazardous; it is rather when combined with a profound and mild temperament that it particularly develops towards its intrinsic worth.

3. On Leonidas' death Cleomenes succeeded to the throne and saw how thoroughly enervated the citizens were by then.[4] Among the rich there was neglect of public affairs in favour of their private pleasures and gains, while ordinary people, because of the wretched state of their domestic affairs, had lost their enthusiasm for campaigning and their motivation for the traditional system of education.[5] He was, however, king merely in name, and all power belonged to the ephors. Thus he at once developed the idea of changing and overturning this current state of affairs; and since he had a friend Xenares, who had been his lover (such love Spartans call 'inspiration'), he began to test him with questions about Agis – what sort of king he had been, what means he had adopted, and what associates he had had in

embarking on the course he took. To begin with Xenares was willing enough to recall those circumstances, and he would relate and explain how each developed. But once it became clear that Cleomenes' emotions were being roused as he listened to him, and that he was tremendously stirred by Agis' reforms and wished to hear the same account of them repeatedly, Xenares reprimanded him furiously for his unhealthy attitude, and eventually he stopped talking to him and visiting him. However, he did not tell anyone the reason for their disagreement, but just said that Cleomenes was aware of it.

With Xenares thus obstructive Cleomenes reckoned that others too would have the same reaction, and began to lay his plans on his own. With the idea that he would stand a better chance of altering the current state of affairs in time of war rather than of peace, he engineered a clash between the city and the Achaeans, who themselves supplied grounds for complaints anyway. For Aratus, who exercised the strongest influence among the Achaeans, had a longstanding desire to draw the Peloponnesians into a single federation. On the many occasions he had been general, and in his long political career, this was his goal, founded upon the conviction that by such means alone would they withstand their external foes. Practically all the rest had joined him, and only the Spartans, Eleans and such Arcadians as were influenced by the Spartans held aloof. Thus from the moment of Leonidas' death Aratus started to provoke the Arcadians and inflicted particular damage on those who shared a common border with the Achaeans, thereby testing the Spartans and Cleomenes, whom he despised as young and inexperienced.[6]

4. As a result the ephors first sent Cleomenes to seize the Athenaeum near Belbina. This spot is one of the gateways to Laconia, and at that time was disputed with the Megalopolitans. Once Cleomenes had seized and fortified it Aratus raised no complaint, but made a night foray to attack the people of Tegea and Orchomenus. Yet when the courage of the local traitors failed them, Aratus withdrew, reckoning that he had not been noticed. But Cleomenes wrote to him in an ironic vein making a friendly

enquiry about the goal of his nocturnal march. Aratus wrote back that, having heard of Cleomenes' plan to fortify Belbina, he had come down to stop it. Cleomenes then sent a second note stating he had been convinced this was the case: 'But,' he said, 'if it's all the same to you, write and tell me why you brought along those torches and ladders.' When Aratus laughed at the joke and asked what sort of person the youngster was, Damocrates the Spartan exile replied: 'If you aim to make any move against the Spartans, your best course is to act quickly before this young cub grows his claws.'

Next, when Cleomenes at the head of a few horsemen and 300 infantry set up camp in Arcadia, the ephors ordered him to pull back, because they feared a war. But once he had pulled back, and Aratus took Caphyae, then the ephors sent Cleomenes out again.[7] After he had seized Methydrium and devastated the territory of Argos, an Achaean force of 20,000 infantry and 1,000 cavalry commanded by Aristomachus moved against him. Cleomenes met it near Pallantium and was willing to give battle, but Aratus was frightened of such daring and did not allow his general to take the risk. Instead he moved off[8] with the Achaeans cursing him, while the Spartans – who did not even number 5,000 – mocked him and despised him. So Cleomenes' spirits were much raised and he became more confident in his attitude towards the citizens. He also reminded them of the remark made by one of their ancient kings that the pointed question Spartans ask about their enemies is not how many of them there are, but where they are.

5. Then, when the Eleans were being attacked by the Achaeans, Cleomenes gave them help. He fell upon the Achaeans near Mount Lycaeum when they were already withdrawing, routed their entire army, and struck panic into it. He slaughtered great numbers and also took many alive, which even gave rise to a rumour throughout Greece that Aratus was dead. But Aratus exploited his opportunity superbly by making a completely unexpected advance against Mantinea immediately after this rout,[9] thus capturing and holding it. The Spartans' morale by contrast was extremely low and they stood out against further

campaigning by Cleomenes. So he moved quickly to recall Agis' brother, Archidamus, from Messene as the man who should rightfully be his fellow king from the other royal house.[10] His thinking was that the ephors' authority would lose its edge more if the kingship became equally balanced and whole again. But those who had murdered Agis earlier found out about this and were frightened of being punished once Archidamus was restored. So while they did welcome him when he slipped secretly into the city, and did co-operate in his return, they then killed him at once – either against Cleomenes' wishes, as Phylarchus believes, or after his friends had prevailed upon him and he had delivered Archidamus to them. Certainly the blame fell mostly on them since it seemed that they had forced Cleomenes' hand.[11]

6. Nevertheless, having once made up his mind to bring about an instant reform of the state, he bribed the ephors to vote him an expedition. He conciliated many others too with the help of his mother Cratesicleia, who unstintingly joined in contributing to his cause and was equally enthusiastic about it. There is a story that even though she had no desire to remarry, all the same for her son's sake she did take as husband a citizen whose reputation and influence were outstanding. After leading out his expedition Cleomenes took a place in the territory of Megalopolis called Leuctra; and once an Achaean relief force commanded by Aratus appeared promptly to oppose him, he was defeated along with some part of his army which he had marshalled right under the town walls.[12] But then Aratus refused to allow the Achaeans to cross a particular deep ravine, and instead ended his pursuit there. Lydiadas the Megalopolitan was incensed at this, however, and spurred on the cavalrymen round him: but when extending the chase into an area cluttered with vines, ditches and walls he charged ahead, got his men scattered among these obstacles, and ended up in difficulties. Cleomenes spotted this and sent in his Tarentines and Cretans[13] against him, and Lydiadas fell to them after putting up a stiff resistance. The Spartans were encouraged at this, fell upon the Achaeans with a roar, and routed the entire army. Cleomenes gave back

under truce the many who were killed – all except Lydiadas, whose body he ordered to be brought to him. He then dressed it in a purple robe, placed a crown on it and sent it off to the gates of Megalopolis. This was the Lydiadas who had abdicated as tyrant, restored the citizens their freedom, and brought the city over to the Achaeans.

7. Following this Cleomenes now felt very self-assured, and was confident that provided he might keep personal control of affairs in the way he desired while waging war on the Achaeans, then he would easily beat them. He began explaining to his mother's husband Megistonous that they needed to be rid of the ephors and to make all their property common for the citizens' benefit: then once Sparta had regained equality, they would rouse her and guide her forward to assume the leadership of Greece. After Megistonous was won over, he brought in two or three of his friends as well. Then, as it happened, around that date one of the ephors had an astonishing dream as he slept in the sanctuary of Pasiphaë.[14] For he had the impression that there was only one seat in position in the spot where the ephors customarily sit to conduct their business, and that the other four had been removed; as he marvelled at this there issued a voice from the sanctuary, declaring that this was better for Sparta. When the ephor gave Cleomenes a full account of this vision, he was initially very perturbed because he had a certain suspicion that he was being tested; but once convinced that the account was not fabricated he felt encouraged. And taking along such citizens as he suspected would be especially opposed to his policy, he captured Heraea and Asea (cities ranged on the Achaean side), brought in food for the people of Orchomenus, pitched camp near Mantinea, and by long marches[15] up and down altogether wore out the Spartans. Then after leaving the majority of them behind in Arcadia at their own request, he proceeded to Sparta himself at the head of his mercenaries. On the journey he also communicated his plan to those he trusted as being particularly loyal to him, and proceeded at a gentle pace so that he might attack the ephors as they were having dinner.

8. When he was close to the city he first sent Eurycleidas to the ephors' mess on the pretence that he had come from the army with some message from the king; Therycion and Phoebis, two of those brought up with Cleomenes (men termed *mothakes*),[16] followed behind with a few soldiers. Then, while Eurycleidas was still talking to the ephors, these dashed in with daggers drawn and stabbed them. The first ephor, Agylaeus, collapsed under the blow and gave the impression of being dead, but quietly rallied and dragged himself out of the room. Quite unnoticed he crept towards a little building which was a shrine of Fear – normally always kept closed, but by chance it happened to be open at that moment. So he hauled himself inside and shut the door. The other four ephors were killed along with at least ten of those who came to their rescue. But people who kept quiet were not killed, nor was anyone who tried to leave the city obstructed. Even Agylaeus was spared when he emerged from the temple the next day.

9. Spartans have shrines not just of Fear, but also of Death and Laughter and other such emotions. They honour Fear, not as something harmful, like the supernatural powers that they seek to ward off, but because in their opinion the state is held together above all by Fear. It was for this reason, too, that the ephors on entering office used to issue a proclamation to the citizens (as Aristotle says) to shave their moustaches and pay attention to the laws so that these might not be irksome to them. They cited moustaches, I suppose, so as to get the young men used to complying over even the most trivial things. Moreover (in my view) the men of old seemed to regard courage not as fearlessness, but as fear of censure and terror of disgrace. For the men who are the most cowardly before the law are the boldest in front of the enemy: those who are particularly nervous of gaining a bad reputation have the least fear of suffering. Thus it has been well said[17] too that:

> 'Where there is fear, there is also a sense of respect.'

And Homer says:

'I respect you, dear father-in-law, and dread you.'

And:

'In silence, in fear of their leaders.'[18]

In fact the most normal pattern is for the majority to respect those whom they fear too. This was also why it was that the Spartans established Fear next to the ephors' mess, once they had invested that magistracy with virtually absolute authority.

10. So when day broke Cleomenes proscribed eighty citizens who were required to leave, and he removed the ephors' seats – except for one in which he intended to sit himself and handle business. Calling an assembly, he spoke in defence of what had been done. Lycurgus, he said, had associated the Elders with the kings, and for a long period the city had been administered in this way and needed no other form of government. But later, when the war against the Messenians became prolonged, and the kings were not free to attend personally to their judicial work because of their campaigning, they picked some of their friends and left them for the citizens as their replacements. These men were called 'ephors', and at first they did continue to be just the kings' assistants, but gradually they diverted authority to themselves and so, before others realized it, they developed a magistracy[19] in its own right. There is proof of that in the practice still current whereby when the ephors send for the king, he refuses the first time and the second, but at their third summons he rises and goes to them.[20] Asteropus, the first ephor to have given the magistracy notable strength and scope, had lived many generations later. So long as the ephors' behaviour had been moderate, he said, it had been better to tolerate them. But now they had become insufferable as they used their usurped authority to break up the traditional form of government – chasing out some kings, putting others to death without trial, and uttering threats against people who yearned to see Sparta return to its loveliest, most divine condition.

Certainly, were it possible not to resort to murder in order to get rid of Sparta's imported pests – luxury, extravagance, debts, loans, and the even older evils of poverty and wealth – then he would reckon himself the most fortunate king of all if he had cured his country painlessly, like a doctor. But now for acting under compulsion he could claim forgiveness from Lycurgus who, while neither king nor magistrate but a private individual, in his attempt to act as a king advanced into the *agora* armed, so that he terrified King Charillus[21] into taking refuge at an altar. However, as a sound and patriotic person Charillus was quick to associate himself with the measures being taken by Lycurgus and approved the reform of the constitution. All the same, Lycurgus' actions testified to the difficulty of effecting constitutional change without resorting to violence and terror. In his own case, Cleomenes said, he had employed such means with the utmost restraint, in removing those who were standing in the way of Sparta's salvation. For everyone else, he went on, all the land would be made public property, debtors freed of their obligations, and a selection and assessment of foreigners held, with the intention that the strongest of them should become Spartiates and give armed protection to the city. Then we should no longer be forced by a lack of defenders to look on as Laconia is treated as an item of plunder by Aetolians and Illyrians![22]

11. Next he handed over his own property to the state first, followed by his father-in-law Megistonous and each of his friends as well, and then by all the rest of the citizens, and thus the land was divided up. He even assigned a lot to each of those whom he had driven into exile, and promised that he would recall them all home once there was peace and quiet. He made up citizen numbers with the most eligible of the *perioeci*, raising 4,000 hoplites and training them to use a *sarissa* gripped by both hands instead of a spear, and to carry their shield by means of an arm-strap[23] rather than with a handle. He then turned to the young men's training and to the so-called *agoge*, where he was helped in most aspects of his work by Sphaerus, who was there in person. As they quickly restored the proper arrangement of both physical training and messes, there were a few people

who had to be forced to co-operate, but the majority willingly took up the famous, economical Spartan way of life. All the same, so as to soften the image of his absolute rule Cleomenes did appoint his brother Eucleidas as his fellow king. And this was the only time it happened that the Spartiates had two kings from the one house.

12. When he realized that the Achaeans and Aratus – because of the instability of his own situation caused by the revolution – did not imagine he would advance out of Lacedaemon or leave the city in a precarious state amidst such great upheaval, it struck him as not at all an ignoble or valueless thing to demonstrate his army's enthusiasm to its enemies. So he invaded the territory of Megalopolis,[24] amassed substantial spoils and caused widespread devastation of the countryside. Finally after capturing some professional actors who were on their way from Messene, erecting a theatre in enemy territory and sponsoring a competition worth forty *minas*,[25] he spent a day sitting and watching – not because he was eager for a spectacle, but in order to ridicule his enemies and to prove by this show of contempt just how much he surpassed them in strength. Normally, of course, the Spartans alone among Greek and royal armies were not accompanied by mimes, conjurors, dancing girls, or harpists, but were entirely free of licentiousness, buffoonery, and general festivity. The young men were mostly engaged in training, and the older ones in instructing them. Whenever they did have spare time, their entertainment consisted of their usual witticisms and of swapping neat Laconic remarks. I have described the value of this kind of entertainment in my *Life of Lycurgus*.

13. Cleomenes personally set an example to everyone by his own economical, plain lifestyle: it had nothing about it that was vulgar, or superior to ordinary people, so that it served as a public model of restraint – something which gave him a certain advantage in the affairs of Greece. For in their encounters with other kings men were not so much taken aback at all their wealth and extravagance, as disgusted by their arrogance and self-importance, together with the offensive, tactless manner in

which they treated those whom they encountered. In contrast those who approached Cleomenes – who really was a king in fact as in title – did not see him surrounded by any purple robes or cloaks, or by the paraphernalia of couches and litters; nor did he make the conduct of affairs difficult and slow with a swarm of messengers and doorkeepers, or by means of secretaries. Instead he came out simply dressed to respond to greetings, and talked at leisure in an affable, considerate way to those who made him requests, so that they were entranced and bowled over, and declared that he alone was descended from Heracles.

As to his meals, the standard daily pattern was for them to be served in a room with three couches, which was distinctly cramped and Spartan. However, if he was entertaining envoys or men with whom he had ties of hospitality, two extra couches were brought in, while the servants brightened up the dinner a bit, not with any rich dishes or desserts, but by offering more generous portions and a more mellow wine. In fact Cleomenes criticized one of his friends when he heard that in acting as host to foreigners the man had served them black broth and barley bread, as would normally be done in the messes. Cleomenes said that there was no need to act in too rigidly Spartan a fashion on these occasions and in front of foreigners. After the table had been removed a tripod was brought in holding a bronze mixing-bowl filled with wine, together with two silver bowls with a capacity of two *cotylae*,[26] and just a few silver cups – from which anyone drank who wished to, though nobody was required to take a cup. There were no recitations, nor were they missed, since by his own conversation Cleomenes made the party an instructive occasion. He would ask questions about some topics and expound others with an enthusiasm which was by no means unattractive, as he spoke with a charming and smooth good humour. As to the way in which other kings would pursue men, lure them with money and presents, and corrupt them, Cleomenes considered this clumsy and wrong. He felt that the best and most regal way for him to win the trust and loyalty of those he dealt with was to mix with them and talk to them in a pleasant fashion, since there is no difference between a friend and a mercenary except that the former is kept by the way he is treated and addressed, and the latter by money.

14. The Mantineans, then, were the first to appeal to him. And when he crept into the city by night, they expelled the Achaean garrison with his help, and then put themselves at his disposal. He restored them both their laws and their constitution, and on the same day marched off to Tegea. A little later he made a detour through Arcadia and descended upon Pharae in Achaea, with the aim of either provoking a battle with the Achaeans or discrediting Aratus for having run away and abandoned the area[27] to him. Though Hyperbatas was general at the time, Aratus in fact exercised complete authority among the Achaeans. The Achaeans came out in full force and pitched camp at Dymae,[28] near the Hecatombaeum. When Cleomenes came up, it did not strike him as a good plan to place his camp between the hostile city of Dymae and the Achaean army. So he took the risk of challenging the Achaeans and forcing them to engage. He won a pitched battle by routing their phalanx: many of them were killed in the fighting, while many survivors were taken prisoner. Cleomenes then made an assault on Lasium,[29] expelled its Achaean garrison and handed the city to the Eleans.

15. With the Achaeans thus crushed, Aratus (whose regular practice it had been to serve as general in alternate years) now declined the office and stuck to his refusal despite appeals and pleas: not an admirable action – when things were in a very stormy state, so to speak, abandoning the tiller to someone else and relinquishing his own authority.[30] Cleomenes at first seemed to make only modest requests of the Achaeans' ambassadors, but when they kept sending others he began to demand that the leadership be handed to him.[31] He promised that he would not dispute any other issue with the Achaeans, but would restore to them both his prisoners and their strongholds. The Achaeans were willing to accept peace on these terms and they invited Cleomenes to Lerna, where they planned to hold their assembly. Cleomenes, however, after making a forced march and taking a drink of water too soon, brought up a quantity of blood and

lost his voice. As a result, while he did restore to the Achaeans the most distinguished of his prisoners, he put off his conference with them and returned to Sparta.

16. This ruined the situation of Greece at a stage when she still had the capacity in one way or another to recover from her current difficulties and to escape Macedonian arrogance and greed. For in the first place Aratus attempted to constrain the Achaeans and block their policy – either because he distrusted Cleomenes and was frightened of him, or because he envied his unexpected success and considered it dreadful that, after occupying the leading position for thirty-three years,[32] his own reputation and at the same time his power should be destroyed by a young man born long after him, who would now take over the control of a cause which he had himself advanced and guided for such a long time. But when the Achaeans in their amazement at Cleomenes' daring paid no attention to Aratus, and instead regarded it as a fair claim on the part of the Spartans to restore the Peloponnese to its traditional organization, he resorted to a step which would be discreditable for any Greek, but was most dishonourable for such a great one and most unworthy of his past activities and policies: he invited Antigonus into Greece and filled the Peloponnese with Macedonians,[33] whom he himself, as a youngster, had expelled from the Peloponnese! It was he who had liberated Acrocorinth,[34] and had become an object of suspicion on the part of all the kings with whom he had had differences. Indeed it was about this very same Antigonus that he made any number of rude remarks in the *Memoirs* he has left! Moreover he says himself that he incurred substantial injuries and risks on the Athenians' behalf in order to free their city from a garrison and from Macedonians.[35] But then he brought them armed into his country, into his own household, and right into its women's quarters![36] In his estimation the descendant of Heracles, the reigning king of the Spartiates, the man who was guiding the traditional constitution, like a melody out of tune, back again to the famous, wise, Doric laws and lifestyle of Lycurgus, was not fit to be termed leader of Sicyonians and Tritaeans.[37] Aratus shunned the barley-bread, the rough cloak,

and – most frightful of all his charges against Cleomenes – his confiscations from the rich and his subventions to the poor. He grovelled himself, and Achaea with him, to a diadem, a purple robe, and decrees of Macedonians and satraps. And in order not to give the impression of carrying out instructions from Cleomenes, at festivals in honour of Antigonus he garlanded himself, made sacrifices and sang paeans – all in honour of a man wasted by consumption. Now while it is with no wish to accuse Aratus that I write this (since in many respects he was a true Greek and a great man), yet I do so with a feeling of pity for the weakness of human nature when it cannot produce a faultless excellence even in characters so notable and so distinguished for virtue.

17. When the Achaeans had arrived[38] at Argos once more for the conference and Cleomenes had come down from Tegea, people were very optimistic that there would be peace. But Aratus had by now reached agreement with Antigonus on the most important points, and he was frightened that Cleomenes would attain all his objectives by winning over the people or by forcing their hand. So he demanded that he should either accept 300 hostages and approach the Achaeans alone, or should come with his forces to the gymnasium called the Cyllarabium outside the city[39] for the discussions. When Cleomenes heard this, he declared that he was being wronged, since he ought to have been informed of this openly before, rather than facing suspicion and expulsion now, when he had come right to their doorstep. He wrote the Achaeans a letter about this, which mostly consisted of accusations of Aratus; and Aratus in turn maligned him at length to the people. Next Cleomenes quickly struck camp and sent a herald to declare war on the Achaeans – not to Argos, but to Aegium[40] (as Aratus mentions), so as to anticipate their preparations.

The Achaeans were now in turmoil and their cities were on the verge of insurrection. The people in them were hoping for division of land and cancellation of debts; in many places the leading citizens were resentful at Aratus, while some were furious with him for inviting Macedonians to the Peloponnese. So, feeling encouraged by these circumstances, Cleomenes invaded Achaea, and first captured Pellene in a sudden assault and expelled its Achaean garrison; after that he won Pheneus and Penteleium[41] over to his side. The Achaeans became afraid that some treachery was developing at Corinth and Sicyon, so they dispatched their cavalry and mercenaries from Argos to keep those cities under surveillance, while they went down to Argos themselves for the Nemean Games.[42] Cleomenes' expectation was that by making a surprise attack on the city when it was crammed with a crowd of festival-goers and spectators, he would cause even greater shock – and such was in fact the case. He moved his army up to the walls at night and seized the rugged, inaccessible area near the Aspis[43] above the theatre. This so terrified the population that not a man considered resistance, but instead they accepted a garrison, handed over twenty citizens as hostages, and became allies of the Spartans under Cleomenes' command.

18. This gave a tremendous boost to his reputation and authority. For despite their many efforts the ancient Spartan kings had not been able to win over Argos securely, while Pyrrhus,[44] that most resourceful of generals, had forced an entry, yet did not hold the city; instead he was killed, and a substantial part of his army died with him. Thus there was astonishment at Cleomenes' swiftness and acumen. Those who previously had laughed at his claims to be imitating Solon[45] and Lycurgus with his cancellation of debts and equalization of property were by now totally convinced that he was responsible for the change in the Spartiates' conduct. For previously they were in such a depressed condition and so incapable of helping themselves that when the Aetolians raided Laconia they took away 50,000 slaves (this was the occasion[46] when one of the older Spartiates is said to have remarked that the enemy did Laconia a service by relieving it of a burden). Just a short time had passed, and they had only just resumed their traditional customs and had got back into the way of the famous *agoge*, yet already – as if Lycurgus were there in person and conducting their policy – they were offering ample proof of their valour and discipline as

they had regained the Peloponnese and were winning back the leadership of Greece for Sparta.

19. Immediately after the capture of Argos, Cleonae and Phlius came over to Cleomenes. At the time Aratus happened to be at Corinth conducting an investigation of people alleged to be supporters of the Spartans. But when the news of these developments assailed him, he was thrown into a panic and imagined that the city was gravitating towards Cleomenes and wanted to be rid of the Achaeans. So while summoning the citizens to the council building, he stole away to the gate unnoticed. His horse was brought there, he mounted, and fled to Sicyon. According to Aratus, the Corinthians were so eager to reach Cleomenes at Argos that all their horses were exhausted, while Cleomenes criticized the Corinthians for not arresting Aratus, but letting him escape. All the same Cleomenes did send Megistonous to him with a request that he hand over Acrocorinth (since it had an Achaean garrison), and with the offer of a large sum of money. He replied, however, that he was not in control of events, but rather he was controlled by events. This is what Aratus has recorded.

But Cleomenes emerged from Argos, brought the people of Troezen, Epidaurus and Hermione over to his side, and arrived at Corinth.[47] Since the Achaeans refused to abandon the citadel, Cleomenes blockaded it. At the same time he summoned Aratus' friends and agents and gave them instructions to take over his house and his property, and to protect and manage these. Then once again he sent off Tritymallus the Messenian to him with a proposal that Acrocorinth should be jointly garrisoned by the Achaeans and Spartans, and with a private assurance to Aratus that he would pay him double the allowance he was getting from King Ptolemy. But Aratus was unresponsive, and instead sent off his son to Antigonus along with the other hostages, and also persuaded the Achaeans to vote for surrendering Acrocorinth to Antigonus. Cleomenes therefore invaded the territory of Sicyon and devastated it, and in addition accepted the gift of Aratus' property when the Corinthians voted it to him.

20. When Antigonus was crossing Geraneia with his considerable force, Cleomenes thought that the real need was to be on guard with stockades and walls in the Oneian hills rather than at the Isthmus, and that it was better to wear out the Macedonians by a war of position rather than to engage their experienced phalanx head-on. Following through with this plan he did indeed put Antigonus in difficulties, since the latter did not have sufficient supplies made ready in advance, nor was it simple to force a way through with Cleomenes dug in. After Antigonus failed in an attempt to slip through Lechaeum at night and lost some of his soldiers, Cleomenes was thoroughly encouraged and his men, excited by the victory, went off to their meal. Antigonus by contrast was discouraged because necessity limited him to plans which would be difficult to carry out. For he was considering shifting camp to the headland of Heraeum and from there ferrying his army over to Sicyon by ship – something that would take a long time and an extraordinary amount of preparation. But then towards evening some men who were friends of Aratus came to him by sea from Argos, inviting him there because the Argives were ready to revolt from Cleomenes. The instigator of the rebellion[48] was Aristoteles, who had no trouble persuading the people since they were irritated that Cleomenes had not effected the cancellation of debts which they had hoped for. So Aratus took 1,500 soldiers from Antigonus and sailed round to Epidaurus. Aristoteles did not wait for him, but at the head of the citizens attacked the garrison on the acropolis, and was reinforced by Timoxenus who came up with the Achaeans from Sicyon.

21. Once Cleomenes heard of this around the second watch of the night[49] he sent for Megistonous and ordered him to save the situation at Argos at once – in some anger because Megistonous, by giving a special assurance about the Argives' loyalty to him, had stopped the expulsion of suspects. So after sending off Megistonous with 2,000 troops, Cleomenes himself kept a watch on Antigonus and maintained the Corinthians' morale by claiming that there was nothing serious going on at Argos, but just some disturbance caused by a handful of men. However,

when Megistonous was killed in the fighting as he made his assault on Argos, and when the garrison only just held out and kept sending a stream of messengers to Cleomenes, he became apprehensive that the enemy might take Argos and by blocking the passes might then devastate Laconia freely and lay siege to Sparta in its undefended state. For these reasons he led his army away from Corinth, with the immediate result that he was deprived of this city, for Antigonus came in and planted a garrison. Then when he reached Argos he tried to make an assault on the walls and marshalled his forces together for this after their march. By hacking through the vaults under the Aspis he made his way up to join the men inside who were still holding out against the Achaeans. Then by bringing up ladders he did gain some areas inside the city and cleared the enemy from the lanes by ordering his Cretan archers to shoot at them. But when he saw Antigonus with his phalanx coming down from the mountains into the plain, and the cavalry in ample numbers already riding into the city, he despaired of winning it. Assembling all his men round him he brought them down safely and withdrew along the wall. Though he had made very great gains in an extremely short time and had come close to attaining control of almost the entire Peloponnese at once in a single expedition, he just as quickly lost everything again. Among those campaigning with him, some abandoned him at once, while others surrendered their cities to Antigonus a little later.

22. After his campaign had met with this outcome and he had led his army off, it was already evening when near Tegea some messengers from Sparta reached him with news of a misfortune at least equal to the one he had just experienced – the death of his wife. She was the reason why he had not been able to endure their separation even on his very successful campaigns, but used to return to Sparta often because of the love and immense esteem he felt for her. Though he was thus stricken with grief, as was natural enough for a young man on the loss of the loveliest, most modest wife, in his sorrow he in no way disgraced or abandoned his resolve and loftiness of mind. Instead he kept his voice, his clothes and his appearance just as they had normally

been before, and even issued orders to his commanders and gave thought to the Tegeates' security. But when day came he went down to Sparta, and after discharging his grief at home with his mother and children, he at once turned to making plans for the welfare of the state.

Ptolemy, the king of Egypt, promised him help, but demanded that his children and his mother be handed over as hostages. For a long time he was ashamed to tell his mother this, and though he frequently went in and was on the point of broaching it, he kept quiet. As a result her suspicions were aroused and she asked his friends if there was something which he could not bring himself to tell her even though he wanted to. When Cleomenes eventually summoned up the courage to speak, she laughed loudly and said: 'Was it this which you frequently meant to tell me but lacked the courage? Why ever don't you hurry to put me on board ship and send me off wherever you think this body of mine will be of the greatest service to Sparta, before old age disposes of it as it just sits here?' So when everything was ready they took a land route to Taenarum with the troops in arms to escort them. Then as Cratesicleia was about to go on board ship she drew aside Cleomenes by himself into the temple of Poseidon. He was very distressed and upset, so she embraced him and kissed him and said: 'Come now, king of the Spartans. When we emerge we want no one to see us in tears nor doing anything unworthy of Sparta. This is all that lies in our power; but our fortunes must be as heaven ordains.'

With these words she composed her features and boarded the ship, taking the little boy with her; then she quickly instructed the helmsman to set sail. When she reached Egypt she discovered that Ptolemy was admitting proposals and embassies from Antigonus, while the news about Cleomenes was that the Achaeans were inviting him to make peace, but that because of her he was afraid of ending the war without Ptolemy's approval. So she sent a message to him declaring that he should act as was fitting and advantageous for Sparta, and should not remain in constant fear of Ptolemy because of a single old woman and a little boy. Such, then, is said to have been her conduct in this predicament.

23. Once Antigonus[50] had taken Tegea and then sacked Orchomenus and Mantinea, Cleomenes was confined just to Laconia itself. After freeing those helots who paid five Attic *minas*, and thus accumulating 500 *talents*,[51] he also armed 2,000 of them in Macedonian style to counter Antigonus' 'White Shields',[52] and began to plan a major, totally unexpected initiative. Now at this date Megalopolis in itself was not at all smaller or weaker than Sparta. It was also enjoying the assistance of the Achaeans and Antigonus, who was in position close beside it and was thought to have been called in by the Achaeans because the Megalopolitans had particularly urged it. It was this city which Cleomenes aimed to pounce on, so to speak – since there is no better word to convey the element of speed and surprise in his plan of action. He ordered his troops to draw five days' rations and led them out towards Sellasia, as if he was going to raid the area around Argos. But from there he went down into the territory of Megalopolis, halted for a meal near Rhoeteium, and then at once made for the city by the route through Helissous.[53] When he was not far away he despatched Panteus with two brigades of Spartans under orders to seize the section between a pair of towers, which he had discovered was the least defended part of the Megalopolitans' walls; meanwhile he followed slowly with the rest of the army. Panteus found not just that spot but also a substantial stretch of the wall to be unguarded: some of it he at once began pulling down, and some he undermined, while all the sentries he encountered he killed. Cleomenes wasted no time in linking up with him, and was in the city[54] with his army before the Megalopolitans realized it.

24. No sooner had this calamity dawned upon those in the city than some fled at once taking with them at random whatever possessions they could, while others grouped together under arms to stand up to the enemy and attack them. They did not have the strength to dislodge them, but they did give those citizens who were fleeing the opportunity to escape in safety, with the result that no more than 1,000 people were caught, whereas all the others along with their children and wives made good their escape to Messene. The majority even of those who

gave assistance and fought survived. Only a few altogether were captured, among them Lysandridas and Thearidas, men of outstanding reputation and authority among the Megalopolitans. So the soldiers, as soon as they apprehended them, immediately brought them to Cleomenes.

When Lysandridas saw Cleomenes from a distance he roared out: 'King of the Spartans, now you have the chance to take a step more noble and more kingly than your present success, and to win the highest glory as a result.' Cleomenes had his suspicions of what he was going to ask, so he replied: 'What do you mean, Lysandridas? After all, you are surely not about to tell me to give you back your city?' And Lysandridas said: 'That is certainly what I mean, and my advice to you is not to destroy a city such as this, but to fill it with friends and loyal, reliable allies by restoring their country to the Megalopolitans and becoming the saviour of so great a people.' After a brief silence Cleomenes said: 'While it is hard to believe this, still my wish is always to give enhancement of my reputation priority over mere advantage.' With these words he despatched the two men to Messene accompanied by a herald, offering to hand the Megalopolitans back their city provided they became his allies and friends, and broke with the Achaeans. Despite this considerate, humane offer on Cleomenes' part, Philopoemen refused to allow the Megalopolitans to abandon their pledge to the Achaeans. Instead he accused Cleomenes of trying not so much to return the city as to gain it *and* its citizens; then he expelled Thearidas and Lysandridas from Messene. This was the Philopoemen who later became leader of the Achaeans and acquired the highest reputation among the Greeks – as I have recorded in a separate account of him.[55]

25. Once this was relayed to Cleomenes, although so far he had carefully guarded the city against damage and looting, so that no one who stole even the smallest item might escape detection, now he became so thoroughly resentful and angry that he did ransack property and send off statues and pictures to Sparta. He demolished and ruined most of the city, including its most important areas, and then moved off home in fear of Antigonus

and the Achaeans. But they took no action since they happened to be holding a council at Aegium.[56] However, when Aratus mounted the rostrum, for a long time he continued crying with his cloak held in front of his face. When those present in their astonishment urged him to speak, he said that Megalopolis had been destroyed by Cleomenes. At this the meeting at once broke up with the Achaeans astounded at the speed and magnitude of the disaster. Antigonus did attempt to go to the rescue, but when his army proved slow in emerging from its winter quarters[57] he ordered it instead to stay put, while he made his own way to Argos accompanied by just a few soldiers.

And this is why the execution of Cleomenes' next exploit, even though it looked like a piece of reckless, even crazy daring, was in fact carried out with considerable advance planning, as Polybius states. For Cleomenes was aware that for their winter quarters the Macedonians were dispersed among various cities, and that Antigonus, spending the winter at Argos with friends, had only a few mercenaries with him. So he invaded the territory of Argos[58] on the reckoning that either shame would provoke Antigonus into fighting and he would defeat him, or he would not dare to fight and would thus alienate the Argives. This is indeed what happened. For once Cleomenes was ravaging the countryside and plundering everything, the Argives were extremely upset and gathered at the king's doors with loud demands that he either fight or hand the leadership over to better men. But Antigonus, as a shrewd general should, considered that taking an unreasonable risk and sacrificing his security would be the shameful course, rather than earning a bad reputation among the crowd outside. So he did not march out, but stuck by his conclusions. Cleomenes came right up to the walls with his army and then, after delivering insults and doing damage, withdrew with impunity.

26. A short time afterwards, however, when he heard that Antigonus was again advancing to Tegea with the intention of invading Laconia from there, he quickly mustered his soldiers and, by taking alternative routes, appeared in front of the city of Argos at dawn. He ravaged the plain, not slashing the grain

with sickles and swords in the usual way, but beating it down with massive pieces of wood shaped like sabres which his men wielded almost playfully as they marched along, thus flattening and destroying the entire crop with no difficulty. However, when they reached the Cyllarabis and attempted to set fire to the gymnasium, Cleomenes stopped them, out of a sense that his measures at Megalopolis had been taken in anger rather than honourably. Antigonus first retreated to Argos at once, and then secured all the heights and passes with patrols. Affecting to show no concern and to feel only contempt for him, Cleomenes then sent heralds with a request to have the keys of the Heraeum,[59] so that he might sacrifice to the goddess and then leave. After thus teasing Antigonus in this ironic fashion, Cleomenes sacrificed to the goddess right next to the locked temple, and then led his army off to Phlius. From there he went on to dislodge the garrison at Olygyrtus and continued down to Orchomenus, where he not only filled the citizens with determination and courage, but even conveyed to his enemies the impression of being a born leader fitted for great things. After all, with no more than a single city as his base he battled on against the combined forces of the Macedonians, all the Peloponnesians and the king's resources. Moreover his ability not only to keep Laconia unscathed, but also to do damage to his enemies' territory and to take such great cities, suggested a man of no ordinary brilliance and greatness of mind.

27. However, my view is that the first person to describe money as 'the sinews of any undertaking' said this with an eye to the conduct of war in particular. For on one occasion when the Athenians, despite having no money, gave orders for the launching and manning of their triremes, Demades[60] said: 'One must knead bread before taking the forward command.' There is also the story about the Archidamus of old,[61] around the outbreak of the Peloponnesian War, when the allies were urging him to fix their contributions, saying that war does not consume set amounts. For just as those athletes who have trained properly eventually weigh down and get the better of those who are merely lithe and skilful, so too Antigonus by devoting substan-

tial resources to the war exhausted and outmatched Cleomenes, who could only just afford to pay the mercenaries and feed the citizens in his army. Yet in other ways time was on Cleomenes' side, because developments at home demanded Antigonus' attention. For in his absence barbarians were ravaging Macedonia and overrunning it, while just at that time a great army of Illyrians had moved in from upcountry, and it was their plundering which prompted the Macedonians to recall Antigonus. As it happened, these letters very nearly reached him before the battle; and if they had, he would have left at once, abandoning the Achaeans completely. But Fortune, which determines the greatest of events by a slim margin, tipped the balance of advantage and demonstrated her influence in such a way that only just after the battle of Sellasia was over, and Cleomenes had lost his army and his city, did those summoning Antigonus appear. This in particular made Cleomenes' misfortune even more distressing. For if he had hung on for only two days and continued to avoid a battle, there would have been no need for him to fight, and after the Macedonians' departure he could have made a truce with the Achaeans on terms of his own choosing. Yet in the event, as I have explained, lack of money forced him to stake everything on an engagement[62] in which, as Polybius says, his 20,000 men confronted 30,000.

28. In the crisis he proved himself a superb general, while the citizens responded to him energetically and even his mercenaries fought faultlessly. But what crushed him was the different style of equipment and the weight of the heavily armoured phalanx. Phylarchus claims that there was also treachery, which did particular damage to Cleomenes' cause. For Antigonus instructed his Illyrians and Acarnanians to make secret manoeuvres, and of the two enemy wings to encircle the one commanded by Cleomenes' brother Eucleidas; then he made the rest of his forces ready for battle.[63] From his observation-point Cleomenes noticed that the arms of the Illyrians and the Acarnanians were nowhere to be seen, and he was afraid that Antigonus might be using them for some such purpose. He called for Damoteles, who was in charge of the *krypteia*,[64] and

instructed him to take a look and investigate the situation at the rear and all around his battle line. The story is that Damoteles had in fact been bribed with money beforehand by Antigonus, and when he told Cleomenes not to worry about those quarters, which were in good shape, but to concentrate on his opponents in front and fight them off, he trusted him and advanced against Antigonus. The impetus of his Spartiates' charge against the phalanx forced the Macedonians to retreat for about five *stades*,[65] while he followed successfully keeping up the pressure. But then, once Eucleidas and his men on the other wing had been surrounded, he came to a halt and realizing the danger they were in he cried out: 'Dearest brother, you are gone from me! You are gone, you noble figure, a model to Spartiate youth, a theme for women's songs!' After Eucleidas and his men had been thus slaughtered and the victorious enemy were now attacking from that direction, Cleomenes looked to his own safety, since he saw that his soldiers were in confusion and no longer had the spirit to stand firm. The accounts state that the majority of his mercenaries fell, as well as all but about 200 of the 6,000 Spartans.

29. When he reached the city he recommended those citizens who met him to accept Antigonus, though he declared that for his own part, whether it meant life or death, he would continue on whatever course might yet benefit Sparta. Once he saw the women running up to those who had fled with him, taking their weapons and offering them drink, he went into his own house. But when the young girl of free status, whom he had taken from Megalopolis and kept since his wife's death, came forward and wanted to attend to him as usual on his return from an expedition, he would neither allow himself to take a drink despite a raging thirst, nor though utterly exhausted to sit down. Instead, just as he was in full armour, he placed his hand at an angle against one of the columns, rested his face on his forearm, and for a short while relaxed his body thus while mentally ranging over every possible scheme. Then he set out for Gytheum[66] with his friends. From there they boarded ships made ready for this specific purpose, and set sail.

30. On his arrival Antigonus took control of the city and dealt humanely with the Spartans. He did not besmirch or insult Sparta's reputation, but restored both her laws and her constitution,[67] and then after sacrificing to the gods left on the third day, once he had learned that warfare was widespread in Macedonia and that the country was being devastated by the barbarians. Moreover his disease by now had a full grip of him, having developed into acute consumption and severe catarrh. All the same he did not give up, but confronted the conflicts at home in a way that led to his meeting his death more gloriously after an overwhelming victory and a massive slaughter of the barbarians.[68] This resulted (as is plausible and vouched for personally by Phylarchus and his circle) from the shout he raised on the battlefield, which caused an internal haemorrhage. In the schools there used to be a version that after shouting for joy following his victory 'O splendid day!', he brought up a quantity of blood, ran a high fever, and died. This, then, was what happened to Antigonus.

31. Cleomenes, on the other hand, landed at another island, Aigilia, on his voyage from Cythera. While he was considering continuing on from there to Cyrene,[69] one of his friends, by the name of Therycion, had a private talk with him. He was a man who adopted a high-minded attitude in all undertakings, and always spoke in a rather elevated and haughty tone. 'O king,' he said, 'we have foregone the finest form of death, that on the battlefield. Yet everyone has heard our declaration that only when the king of the Spartiates is a corpse will Antigonus overcome him. But the form of death which ranks second in terms of glory and merit still remains open to us now. What is the destination of our aimless voyage, as we flee from troubles close by and dash far away? For if there is no disgrace in the descendants of Heracles being slaves to those of Philip and Alexander, we shall save ourselves a long voyage by surrendering to Antigonus, who in all likelihood is as superior to Ptolemy as Macedonians are to Egyptians. But if we do not think it right to be ruled by those who have beaten us in battle, why do we accept as our master a man who has not conquered

us, so that we may appear inferior not to one, but to two kings, because of our flight from Antigonus and our flattery of Ptolemy? Or shall we claim that we have come to Egypt because of your mother? Yet when she shows you off to Ptolemy's wives, what a wonderful and admirable sight you would be – her son who was a king, but is now a captive and a refugee! Instead, while we still retain control of our own swords and are in sight of Laconia, shall we not free ourselves from misfortune here, and thus justify ourselves to those who lie at Sellasia for Sparta's sake, rather than lounging in Egypt inquiring who Antigonus has left as satrap of Sparta?'

Cleomenes replied as follows to this speech by Therycion: 'Poor man, dying is the easiest of mortal actions and one which everybody may readily perform. But do you consider yourself brave in resorting to this form of escape, more shameful as it is than our earlier one? Even better men than we have yielded to their enemies before now, either tripped up by bad luck or overcome by force of numbers. The man who despairs in the face of difficulties and hardships, or of public censure and opinion, is defeated by his own feebleness. For a death that is self-inflicted ought not to be an escape from action, but an action in its own right, since it is despicable that men should live, and die, just for themselves. Yet this is what you are now inviting us to do in your eagerness to be free of our current plight, though the act is one which will have no further merit or value. But my opinion is that neither you nor I should abandon our hopes for our country. Yet whenever those hopes abandon us, then death will come very easily to such as desire it.'

Therycion made no reply to this, but at his first opportunity left Cleomenes, walked off along the seashore and committed suicide.

32. Cleomenes for his part sailed from Aigilia, reached Libya, and by making his way through the king's territory arrived in Alexandria. When they first met, he found Ptolemy's[70] attitude towards him guarded, and just routinely agreeable. Yet this was to change as he personally proved his ability and demonstrated his shrewdness, while his plain, Spartan temperament retained

its independent charm in his everyday dealings; he did not disgrace his noble background at all, or seem crushed by his plight, but showed himself a more reliable character than those whose every word is designed to please and to flatter. Therefore Ptolemy came to respect him greatly and to regret that by disregarding such a fine man he had abandoned him to Antigonus, who had thereby won so much glory and at the same time power. So now Ptolemy began trying to recompense Cleomenes with distinctions and kindnesses, and kept making encouraging declarations that he would send him back to Greece with ships and money and would restore him to his kingdom. He also offered him an allowance of twenty-four *talents* annually. From this Cleomenes made provision for himself and those close to him on an economical, reasonable scale, but he used up most of it on charity and grants to those who had escaped to Egypt from Greece.

33. However, before he could make good his promise to send Cleomenes home, the elder Ptolemy died. At once the kingdom was plunged into such a lax, drunken state, with women wielding extensive power, that Cleomenes' concerns too were neglected. For the king[71] personally suffered so much mental damage from women and liquor that whenever he was particularly sober and in full possession of his faculties he would celebrate rites at which he used a drum to assemble people in the palace. In consequence the most important matters of government were handled by his mistress Agathocleia and by her mother, the procuress Oenanthe. Nonetheless initially there did really seem to be some role for Cleomenes as well. This was because of Ptolemy's fear of his brother Magas, who was influential in military circles, thanks to his mother. So Ptolemy enlisted Cleomenes' help and made him privy to his secret councils as he plotted to do away with his brother. Despite the fact that everyone else was urging him to put this plot into effect, Cleomenes alone argued against it, saying that instead, were it possible, more brothers should be produced for the king to make his position really secure and stable. Whenever Sosibius, the most influential of the king's friends, maintained that it was

impossible for them to rely on the mercenaries so long as Magas was still alive, Cleomenes would tell him to have no worries on that score since more than 3,000 of the mercenaries were Peloponnesians – men loyal to himself who at a mere nod from him would spring to his side in battle gear. At the time it was made, this claim substantially enhanced confidence in Cleomenes' loyalty as well as his reputation as a strong figure. Later, however, when Ptolemy's feebleness aggravated his apprehensions, and (as tends to happen in the absence of rational thinking) it seemed to him safest to be frightened of everything and distrustful of everybody, the claim made Cleomenes an object of fear to the courtiers because of his influence over the mercenaries. And many could be heard to remark that 'This is a lion living among these sheep.' That was indeed the kind of impression which he made on the king's men as he observed the course of events with a quietly suspicious air.

34. So he gave up asking for ships and an army. But then he learned that Antigonus was dead, that the Achaeans were embroiled in a war against the Aetolians, and that the situation itself expressed a longing and a call for his return, since the Peloponnese had become so confused and torn apart. So he asked to be despatched as a single individual with his friends, but the plea met with no success: the king was deaf to it since he was completely preoccupied with his women and festivities and revelry, while Sosibius, who was placed in complete control and was chief adviser, reckoned that even though Cleomenes would be an intractable and formidable figure if he remained in Egypt against his will, he might prove even more formidable if he was allowed to leave, given his daring and his grand designs and the fact that he had observed that the kingdom was ailing. Not even gifts mollified him. He was like Apis,[72] who spends his days in plenty and apparent luxury but whose natural inclination is to long for a life of running and jumping freely, and who plainly is irked by the way of life prescribed for him by the priests. Cleomenes likewise was displeased by being pampered, but

Continued to pine in his inmost heart,

like Achilles

As he stayed there, and went on longing for the battle-cry and fighting.[73]

35. Such was Cleomenes' situation when there arrived in Alexandria a Messenian called Nicagoras,[74] a man who detested him though he pretended to be his friend. Nicagoras had once sold Cleomenes a fine estate, but then because of financial straits, I imagine, and apparently other preoccupations, and wars, he had not received his money. So when Cleomenes happened to be taking a walk along the quay at the harbour and at that moment spotted him disembarking from his trading vessel, he welcomed him warmly and asked him what prompted his visit to Egypt. Nicagoras was similarly genial in his response and said that he was bringing the king some splendid war-horses. At this Cleomenes laughed and said: 'To my mind it would have been better for you to arrive with a cargo of girls who play the sambuca and of boy prostitutes, since these currently preoccupy the king most of all.' Nicagoras smiled at this at the time. Yet a few days later he reminded Cleomenes about the estate and asked if now at last he might be paid for it – something he would not have bothered him about, he claimed, had he not incurred a considerable loss on the sale of his wares. When Cleomenes declared that he had nothing left of what he had been given, Nicagoras in his annoyance disclosed Cleomenes' jibe to Sosibius. The latter, while delighted to learn of it, was at the same time casting round for a more serious charge with which to arouse the king, and so persuaded Nicagoras to write and leave behind a letter accusing Cleomenes of having planned to occupy Cyrene, if only he could obtain triremes and soldiers from him. So Nicagoras put this in writing and sailed away. Four days later Sosibius brought the letter to Ptolemy as if it had just been handed to him, and so roused the young man to make the decision that Cleomenes should be installed in a large mansion where he would be afforded the same style of living, except that he would be kept there under house arrest.

36. This, then, was distressing enough to Cleomenes, but his outlook for the future was now made more depressing by the following incident. Ptolemy, the son of Chrysermus and a friend of the king, had maintained a consistently cordial attitude towards Cleomenes: the two had struck up something of a familiar relationship and would exchange views with frankness. So at this stage when Cleomenes asked him to visit him, he did come, and adopted a moderate tone, disarming his suspicions and taking a defensive line about the king. But as he was on his way out of the house again, having failed to notice that Cleomenes was following right behind as far as the doors, he reprimanded the guards sharply for the careless, lazy watch they were keeping on such a great monster who was so hard to confine. After hearing this with his own ears Cleomenes turned back – before Ptolemy could observe him – and informed his friends. In consequence all of them abandoned their earlier hopes and angrily resolved to take revenge for Ptolemy's unjust, outrageous treatment of them, and then to meet their deaths in a style worthy of Sparta rather than to hang around like sacrificial victims to be fattened and chopped down. In their view it was a dreadful thing that Cleomenes, after spurning any peace with Antigonus, that man of war and of action, should sit waiting until a free moment might be found by a king who was a beggarly priest of Cybele[75] and who intended to kill him just as soon as he should put down his drum and break off his ecstatic worship.

37. After they had made this decision Ptolemy happened to leave for Canopus.[76] So first they spread a rumour that Cleomenes' guard was going to be withdrawn by the king, and then in conformity with the royal custom of sending a dinner and presents to those on the point of being released from confinement, Cleomenes' friends made ready a quantity of such things for him and sent them in from outside, thereby deceiving the guards into thinking that the things had been despatched by the king. Moreover Cleomenes performed sacrifices, divided his gifts generously with his guards, put on garlands and reclined to have a feast with his friends. The story is that he put his

scheme into action earlier than planned, once he realized that a servant who was one of those in the plot had been sleeping outside with a woman of whom he was enamoured. And so, in fear of being informed against, when it was midday and he saw that the guards were in a drunken sleep, he put on his tunic, loosened its seam from the right shoulder downwards, and then with drawn sword dashed out accompanied by thirteen friends in the same gear. Hippitas, who was lame, joined enthusiastically in the initial rush, but when he saw that he was slowing down their progress, he told them to kill him and not to ruin the scheme by waiting for a man who was useless. But by chance one of the Alexandrians was leading a horse past the doors, so they commandeered it and mounted Hippitas, then charged through the streets at the double, inviting the populace to claim its liberty. While it seems that people did evidently have sufficient nerve to praise and admire Cleomenes' daring, nobody had the courage to follow him and help.

At any rate three of his men did straight away assault and kill Ptolemy the son of Chrysermus as he was leaving the palace. Then when another Ptolemy, the city guard commander, drove towards them in a chariot, they turned and faced him: after scattering his servants and bodyguards, they pulled him from his chariot and killed him. They made for the citadel next, with the intention of smashing open the prison and employing the great mob of prisoners. But the warders forestalled them by smartly barricading themselves in, so that once this initiative on his part was repulsed Cleomenes found himself ranging all over the city, and wandering about with nobody joining him but rather the entire population shunning him in terror. So in these circumstances he gave up, remarking to his friends: 'It certainly is no surprise that women take control of these men who shun liberty'; and he urged them all to die in a fashion worthy of himself and of their achievements. And first Hippitas at his own request was struck down by one of the younger men, and next each of the others calmly and fearlessly stabbed himself, except Panteus who was the first to break into Megalopolis. As a youth he had been extremely handsome and was the young man best suited to the *agoge*. The king had been his lover, and now gave him the order to commit suicide as soon as he saw that he himself and the others were dead. When they had all fallen, Panteus jabbed each one with his dagger to check that there was none still left alive undetected. And when he touched Cleomenes on the ankle he noticed that his face twitched; so he kissed him and then sat down beside him. And when Cleomenes had finally expired, he embraced his corpse and stabbed himself to death over it.

38. This, then, shows the kind of man Cleomenes was, and this was how he met his death after being king of Sparta for sixteen years.[77] Once the news spread through the entire city Cratesicleia, noble woman though she was, broke down at the magnitude of the catastrophe, put her arms around Cleomenes' children, and wept. But the elder of the two children broke away when no one could have expected it and threw himself head-first off the roof: and while he was seriously injured, yet still he was not killed, but was picked up screaming and complaining at his being prevented from dying. When Ptolemy was informed of all this, he gave orders that Cleomenes' body should be placed inside a leather bag and strung up, while his children, his mother and the ladies of her suite should be executed. Among the latter was Panteus' wife too, the loveliest, noblest-looking woman. These disasters struck them when they were still newly married and most deeply in love. Now though she naturally wanted to sail off at once with Panteus, her parents had not permitted it, but forcibly confined her and placed a guard on her. Yet a short while later, after procuring herself a horse and a small amount of gold, she escaped at night and galloped fast to Taenarum, where she boarded a ship bound for Egypt. Thus conveyed to her husband, she shared his life in a foreign country cheerfully and with no regrets.

It was she who now held Cratesicleia's hand as she was being conducted away by the soldiers, lifted her robe and urged her to keep her spirits up. Cratesicleia personally in no sense dreaded death, but did make just the one request that she might die before the children. However, when they reached the spot where the warders normally carried out these sentences, they slaughtered the children first in full view of Cratesicleia, and then her. The only words she uttered in the face of such agonies were: 'Children, where have you gone to?' Being strong and well-built, Panteus' wife hitched up her dress, and quietly and calmly attended to each of the dying women, covering them with whatever lay to hand. Finally after all the others, she made herself neat, let down her dress, and permitted no one to come close or touch her except the man deputed to carry out the execution: thus she met her end in heroic style, without having made anyone a request to tidy and cover her after she had passed away. So her discretion endured in death, and she maintained the watch over her person which she kept in her lifetime.

39. In short, during these final stages Sparta played her role through the prowess of women which was equally matched with that of the men, and she thus demonstrated that true virtue cannot be undermined by Fortune. A few days subsequently those on guard over Cleomenes' crucified body saw an enormous snake coiled about his head and shielding his face so that no carrion bird might swoop down on it. In consequence the king was gripped by superstition and fear, which in turn gave the women the opportunity to perform various purification rituals in recognition of the fact that it was a favourite of the gods, a man of superior powers, who had met his death. The Alexandrians even began to regard Cleomenes as divine, visiting the spot constantly and invoking him as a hero and a child of gods. Eventually the more learned citizens stopped them from doing this with the explanation that just as putrefying cattle produce bees, and horses produce wasps, while beetles are propagated by asses in the same state, so human bodies yield serpents once the juices around the marrow have gradually run together and coagulated. And it was their observation of this which prompted the men of old to regard the snake as the creature particularly associated with heroes.

SAYINGS

INTRODUCTION

As Plutarch explained and illustrated at some length in his *Life of Lycurgus*, to develop 'the technique of expressing a range of ideas in just a few, spare words' was an important part of every Spartiate's upbringing. Such Spartan 'sayings' caught the imagination of other Greeks and featured in written accounts as early as that of Herodotus in the fifth century. By the late fourth century Aristotle in his *Rhetoric* can mention 'Laconic sayings' as a distinct type of maxim which an orator will find useful. At the same period such sayings also came to have special appeal for Diogenes and his followers in their 'Cynic' way of life, which spurned material possessions and questioned conventions of every kind. The Cynics' vision of Spartan society and traditional Spartan attitudes so tremendously stirred their admiration that they were active in developing – or perhaps even establishing – collections of Spartan sayings which continued to enjoy a wide popularity for centuries.

Plutarch's interest in the saying of Spartans and others derives to a marked extent from his concern for the character of his subjects in the *Lives*. Thus he acknowledges his failure to give a full account of the careers of Alexander the Great and Julius Caesar, and goes on to excuse it in the following terms:

> For neither is it histories we are writing, but lives, nor is there by any means display of merit or vice in the most outstanding actions, but often a trivial matter as well as a remark and some joke have offered a better illustration of character than clashes with countless casualties and the biggest battalions and sieges of cities.

Elsewhere Plutarch mentions that he made a practice of collecting anecdotes and sayings, and it is entirely understandable that various sets of such material should have been attributed to him and preserved among his *Moralia*. The two most immediately relevant to this volume are what editors have called *Sayings of Spartans* and *Sayings of Spartan Women*. The second of these is much the shorter, as well as being separated from the first by a brief compilation of material outlining Spartan customs. In addition, considerable duplication occurs between *Sayings of Spartans* and the Spartan section of a further collection called *Sayings of Kings and Generals*.

Sayings of Spartans preserves something over 340 sayings of 68 named Spartiates arranged in (Greek) alphabetical order, followed by 72 anonymous sayings. 'Saying' here admits no strict definition. Most are indeed pointed remarks, but wide variations remain in their length and in the explanation of their context. Other sayings are in fact anecdotes of notable exploits or attitudes on the part of Spartiates. The spread of material among named Spartiates is very uneven. While as many as 79 sayings are attributed to Agesilaus, next in order is Lycurgus with 31, then Agis son of Archidamus and Cleomenes son of Anaxandridas with 18 each; at the other end of the scale the majority have no more than one or two sayings attributed to them. In *Sayings of Spartan Women* a mere ten sayings are attributed to four named women (even the last name beginning with no more than the fourth letter of the alphabet), followed by 30 anonymous sayings.

Sufficient accounts of Sparta and Spartan history survive to prove how the sayings in these collections derive from a wide variety of sources followed with varying degrees of conscientiousness. Historical accuracy, however, was considered much less important than sharp, attractive presentation: occasionally even the Doric forms of Greek, which Spartans would have used, are introduced for the sake of 'authenticity'. Attribution of versions of the same saying to two or more Spartans (legendary figures among them!) is commonplace, but again unimportant to their inventors. The same applies to the confusion and anachronism which can occur in historical details. How different sayings were formulated and embroidered over the centuries can no longer be traced.

From all this it follows that the sayings are to be relied upon as historical sources only with the greatest caution. The sayings are mostly intended to reflect what were considered excellent features of the Spartan character, and their value lies rather in the demonstration they offer of how Sparta's admirers from the fourth century onwards (Plutarch among them) liked to dream of her citizens in bygone days – bold, wise, just, free, unworldly.

Scholars continue to debate what part, if any, Plutarch himself played in the compilation of either collection translated here. It is striking, however, that those sayings in *Sayings of Spartans* attributed to Agesilaus, Lycurgus and Lysander that also feature in the corresponding *Life* by Plutarch appear in the same order in both works. To be sure, the explanation may be that whoever complied *Sayings of Spartans* did so *after* the appearance of the *Lives*, and was able to excerpt from them. But this hypothesis is rendered less persuasive, among other reasons, by the presence of further sayings – not appearing in the relevant *Life* – interspersed among those that do occur in the *Lives*. It seems distinctly more likely that *Sayings of Spartans* (in part at least, if not as a whole) represents preliminary research material gathered by Plutarch in preparation for writing Lives. Whenever he turned to the latter task, he could select from the collection of sayings he had already assembled himself. It is conceivable, too, that he had expanded or adapted one or other pre-existing collections of Spartan sayings. His role in the compilation of *Sayings of Spartan Women* must remain a more open question.

This translation omits those sayings attributed to Lycurgus and Agesilaus which largely duplicate passages in the corresponding *Life* by Plutarch. Since most of the Sayings of Unnamed Spartans likewise repeat what may be found elsewhere in this volume, they are omitted also. A few other sayings are omitted because the text is in too poor a condition to render them comprehensible.

SAYINGS OF SPARTANS

AGASICLES
(Sixth-century Eurypontid king)

1. Agasicles, king of the Spartans, despite his fondness for
208B intellectual discourse, would not entertain the sophist Philophanes. When someone expressed surprise at this, he declared: 'I want to be the student of men whose son I should like to be as well.'

2. When asked how anyone could rule the citizens safely without having a bodyguard, he said: 'By ruling them in the way that fathers do their sons.'

AGESILAUS
(Eurypontid king, 400–360)

1. When the great Agesilaus was once chosen by lot to preside at a drinking session, and the cupbearer asked him how much to serve each man, his answer was: 'If plenty of wine has been provided, then as much as each requests; but if there is only a little, then give everyone an equal amount.'

2. When some criminal submitted calmly to torture, he remarked: 'What an exceptionally wicked man he is to apply such endurance and fortitude to evil and disreputable ends.'

3. When somebody was praising an orator for his ability to magnify small points, he said: 'In my opinion it's not a good cobbler who fits large shoes on small feet.'

4. When somebody once said to him, 'You did agree,' and frequently repeated the point, he responded: 'Yes, by Zeus, I did, if it's right to; if not, though I spoke the words, I did not agree.' When the other added: 'But surely kings should fulfil "whate'er they assent to with a nod of the head",'[1] he replied: 'No more than those who approach kings should make proper requests and statements, aiming both for the right moment and for something appropriate to kings.'

5. Whenever he heard people being critical or complimentary, he considered it just as important to establish the characters of those talking as of those being talked about.

6. When he was still a boy, at a celebration of the Gymnopaediae the choral director put him in an inconspicuous position. Even though he was already in line to become king,[2] he complied, and remarked: 'That's fine, for I shall show that it isn't positions which lend men distinction, but men who enhance positions.'

7. When some doctor prescribed for him a rather elaborate and complicated course of treatment, he declared: 'By the two gods,[3] I surely have no prospect of remaining alive if I have to put up with all that.'

8. Once he was standing sacrificing an ox at the altar of Athena of the Bronze House and a louse bit him, but he was not upset. Quite openly in front of everybody he caught and killed it, with the remark: 'By the gods, what a pleasure to eliminate the conspirator even at the altar.'

9. Another time he watched a mouse being pulled from its hole by a small boy. When the mouse turned round, bit the hand of its captor and escaped, he pointed this out to those present and said: 'When the tiniest creature defends itself like this against aggressors, what ought men to do, do you reckon?'

10. When he wanted to go to war against Persia with the aim of liberating the Greeks living in Asia, he consulted the oracle of Zeus at Dodona. Its instructions were to launch the campaign if the person responsible for the decision considered it feasible.
He informed the ephors of this response, and they told him to 209

go to Delphi and repeat his inquiry. So when he entered the shrine of the oracle, he framed his question like this: 'Apollo, is your opinion the same as your father's?' When Apollo concurred, Agesilaus was selected and thus did go on the campaign.

15. When Megabates the son of Spithridates, who had a most handsome figure, came up to embrace Agesilaus and kiss him – under the impression that he was extremely fond of him – Agesilaus recoiled. Since Megabates then ceased to approach him, Agesilaus asked after him. His friends told him that it was his own fault for being frightened of a kiss from the handsome youth, but that if he were willing and wouldn't flinch, then Megabates would return. Agesilaus thought this over in silence for a while and declared: 'You needn't try to persuade him, since my view is that I should prefer to be above such things than to take by storm the best-manned city of my opponents. For it is better to maintain one's own freedom than to deprive others of theirs.'

18. His personal lifestyle was in no way superior to that of his comrades. He totally abstained from eating and drinking to excess, while he treated sleep not as his master, but rather as a subject governed by his own activities. His reactions to heat and cold were such that he alone always took advantage of the changing seasons. He would pitch his tent in the midst of his troops and had bedding of no better quality than anyone else.

19. He frequently remarked that the commander should outclass his troops not in fastidiousness and high living, but in stamina and courage.

20. Certainly when somebody asked what gain the laws of Lycurgus had brought Sparta, he said: 'Contempt for pleasures.'

21. To the man who was amazed at how modest his clothes and his meals were, and those of the other Spartans as well, he said: 'Freedom is what we reap from this way of life, my friend.'

23. Even when he had grown old he maintained the same regime. So to the man who inquired why on attaining such an age he still went about without any undergarment in the depths of

winter, he said: 'So that the young men may do the same, with the oldest men and office-holders as their example.'

24. As he was traversing the Thasians'[4] territory with his army, they sent him barley-meal, geese, dried fruits, honey cakes, and all sorts of expensive things to eat and drink. He accepted just the barley-meal, but as for everything else he instructed those who had brought it to take it back, since his men would have no use for it. Yet when they begged and pleaded with him to accept it all the same, he told them to hand it over to the helots. When they asked why, he said: 'It's quite inappropriate for those who profess true manly qualities to accept such delicacies. Things which attract slavish characters are alien to free men.'

25. The Thasians again, because of their belief that he was bringing them such notable benefits, had honoured him with temples and deification and had despatched an embassy to him in this connection. He read the list of honours conveyed to him by the envoys and enquired whether their country had power to deify humans. When they said it did, he replied: 'Very well, make yourselves gods first, and when you have achieved that, then I shall believe your claim that you will be able to make me a god too.'

26. When the Greek peoples in Asia voted to erect statues of him in their most famous cities, he was quick in writing to them: 'There is to be no image of me, either painted or modelled or constructed.'

27. On noticing a house in Asia roofed with square beams, he asked the owner whether timber grew square in that area. When told no, it grew round, he said: 'What then? If it were square, would you make it round?'

28. Asked once how far Sparta's boundaries stretched, he brandished his spear and said: 'As far as this can reach.'

29. When somebody else asked why Sparta lacked fortification walls, he pointed to the citizens under arms and said: 'These are the Spartans' walls.'

30. When another person put the same question to him, his reply was: 'Cities shouldn't be fortified with stones or timbers, but with the valour of their inhabitants.'

31. He recommended his friends to strive to be rich not in possessions, but in courage and merit.

32. Whenever he wanted some job done promptly by his troops, he first got down to it personally in full view of everyone.

33. He was prouder of working just as hard as anyone, and in exercising self-discipline, than he was of being king.

34. Noticing a lame Spartan setting off to fight and looking for a horse, he said: 'Don't you realize that war requires not men who flee, but those who stand their ground?'

35. Questioned as to how he had gained his great reputation, he said: 'By having despised death.'

211 36. When someone asked why Spartiates go into battle to the music of pipes, he said: 'So that, as they proceed in step to the music, both the cowards and the brave may be clearly distinguished.'[5]

37. When someone was extolling the happy circumstances of the king of the Persians, who was quite a young man, he remarked: 'But at that age not even Priam had met with disaster.'

38. After gaining much of Asia he decided to advance against the Great King himself with the intention of putting an end to his leisure and his bribery of the Greeks' popular leaders.

39. When the ephors recalled him[6] because Sparta was ringed by Greek enemies thanks to the money sent over by the Persians, he declared that the good commander should be commanded by the laws, and sailed from Asia, leaving behind deep longing for him among the Greeks there.

40. Since it was an archer that was stamped on the Persian coinage, as he struck camp he remarked that he was being expelled from Asia by the Great King with 30,000 archers – because it was the fact that Timocrates had arranged for this

number of gold *darics* to be conveyed to Athens and Thebes and distributed to their popular leaders which had caused the citizen bodies there to declare war on the Spartiates.

41. He also wrote this letter[7] back to the ephors: 'Agesilaus to the ephors, greetings. We have subjugated the greater part of Asia, routed the Persians, and established many strongholds in Ionia. But since your orders are that I come over by the date set, I am following after this letter, and shall nearly be there first. I do not hold the command in my own interest, but in that of our city and allies. After all, a genuinely dutiful commander is one who always exercises his command subject to the instructions of both laws and ephors, or of whatever other authorities a city may have.'

47. After Diphridas brought him from home the message that 212
he should immediately turn aside to invade Boeotia (something which he had planned to do – though later, when he was better prepared), he was not disobedient to the magistrates but sent for two of the *moras*[8] on service near Corinth and entered Boeotia. At Coronea he engaged Thebans, Athenians, Argives, Corinthians and both Locrian peoples, and despite the fact that his many wounds had put him in bad physical shape, he won what was (as Xenophon[9] states) the greatest of all the battles in his own day.

48. Once he returned home, such great success and victories did not prompt him to make any changes in his personal habits and lifestyle.

51. When asked another time for what particular reason the Spartiates enjoyed notably more success than others, he said: 'Because more than others they train to give orders and to take them.'

54. When somebody asked him to write to his friends in Asia so that he might gain justice there, he replied: 'But my friends do what is right of their own accord, even without a letter from me.'

55. Somebody drew his attention to the solid city-wall with its exceptionally strong construction and inquired if it made a

favourable impression on him. 'By Zeus,' he said, 'favourable, but for women to live inside, not men.'

56. He said to some Megarian who was bragging about his city to him: 'Young man, a great deal of force is required to back up your remarks.'

213C 64. He used to remark that those living in Asia were worthless as free men, but good slaves.

65. When he was asked how someone might most surely earn people's esteem, he replied: 'By the best words and the finest actions.'

66. He used to say that a general needs to show daring towards his opponents, goodwill towards his subordinates and a cool head in crises.

67. When someone inquired of him what children should learn, he said: 'What they will also use when they become men.'

68. When he was trying a case and the prosecutor had spoken well, but the defendant feebly – just stating with reference to each point, 'Agesilaus, the king must uphold the laws' – he said: 'And supposing somebody dug their way into your house and took your cloak, would you expect the builder or the weaver of the cloak to help you?'

69. When – after the conclusion of peace – there was brought to him from the Persian king a letter offering ties of hospitality and friendship, conveyed by the Persian accompanying the Spartan Callias, he rejected it, and gave instructions for it to be reported back to the king that there was no need to send him letters privately; instead, if he proved a genuine friend of Sparta and meant well towards Greece, then to the utmost Agesilaus too would himself be his friend. 'However, should he be caught scheming against us, then not even if I receive ever so many letters, should he believe that he will have me for a friend.'

214B 73. When many Spartans had run away at the battle near Leuctra and thus by law were liable to loss of status,[10] the ephors saw the city deprived of men yet desperate for soldiers, and so wanted to annul the loss of status as well as uphold the laws. Thus they picked Agesilaus as lawgiver. He came into the public gathering and said: 'I would not become a lawgiver to make laws different from the present ones, nor would I add, subtract or alter anything. On the contrary, it is fine for these current laws of ours to be valid – from tomorrow.'

74. Even though Epaminondas had swept in with the surging force of a breaking wave, and the Thebans and their allies were boasting about their victory, Agesilaus still kept him out of the city and made him withdraw, despite the small number of men in the city.

75. At the battle near Mantinea[11] he urged the Spartans to ignore the rest and fight Epaminondas, asserting that only the intelligent are brave and they alone are responsible for a victory: so if they should kill him, it would be very easy for them to overcome the rest, since these were unintelligent and negligible. And so it turned out. For just when victory was going to Epaminondas and a rout was under way, one of the Spartans struck him a mortal blow as he had turned round and was urging on his own men. Once he had fallen, Agesilaus' men reversed their retreat and put the victory in the balance again, with the Thebans now making a much worse showing and the Spartans a much better one.

76. Because Sparta needed funds for war and for the maintenance of mercenaries Agesilaus responded, for a fee, to a call from the king of the Egyptians.[12] But the plainness of his dress led the natives to regard him with contempt, since they were expecting to see the person of the Spartan king, like the Persian one, superbly attired – a misguided notion to have of kings. At any rate, in the meantime Agesilaus did demonstrate to them that brains and courage are needed to achieve greatness and importance.

77. When he saw that his men were on the verge of giving way in their fear of the impending danger created by the mass of the enemy (200,000 of them) and the small number of men he had, he decided to make a sacrifice before marshalling his forces.

And without the others' knowledge he wrote on his hand the word 'Victory' with the letters facing left. Then, when the diviner gave him the liver, he placed it on the hand with the writing on it and held it there for a suitable period while appearing puzzled and pretending to be at a loss, until the marks of the letters should have stained the liver and been imprinted on it. And then he displayed it to the men who were about to accompany him into battle, declaring that by means of what had been written the gods had foretold a victory. Thus his men's morale was high as they went into battle believing it had been proved convincingly that they would win.

78. When the enemy, thanks to their huge numbers, were digging a trench around his camp and his ally Nectanabius demanded to make a sortie and do battle with them, he said that he would not obstruct the enemy in their wish to become equal to
215 themselves. But once the trench was almost complete all round, then he marshalled his men in front of the remaining space and in a fight where both sides were equally matched he achieved a rout, and with his few soldiers caused widespread slaughter of the enemy as well as sending back plenty of money to his city.

79. As he was dying on the voyage back from Egypt, he gave instructions to those close to him that they should not be responsible for making any image of his person, be it modelled or painted or copied: 'For if I have accomplished any glorious feat, that will be my memorial. But if I have not, not even all the statues in the world – the products of vulgar, worthless men – would make any difference.'

AGESIPOLIS SON OF CLEOMBROTUS
(Agiad king, 371–370)

1. When someone remarked that Philip had demolished Olynthus in a few days,[13] Agesipolis son of Cleombrotus said: 'By the gods, it will take him much longer than that to build another equal to it.'

2. When someone else remarked that during his reign he, along with other men in their prime, had served as hostage, while their

children and wives had not, he responded: 'That was fair, since it is entirely proper that we should personally suffer for our own mistakes.'

3. When he wanted to send for young dogs from home and someone said: 'We don't permit their export,' he remarked: 'Previously the same was true of men too, but it's happened now.'

AGESIPOLIS SON OF PAUSANIAS
(Agiad king, 395–380)

When the Athenians put to Agesipolis son of Pausanias the proposal that the city of Megara should arbitrate complaints which each had against the other, he said: 'Athenians, it is a disgrace that those who have been the leaders of the Greeks should have a slighter knowledge of justice than Megarians.'

AGIS SON OF ARCHIDAMUS
(Eurypontid king, 427–400)

1. Once when the ephors said to him: 'Take the young men and march against this man's country: he will personally conduct you to the acropolis,' Agis son of Archidamus replied: 'And how is it proper, ephors, for so many young men to trust this one man who is betraying his own country?'

2. When asked what form of training was most practised at Sparta, he said: 'Understanding of how to take orders and to give them.'

3. He remarked that the Spartans do not ask how many the enemy are, but where they are.

4. When at Mantinea he was prevented from doing battle with the enemy, who were superior in numbers, he said: 'The man who wants to rule many men must fight many.'

5. When someone was inquiring what the number of Spartans was, he said: 'One sufficient to keep out undesirables.'

6. As he was passing through the Corinthians' walls and

observed their height and strength and great extent, he said: 'What women live in this place?'

7. When some sophist stated: 'Speech is the most powerful thing of all,' he said: 'In that case you, if you're silent, are worthless.'

8. When after their defeat the Argives met him again with a bolder air, and he saw that his allies were disturbed, he said: 'Keep your spirits up, men! For when we the victors are afraid, what do you think those we have defeated are feeling?'

9. When the envoy from the Abderans had stopped after a lengthy speech and was asking what he should report back to his fellow citizens, he said: 'Say that throughout the entire time you needed for speaking, I continued listening in silence.'

10. When some people were praising the Eleans' outstanding fairness in connection with the Olympic Games, he said: 'What great or wonderful achievement is it on their part if they act fairly on just one day every four years?'

11. To those claiming that some members of the other royal house envied him, he said: 'Then they will be distressed by their own troubles, and also by my good fortune and that of my friends.'

12. When someone was recommending that those of the enemy who were fleeing should be allowed to escape, he said: 'Yet if we don't fight those who are fleeing out of cowardice, how shall we fight those brave enough to stand firm?'

216 13. When someone was presenting proposals for the liberty of the Greeks which, while not ignoble, were difficult to put into effect, he said: 'My friend, your words need to be complemented by force and money.'

14. When someone was remarking that Philip would make Greece beyond the Isthmus inaccessible to them,[14] he said: 'Stranger, it is sufficient for us to have freedom of movement in our own land.'

15. An envoy who came to Sparta from Perinthus delivered a lengthy speech; when he had finished talking and asked Agis

what he should report back to the Perinthians, he said: 'What else except that you barely managed to stop talking, while I remained silent?'

16. He came alone on an embassy to Philip. When the latter said: 'What's this? Have you come alone?', he replied: 'Yes, since I've come to see one man.'

17. When he was old, one of the more elderly men remarked to him that he kept observing the abandonment of old customs and the infiltration of other, harmful ones, and as a result of this Sparta was now all upside down. Agis replied jokingly: 'If that is so, then things are developing logically, because when I was a boy I used to hear my father declaring that their situation then was all upside down, and he said that when he was a boy *his* father had told him this too. And so we shouldn't be surprised if things later get worse than they were earlier; but we should be, if they get any better or remain much the same.'

18. When asked how one should remain a free man, he said: 'By despising death.'

AGIS THE YOUNGER
(Eurypontid king, 338–331)

1. When Demades[15] was remarking that conjurors swallow Spartan swords because they are so small, Agis the Younger said: 'All the same, the Spartans do reach the enemy with their swords.'

2. To the wretched character who frequently kept asking him who was the best Spartiate, his response was: 'The one least like you.'

THE LAST AGIS
(Eurypontid king, 244/3–241)

Agis the last Spartan king[16] was arrested by means of a trap and condemned by the ephors without trial. As he was being led off to the noose, he noticed one of the attendants in tears and said: 'Man, stop crying for me, since my death in defiance of law and justice makes me superior to my murderers.' With these words he readily allowed the noose to be placed around his neck.

ACROTATUS

(Elder son of the Agiad King Cleomenes II (370–309), who died before his father. See *Agis*, Ch. 3)

When his parents required him to be their accomplice in some wrongdoing, up to a point Acrotatus voiced his opposition. But once they became insistent, he said: 'So long as I was under your care I didn't have the slightest notion or grasp of justice. But now that you have handed me over to my country and its customs, and moreover have had me instructed to the best of your ability in both justice and honourable behaviour, I shall attempt to follow these principles no less than you. And since you wish me to adopt the best course, and the best course is the just one both in the case of a private person, and much more so in that of a ruler, I shall do what you wish; but as for what you are proposing, I shall decline.'

ALCAMENES SON OF TELECLUS

(Eighth-century Agiad king)

1. When somebody asked how one might best maintain the position of king, Alcamenes son of Teleclus said: 'By not attaching undue importance to self-advantage.'

2. When someone else wanted to know why he declined gifts from the Messenians, he said: 'Because if I accepted them it would be impossible to live at peace with the laws.'

3. When someone was remarking that he lived modestly although possessing adequate means, he said: 'Yes, for it is well that reason, not passion, should govern the life of a man who is well-off.'

ANAXANDRIDAS
(Sixth-century Agiad king)

1. Anaxandridas the son of Leon said to a man who resented being exiled from his city: 'Good friend, it's exile from justice, not from your city, that you should dread.'

2. He said to the man who, while giving necessary information to the ephors, used more than enough words: 'Stranger, you meet the need, but at needless length.'

3. When someone was inquiring why their practice was to hand
their landholdings over to the helots and not to care for them 217
personally, he said: 'Because we acquired them by caring for
ourselves, not for land.'

4. When someone else was maintaining that good reputations are harmful and that the man who is freed of such considerations will be happy, he said: 'Then on your argument criminals would be happy, since how would any temple-robber or other offender be bothered about his reputation?'

5. When another person was inquiring why in their wars Spartiates confidently face danger, he said: 'Because we practise proper respect for life, not fear of it like the rest of mankind.'

6. When someone was asking him why the Elders hear capital cases over several days, and why anyone should still be liable to a further trial even if acquitted, he said: 'They take many days reaching a verdict because in capital cases errors cannot be rectified, while by law a person will have to remain liable for trial because according to this law the possibility of reaching better decisions would also be open.'[17]

ANAXANDER SON OF EURYCRATES
(Seventh-century Agiad king)

When someone was asking why they do not collect money for the treasury, Anaxander son of Eurycrates said: 'So that those who have become its custodians are not corrupted.'

ANAXILAS

(Seventh-century Eurypontid king)

To the man who was wondering why the ephors do not stand up to show respect to the kings, even though they are appointed to this office by the kings, Anaxilas said: 'For the same reason that they are also ephors ('overseers').'[18]

ANDROCLEIDAS

The Spartan Androcleidas, who had a crippled leg, enlisted himself among the fighting men. When some were determined to debar him because he was crippled, he said: 'But what's needed to fight our foes is a man who stands his ground, not one who runs away.'

ANTALCIDAS

(Prominent Spartiate of the early fourth century, especially noted as a negotiator with the Persians. See *Agesilaus*, Ch. 23)

1. When Antalcidas was being initiated into the Mysteries on Samothrace, and was asked by the priest what really frightful act he had committed in the course of his life, he replied: 'If I have done any such thing, the gods will know of it themselves.'

2. To the Athenian who was calling the Spartans uneducated, he said: 'At least we are the only ones who have learned nothing wicked from you.'

3. When another Athenian said to him: 'We have indeed often driven you from the Cephisus,' he replied: 'But we have never driven you from the Eurotas.'

4. When asked how one might best please people, he said: 'By talking to them very pleasantly while dealing with them most helpfully.'

5. When some sophist was about to read a eulogy of Heracles, he said: 'But who finds fault with him?'

6. After Agesilaus had been wounded in battle by the Thebans[19] he said to him: 'You are receiving your fee for having taught

people to fight who had neither the wish nor the knowledge to do so.' For it was thought that they became warlike as a result of Agesilaus' continual campaigns against them.

7. He used to say that Sparta's young men were her walls, and the points of their spears her frontiers.

8. To the person who was wanting to know why Spartans use short daggers in warfare, he said: 'Because we fight our enemies at close quarters.'

ANTIOCHUS

(Presumably ephor in 338/7. Otherwise unknown)

When Antiochus, as ephor, heard that Philip had granted their country to the Messenians, he inquired if he had also equipped them with the strength to win in a fight over the country.

AREUS

(Agiad king, 309–265)

1. When some men were expressing admiration not for their own wives but for some other people's, Areus said: 'By the gods, not an idle word should be spoken about respectable women, but their characters should be completely unknown except just to their families.'

2. Once when he was passing through Selinus in Sicily, he saw this couplet inscribed on a monument:

> These men were once cut down by brazen Ares as they were
> Extinguishing tyranny: they died around the gates of Selinus,

and said: 'You deserved to die for trying to extinguish a tyranny which was on fire, because instead you should have let it burn out totally.'

ARISTON 218

(Sixth-century Eurypontid king, who reigned with the Agiad Cleomenes I)

1. When someone was expressing approval of Cleomenes' maxim (asked how the good king should behave, he said: 'Do good to his friends and harm to his enemies'), Ariston said: 'And how much better wouldn't it be, dear fellow, to do good to friends and make enemies into friends?'

2. When someone was inquiring what the total number of Spartiates was, he said: 'One sufficient to keep off our enemies.'

3. As some Athenian was reading a funeral eulogy in praise of men killed by Spartans, he said: 'What, then, do you think was the quality of our men who defeated them?'

ARCHIDAMIDAS
(For possible identification of him and of Hecataeus in no. 2 below, see *Lycurgus*, Ch. 20, note 60)

1. Archidamidas said to the man who was praising Charilaus because he behaved kindly to all alike: 'And how might anyone properly be praised if he behaves gently towards scoundrels too?'

2. When someone was criticizing the sophist Hecataeus because he had been invited to their mess and would then say nothing, he remarked: 'Evidently you don't understand that an expert at speaking also knows when to speak.'

ARCHIDAMUS SON OF ZEUXIDAMUS
(Eurypontid king, *c*. 469–427)

1. When somebody asked him who were in charge at Sparta, Archidamus son of Zeuxidamus said: 'The laws and the magistrates in accordance with the laws.'

2. To the man who was praising a lyre-player and marvelling at his ability, he said: 'Dear friend, what kind of compliment will you find to bestow on true men, when you praise a lyre-player in these terms?'

3. When someone introduced a harpist to him by saying: 'This man is a good harpist,' he replied: 'In *our* country that man is a

good maker of broth' – so as to stress the lack of any difference between affording pleasure through the sound of instruments and through the preparation of meat dishes and broth.

4. When someone was guaranteeing him that he would make their wine sweet, he said: 'What for? More wine will then certainly be consumed and it will reduce the value of the messes.'

5. As he was approaching the city of Corinth with an army, he saw hares start up from the area near the wall. So he said to the troops with him: 'The enemy are easy for us to capture.'

6. After two people had accepted him as arbitrator he brought them to the sanctuary of Athena of the Bronze House and made them swear to abide by his judgements. Once they had sworn, he said: 'My verdict is, then, that you should not leave the sanctuary until you have resolved your mutual differences.'

7. When Dionysius the tyrant of Sicily sent expensive clothes for his daughters, he declined them with the words: 'I'm afraid that if they wore them the girls might look disreputable to me.'[20]

8. When he observed his son fighting the Athenians recklessly, he said: 'Either increase your strength, or reduce your self-confidence.'

ARCHIDAMUS SON OF AGESILAUS
(Eurypontid king, 360–338)

1. When Philip wrote him a rather arrogant letter after the battle of Chaeronea,[21] Archidamus son of Agesilaus wrote back: 'Were you to measure your own shadow, you wouldn't find that it had grown any bigger than before your victory.'

2. When asked the extent of territory controlled by the Spartiates, he said: 'As much as they may reach with their spears.'

3. Since Periander the doctor was professionally well respected and very highly recommended, but used to write dreadful poetry, he said to him: 'Why ever is it, Periander, that you are so keen to be called a bad poet instead of an expert doctor?'

4. In the war against Philip, when some people were advising that they should join battle far from home, he said: 'No, we shouldn't be looking at that question, but instead whether we shall be superior to the enemy in battle.'

5. To those who congratulated him on his victory in the battle against the Arcadians,[22] he said: 'It would be better if our intelligence were beating them rather than our strength.'

219 6. When he discovered, after invading Arcadia, that the Eleans were aiding the Arcadians, he sent them a message: 'Archidamus to the Eleans: Inaction is good.'

7. In the Peloponnesian War when the allies were inquiring how much money would suffice and were demanding that he fix their contributions, he said: 'War does not call for set amounts.'[23]

8. On seeing an arrow shot from a catapult when it was first brought from Sicily, he exclaimed: 'By Heracles, man's valour is done for.'

9. When the Greeks were unwilling to listen to him, to terminate their agreements with the Macedonians Antipater and Craterus and so to be free (because they thought Spartans would prove more oppressive than Macedonians), he said: 'While a sheep always utters the same cry, a human makes a great variety until he achieves his object.'[24]

ASTYCRATIDAS

(Otherwise unknown. The battle occurred in 331)

After the defeat of King Agis in the battle against Antipater near Megalopolis, when somebody said to Astycratidas: 'What will you do, Spartans? Surely you won't become slaves to Macedonians?', he replied: 'What? Could Antipater stop us from dying fighting for Sparta?'

ANAXIBIUS[25]

When he was trapped in an ambush by the Athenian general Iphicrates and his soldiers asked what was to be done, Anaxibius replied: 'What else, except that you save yourselves, while I die fighting?'

BRASIDAS

(Distinguished commander in the early years of the Peloponnesian War. Killed in 422)

1. Brasidas, after catching a mouse among some dried figs, got bitten and let it go; then he said to those who were there: 'There is nothing so tiny that it lacks the courage to repel its assailants and save itself.'

2. After a spear had penetrated through his shield in some battle and wounded him, he pulled it out and with the very same weapon killed his opponent. And when asked how he had been wounded, he said: 'When my shield betrayed me.'

3. After departing on campaign he wrote[26] to the ephors: 'I'll achieve my wishes in this war or I'll die.'

4. When it happened that he met his death while liberating the Greeks in the Thraceward area, they despatched envoys to Sparta who approached his mother Archileonis. She inquired first if Brasidas' death had been a noble one, to which the Thracians responded by praising him and declaring that there was no one else to match him. She declared: 'Strangers, you don't know that. Brasidas was a brave man, but Sparta has many better than he.'

DAMONIDAS

When he was assigned the last place in the chorus by the man who was organizing the dancing, Damonidas said: 'Splendid, director! You have discovered how even this undistinguished place may become distinguished.'

DAMIS

(Otherwise unknown. The incident can be dated to 324)

With reference to the instructions about voting that Alexander was a god, Damis said: 'Let us agree that Alexander be called a god, if he so wishes.'

DAMINDAS

(Otherwise unknown. Philip's invasion occurred in 338)

After Philip had invaded the Peloponnese and someone remarked: 'The Spartans are running the risk of a terrible disaster if they won't make terms with him,' Damindas said: 'You effeminate man, since we have despised death, what terrible thing could we suffer?'

DERCYLLIDAS

When Pyrrhus was on Spartan territory with his army, and Dercyllidas had been sent to him as an envoy, Pyrrhus was demanding that they take back their king Cleonymus or else they would discover that they were no braver than other men; Dercyllidas interjected the remark: 'If he is a god, we are not afraid, for we are not guilty of anything; but if he's human, he isn't superior to *us*.'[27]

DEMARATUS

(Eurypontid king deposed in 491. He accompanied Xerxes' invasion of Greece in 480)

1. After Orontes had conversed with him rather rudely and
220 somebody remarked: 'Demaratus, Orontes has treated you rudely,' Demaratus replied: 'He has done me no wrong, since it's those who converse to curry favour who do harm, not those who show their enmity.'

2. When someone asked him why they deprive of their status those among them who discarded their shields, but not those who discarded their helmets and breastplates, he said: 'Because they put on the latter for their own benefit, but their shields for the sake of the battle-line as a whole.'

3. As he was listening to a harpist, he remarked: 'To me it's just foolery, but he does it pretty well.'

4. At a council meeting he was asked whether he was keeping quiet because he was stupid or because he was at a loss for words. 'Well certainly,' he said, 'a stupid person wouldn't be able to keep quiet.'

5. When someone asked why he, a king, was an exile from Sparta, he said: 'Because her laws are more powerful than I am.'

6. When one of the Persians by persistent bribery had lured away the person Demaratus was in love with and was saying: 'Spartan, I have hunted down your beloved,' he replied: 'By the gods, it's not you, it's the fact that you have bought him.'

7. One of the Persians had revolted from the Great King and had been persuaded by Demaratus to return to him. The King was about to have this Persian disposed of when Demaratus said: 'O King, what a disgrace it is that when this man was your enemy you could not punish him for his revolt, but now that he's become your friend, you are executing him!'

8. To the King's parasite[28] who used to make fun of him frequently about his exile, he said: 'I shall not take issue with you, my friend, since I have squandered my position in life.'

ECPREPES

(Fifth-century Spartiate, otherwise unknown)

Ecprepes, when ephor, took an adze and cut away two of the nine strings from the musician Phrynis' lyre, declaring: 'Don't do harm to music.'

EPAENETUS

Epaenetus said that liars are responsible for all faults and wrongs.

EUBOEDAS

Euboedas would not tolerate hearing some men praising someone else's wife, but declared that not a word should be said about a wife's character among those outside her family.

EUDAMIDAS SON OF ARCHIDAMUS
(Late fourth-century Eurypontid king)

1. After he had seen Xenocrates,[29] by now quite elderly, having a philosophical discussion with his pupils in the Academy, Eudamidas son of Archidamus, the brother of Agis, inquired who the old man was. When somebody said that he was a wise man and one of those who search for virtue, Eudamidas said: 'And when will he make use of it if he is still searching for it?'

2. After hearing a philosopher who had argued that the wise man is the only good general, he said: 'It's a wonderful claim, but the man who makes it is untrustworthy, because he has not heard the battle-trumpets sound.'

3. At the point when Xenocrates had expounded his argument and was drawing to a close, Eudamidas arrived. When one of those with him commented on this: 'The moment we arrive is the moment he has stopped,' Eudamidas said: 'That's fine, if he has already said what he wanted to.' To the other's remark: 'It would be pleasant to hear him,' Eudamidas replied: 'And if we joined a man who had just had a meal, surely we wouldn't expect him to have another one?'

4. When someone was inquiring why it was that he saw fit to keep quiet himself when the citizens were in favour of the war against the Macedonians, he said: 'Because I have no desire to show them up as liars.'

5. When another person was citing their glorious deeds against the Persians and strongly advocating the war, he said: 'In my opinion you are not aware that this proposition is the same as taking on fifty wolves after overcoming a thousand sheep.'

6. When some harpist had been a great success, Eudamidas was asked his impression of him and said: 'In his own small line he puts on a great show.'

7. When somebody was praising Athens, he said: 'And who could appositely praise that city, for which no one has felt affection because it made them better?'

8. When an Argive was maintaining that once they go abroad
Spartans degenerate because they are detached from their tra-
ditional way of life, he said: 'But you Argives, after coming to 221
Sparta, don't become worse, you become better.'

9. After Alexander had announced at Olympia that all exiles except Thebans[30] should return home, he said: 'While this announcement is unfortunate for you, Thebans, it is an honour nonetheless, since Alexander is frightened only of you.'

10. When asked what purpose they had in sacrificing to the Muses before their ventures, he said: 'So that our actions may attract good reports.'

EURYCRATIDAS SON OF ANAXANDRIDAS

(Late seventh/early sixth-century Agiad king. 'Anaxandridas' is presumably a slip for 'Anaxander')

When someone was inquiring why the ephors try cases relating to contracts daily, Eurycratidas son of Anaxandridas said: 'So that even in the face of our enemies we may trust each other.'

ZEUXIDAMUS

(Probably son of Leotychidas II, Eurypontid king 491–*c.* 469)

1. When someone was inquiring why they keep their laws about bravery unwritten, without setting them down and handing them to the young men to read, he said: 'Because it's better for them to get used to acts of bravery rather than to study written documents.'

2. When some Aetolian was claiming that for men eager to display courage war was better than peace, he said: 'No, by the gods; rather for those men death is better than life.'

HERONDAS

Herondas was at Athens when a man was convicted on a charge of having no work. After hearing about this he asked people to point out to him the man who had been required to pay this penalty for his freedom.

THEARIDAS

As Thearidas was honing his sword and was asked if it was sharp, he said: 'Sharper than slander.'

THEMISTEAS

(Otherwise unknown. Herodotus (7.221) calls him Megistias and makes him an Acarnanian)

As a seer Themisteas forewarned King Leonidas of the future destruction near Thermopylae[31] of both himself and the troops with him. But he was despatched to Sparta by Leonidas, ostensibly in order to report what would happen, though really so that he should not perish too. He would not tolerate this, but declared: 'I was sent out as a fighting man, not as a message-bearer.'

THEOPOMPUS

(Late eighth/early seventh-century Eurypontid king)

1. To the person who asked him what was the safest way for a king to maintain his rule, Theopompus said: 'By permitting his friends to be properly frank, while so far as he is able not overlooking injuries to his subjects.'

2. To the stranger who was claiming that among his own citizens he was called a friend of Sparta, he said: 'It would be better for you to be called a friend of your fellow citizens rather than a friend of Sparta.'

3. When the ambassador from Elis stated that the citizens had dispatched him for the specific reason that he alone emulated the Spartan way of life, he said: 'And which of the two ways of life is better, Elean – yours, or that of your fellow citizens?' When he declared that his was, Theopompus said: 'How then could this city of yours keep itself safe when among a numerous population there is only one brave man?'

4. When someone was saying that Sparta was preserved by her kings' talent for command, he said: 'No, rather by her citizens' readiness to obey.'

5. When the Pylians voted him quite exceptional honours, he wrote back: 'While time will magnify moderate ones, it obliterates excessive ones.'

THERYCION

(Otherwise unknown. The incident dates to 338)

When he arrived from Delphi and saw that Philip with his army had already seized the narrow passage at the Isthmus, Therycion said: 'Corinthians, you make poor gatekeepers of the Peloponnese.'

THECTAMENES

After the ephors had condemned him to death, Thectamenes left smiling. And when one of those present asked if he had contempt for Spartan regulations, he said: 'No. Instead I'm delighted that I should pay this penalty without requesting or borrowing anything from anyone.'

HIPPODAMUS 222

(Otherwise unknown. Possibly the battle against Megalopolis in 352 is meant)

When Agis was lining up for battle next to Archidamus, Hippodamus was sent by Agis to Sparta to carry out duties there. 'But,' he said, 'won't I die more nobly here, battling manfully for Sparta?' (He was over eighty years of age.) And with those words he took up his arms, stood on the king's right, and died fighting.

HIPPOCRATIDAS

(Otherwise unknown. The incident is most likely to date to the early fourth century)

1. Because a Spartan had known of the conspiracy formed by a certain group, but had kept quiet about it, the satrap of Caria wrote to Hippocratidas and in a postscript asked how he should deal with the man. He answered: 'If you have bestowed any special benefit on him, execute him; but if not, expel him

from your territory as someone completely lacking in good qualities.'

2. Once when a youth followed by a lover met Hippocratidas and could not face him, he said: 'You ought to go around with the sort of people who won't cause you to change colour when observed.'

CALLICRATIDAS

(*Navarch*, or commander, of the Spartan fleet against Athens in 407/6. Defeated and killed at the battle of Arginusae)

1. When Lysander's friends were asking him to allow them to do away with one particular opponent of theirs in exchange for fifty *talents*, Callicratidas as *navarch* refused, even though he was desperate for money to provide rations for his sailors. His adviser Cleander said: 'But I would certainly have accepted if I were you.' To which Callicratidas replied: 'I would have too, if I were you.'

2. When he approached the Spartans' ally, Cyrus the Younger, at Sardis to get money for his fleet, on the first day he gave instructions for the message to be conveyed that he wished to meet Cyrus; but when told that he was drinking, he said: 'I'll wait until he's finished.' And then, once he realized that there would be no possibility of conferring with him that day, he departed, giving the impression of being rather ill-mannered. But on the following day, when again informed that Cyrus was drinking and would not appear, he declared: 'Surely my eagerness to obtain money ought not to be so great as my concern to do nothing unworthy of Sparta?' So he departed to Ephesus after calling down many curses on those who had first been treated with contempt by barbarians and who had then taught them to behave arrogantly because of their wealth; and he swore to those with him that from the moment he arrived in Sparta he would make every effort to reconcile the Greeks, so that they might be more of a threat to the barbarians and would no longer require the resources of the latter to use against each other.

3. When asked what sort of men the Ionians were, he said: 'Good slaves, but worthless as free men.'

4. When Cyrus forwarded the pay for his soldiers and gifts of friendship for himself, he accepted only the pay and returned the gifts, with a statement that he had no need of personal friendship with him, but regarded the general one concluded with all Spartans as sufficient for himself too.

5. As he was about to engage in the naval battle near the Arginusae Islands and the helmsman Hermon remarked to him that it would be a good idea to sail away because the Athenians had many more triremes, he said: 'And what of that? Surely to flee would be disgraceful as well as damaging to Sparta, so the best course is to stay here and either die or win.'

6. When in sacrificing before battle he heard from the seer that the burnt offerings predicted victory for his forces but death for their commander, he said quite unperturbed: 'Sparta's fate does not depend on one man. For if I die my country will not be worsted, but if I yielded to the enemy it would be.' So after designating Cleander to succeed him as commander, he engaged in the naval battle and died fighting.

CLEOMBROTUS SON OF PAUSANIAS 223
(Agiad king, 380–371)

When some stranger was arguing about virtue with his father, Cleombrotus son of Pausanias said: 'My father will always be superior to you – until you too have had sons.'

CLEOMENES SON OF ANAXANDRIDAS
(Agiad king, *c.* 520–491)

1. Cleomenes son of Anaxandridas said that Homer was the poet of the Spartans and Hesiod[32] that of the helots, because the former encouraged men to make war, and the latter to farm.

2. After making a seven-day truce with the Argives he kept to it for two days and then during the third night, when they were

asleep because of their confidence in the agreement, he made an assault, killing some and taking the rest prisoner.

3. When he was taken to task for breaking his oaths he said he had not sworn to include the nights as well as the days; and in any case among both gods and humans whatever harm one may inflict upon the enemy is considered to be something superior to strict equity.

4. As it turned out, he failed in his bid to take Argos (for the sake of which he had broken the truce) because the women took down the weapons from the shrines and used these to repel him. And later, when he was out of his mind, he grabbed a little dagger, slashed himself from his ankles all the way up to his vital parts, and by this means ended his life laughing and grimacing.

5. Though the seer was discouraging him from leading his army against the city of Argos (on the grounds that the return march would prove shameful), he did advance against the city and so observed that the gates were barred and the women on the walls. At this he said: 'Do you really believe that the return march will be shameful, when the men here are dead and it's the women who have barred the gates?'

6. He said to those Argives who were execrating him as an ungodly perjurer: 'You may have the power to utter abusive words, but I'm able to do you real harm.'

7. When envoys from Samos were urging him to go to war against the tyrant Polycrates[33] and made protracted speeches for the purpose, he said: 'I don't recall the beginning of what you said, and consequently I also don't grasp the middle sections, while the part at the end I don't approve of.'

8. A brigand overran the country and after his capture declared that: 'I did not have the means to support my soldiers, so I attacked those who did have it but wouldn't be willing to provide it, with the intention of taking it by force.' Cleomenes said: 'By the gods, crime is concise.'

9. As some vulgar character was insulting Cleomenes, he said: 'Do you insult all of us with the intention that while defending ourselves we shouldn't find time to point out your faults?'

10. When one of the citizens was maintaining that the good king should be altogether mild in every way, he said: 'Yes, but not to the extent of being contemptible.'

11. When he was dragged down by a long bout of illness and turned to ritual healers and seers (which he had not done previously), somebody expressed amazement. But he said: 'What are you amazed at? I'm not the same person that I was before, and not being the same, what I approve of isn't the same either.'

12. While some sophist was talking at length about bravery, he burst into laughter. When the sophist said: 'Why does hearing a man talk about bravery make you laugh, Cleomenes, especially when you're a king?', he replied: 'Because, my friend, if the swallow were talking about it also, I should do the same; but were it an eagle, I would keep very quiet.'

13. When the Argives were claiming that they would retrieve their previous defeat, he said: 'I am surprised if substituting one syllable[34] has made you stronger than you were before.'

14. When someone was insulting him and said: 'Cleomenes, you're soft,' he replied: 'Well, that's an improvement on being unjust. Look at you, you're avaricious even though you have adequate means.'

16. After Maeandrius the tyrant of Samos had fled to Sparta[35] 224
because of the Persians' onslaught and had displayed all the gold and silver goblets which he had brought, he freely offered Cleomenes as many as he wanted. But he accepted none, and took equal care that Maeandrius should not present them to any other citizens: he went to the ephors and said that it would be better for Sparta if his Samian guest should leave the Peloponnese so as not to influence any of the Spartiates into becoming a bad character. They took his advice and proclaimed Maeandrius' banishment the same day.

17. When someone said: 'After your frequent victories over the Argives in their wars against you, why haven't you wiped them out?', he replied: 'We wouldn't wish to wipe them out, because we want sparring-partners for our young men.'

18. When someone was asking him why Spartiates do not dedicate the spoils from their enemies to the gods, he said: 'Because they come from cowards.'

CLEOMENES SON OF CLEOMBROTUS
(Agiad king, 370–309)

When someone was presenting him with fighting cocks and claiming they would die in the struggle for victory, Cleomenes son of Cleombrotus said: 'Then give me some of those which kill them, since they'll be much better.'

LABOTAS
(Early Agiad king)

When someone was speaking at length Labotas said: 'Why do you give me such a long introduction to a small matter? The speech you make should be in proportion to the topic.'

LEOTYCHIDAS
(Seventh-century Eurypontid king)

1. When someone was remarking on how readily he changed his mind, Leotychidas the First said: 'Yes, but in accordance with the circumstances and not (like you people) because of a weak character.'

2. To the person who was asking how a man might best maintain his present favourable circumstances, he said: 'By not trusting everything to Fortune.'

3. When asked what freeborn boys should learn in particular, he said: 'The things that should be advantageous to them when they become men.'

4. When someone was asking the reason why the Spartiates drank so sparingly, he said: 'So that others may not make decisions on our behalf, but we may for others.'

LEOTYCHIDAS SON OF ARISTON
(Eurypontid king, 491–*c.* 469)

1. Leotychidas son of Ariston said to the man who mentioned that Demaratus'[36] sons were spreading bad reports about him: 'By the gods, I'm not surprised, since none of them could ever find a good word to say.'

2. When a snake had coiled round the key on the inside of the gate and the seers were declaring this to be a portent, he remarked: 'It doesn't look like that to me. If instead the key had coiled round the snake, that would be a portent.'

3. The Orphic priest Philip was completely destitute, but used to claim that those initiated by him would find happiness after their life's end. Leotychidas said to him: 'Well then, you fool, why don't you die as quickly as possible, so that you may thereby put an end to moaning about your ill-fortune and poverty?'

4. When somebody asked why they do not dedicate weapons won from their enemies to the gods, he said: 'Because there is nothing honourable in the young men seeing things seized through their owners' cowardice, or in dedicating them to the gods.'

LEON SON OF EURYCRATIDAS
(Sixth-century Agiad king)

1. When asked what sort of city one should live in to live safely, Leon son of Eurycratidas said: 'One whose inhabitants will possess neither too much nor too little; and where justice will be strong and injustice weak.'

2. As he saw the runners at Olympia eagerly seeking to gain an advantage at the starting-line, he remarked: 'How much more concerned the runners are about speed than about fairness.'

3. When someone engaged him at an inappropriate moment about business which was by no means trivial, he said: 'Friend, the question you raise is a good one, but your timing is not good.'

LEONIDAS SON OF ANAXANDRIDAS

(Agiad king, 491–480. Killed at the battle of Thermopylae against Xerxes)

225 1. When someone said to him: 'Except for being king you are not at all superior to us,' Leonidas son of Anaxandridas and brother of Cleomenes replied: 'But were I not better than you, I should not be king.'

2. When he was leaving for Thermopylae to fight the Persians, his wife Gorgo inquired if he had any instruction for her, and he said: 'To marry good men and bear good children.'

4. When the ephors said: 'Haven't you decided to take any action beyond blocking the passes against the Persians?', 'In theory, no,' he said, 'but in fact I plan to die for the Greeks.'

5. Once at Thermopylae he said to his men: 'They say that the Persians are close by while we are wasting time. Not so; for now we either kill the Persians or die willingly ourselves.'

6. When someone was saying: 'It isn't even possible to see the sun because of the Persians' arrows,' he said: 'How pleasant then, if we're going to fight them in the shade.'

7. When another person said: 'They are close to us,' he replied: 'Then we're also close to them.'

8. When someone said: 'Leonidas, are you here like this, to run such a risk with a few men against many?', he replied: 'If you think that I should rely on numbers, then not even the whole of Greece is enough, since it is a small fraction of their horde; but if I am to rely on courage, then even this number is quite adequate.'

9. When another person was asking him the same question, he said: 'I'm certainly bringing plenty of men to meet their deaths.'

10. When Xerxes wrote to him: 'It is possible for you not to fight the gods but to side with me and be monarch of Greece,' he wrote back: 'If you understood what is honourable in life, you would avoid lusting after what belongs to others. For me, it is better to die for Greece than to be monarch of the people of my race.'

11. When Xerxes wrote again: 'Deliver up your arms,' he wrote back: 'Come and take them.'

12. Just at the time when he was eager to attack the enemy the *polemarchs* told him that he must wait for the other allies. He said: 'But aren't those who intend to fight already here? Or aren't you aware that the only men who fight against the enemy are those who respect and fear their kings?'

13. He passed the word to his soldiers to eat breakfast in the expectation that they would be having dinner in Hades.

14. When asked why the best men prefer an honourable death to a life without honour, he said: 'Because they regard the latter as the gift of Nature, and the former as being in their own hands.'

15. Wishing to save the youths, but knowing that they would absolutely reject this, he gave each of them a dispatch[37] and sent them to the ephors. He wanted to save three of the mature men too, but they read his mind and refused to take the dispatches. One of them said: 'I joined you as a fighting-man, not a herald.' The second said: 'I would be a better man for staying here.' The third said: 'I won't be behind these others, but first into battle.'

LOCHAGUS

Lochagus, the father of Polyaenides and Seiron, when informed by somebody that one of his two sons was dead, said: 'I have long been aware that he had to die.'

LYCURGUS

1. Lycurgus the lawgiver, in his wish to convert the citizens from their existing habits to a more disciplined way of life and to make them brave and honourable (since they were living a soft life), reared two puppies born of the same father and mother; and one he conditioned to a life of luxury, allowing it to stay at home, while the other he took out and taught to hunt. Next he brought them into the assembly, put down some bones and delicious tidbits, and then released a hare. Each of the two dogs went after what it was used to; when the second of them had caught and killed the hare, Lycurgus said: 'Citizens, do you see how, although these dogs belong to the same family, their upbringing for life has made them turn out very different indeed
226 from each other? Do you see, too, how education is more effective than birth for producing noble behaviour?'

However, some people say that he did not produce puppies born of the same parents; instead one was from a domestic breed, the other from hunters. And then he trained the puppy of inferior stock to hunt, while merely conditioning the better-bred one to a life of luxury. So, when each of the two went after what it was used to, he highlighted the extent to which improvement or deterioration is the product of upbringing, and said: 'In our case, too, citizens, neither noble birth (which the masses so admire) nor descent from Heracles is of any value unless we perform the kind of actions with which he proved himself more worthy of fame and more nobly born than any other mortal, by training ourselves and learning what is good throughout our lives.'

227F 15. He said to someone who was inquiring why he made a law that girls should be given in marriage without a dowry: 'So that none should be left unmarried because of poverty nor any pursued for their wealth, but that each man should study the girl's character and make his choice on the basis of her good qualities.' For this reason he also outlawed the use of make-up from the city.

18. Perfume he banned too because it wasted and spoilt olive-oil, and dyeing because it pandered to the senses.

23. When someone asked the reason why he would permit 228D
citizens to take part only in those games where a hand is not raised, he said: 'So that none of them may acquire the habit of crying off when in difficulties.'[38]

24. When someone was inquiring why his orders were to shift camp frequently, he said: 'So that we may do the enemy greater harm.'

25. When someone else was keen to know why he ruled out attacks on forts, he said: 'So that a woman or child or some such creature should not kill men, who are better than they.'

31. When someone was asking why he had ordered that enemy corpses were not to be despoiled, he said: 'So that the men's
attention may not wander from the fighting as they peer about 229
for spoils, but also so that they may remain poor as well as in battle-order.'

LYSANDER

(Outstanding commander of the late fifth and early fourth centuries. Killed in battle in 395)

1. When Dionysius the tyrant of Sicily sent expensive clothes for his daughters, Lysander declined them, remarking that he was afraid these might instead make them look disreputable. But soon afterwards when he was sent as envoy[39] from the same city to the same tyrant, Dionysius forwarded him two dresses with instructions that he should pick the one he liked and take it for his daughter. But he said that she would choose better, and so he left taking both.

2. Lysander became an awfully clever trickster who did a great deal of fraudulent 'fixing'. He showed regard for justice only when it was to his advantage and for honour only when it suited him. He used to say that the truth is better than a lie, though in each case it is how they are used which determines their worth and value.

3. When he was censured for operating mostly by trickery and fraud in a way unworthy of Heracles, and for achieving no honest success, he used to laugh and say that fox-skin had to be stitched on wherever lion-skin wouldn't stretch.

4. When others were criticizing him for breaking the oaths which he gave at Miletus, he would say: 'Children have to be tricked with dice, but men with oaths.'

5. After defeating the Athenians by a ruse at Aegospotami[40] and making them feel the pinch of hunger, he forced them to surrender their city and wrote to the ephors: 'Athens is taken.'

6. When the Argives were disputing land boundaries with the Spartans and were maintaining that theirs was the fairer claim, he drew his sword and said: 'The man who has this within his grasp argues best about land boundaries.'

7. Noticing that the Boeotians' reaction to his crossing their territory was ambiguous, he sent a message to inquire whether he should march through their territory with spears ready for action or at the slope.

8. When a man from Megara was rather outspoken towards him in the general assembly, he said: 'My friend, your words require the backing of a city.'

9. While passing by the walls of Corinth when it had revolted, he noticed the Spartans' reluctance to attack; and when a hare was seen leaping over the ditch, he said: 'Spartiates, aren't you ashamed of your fear of enemies like this, who are so lazy that hares sleep on their walls?'

10. When he was consulting the oracle on Samothrace the priest instructed him to state the most criminal act he had ever perpetrated in his life. His reaction was to inquire: 'Is it on your orders that I have to do this, or on those of the gods?' When the priest declared: 'The gods,' he said: 'Then you move out of my way, and I'll tell *them* should they ask.'

11. When a Persian inquired what type of constitution met with his greatest approval, he said: 'Whichever gives brave men and cowards their due.'

12. He said to the man who declared his admiration and special affection for him: 'I have two oxen in a field; even though neither says anything, I'm fully aware of which one idles and which one works.'

13. When someone was abusing him he said: 'Say all you want, miserable little foreigner, and leave nothing unsaid, should that enable you to evacuate from your spirit the nastiness you seem to be full of.'

14. At a later date, after his death, a dispute developed over an alliance and Agesilaus came to Lysander's house to examine his records of it, since Lysander kept these at home. But he also discovered a pamphlet about the constitution written for Lysander. The thesis was that the kingship be removed from the Eurypontids and Agiads and be thrown open, and that the selection be made from among the best individuals, so that this privilege would be bestowed not upon Heracles' descendants but upon those who like Heracles were chosen for their merit (that being the reason why he too was raised to divine status). Agesilaus intended to make this work known to the citizens and to demonstrate what sort of citizen Lysander had secretly been, as well as to create prejudice against Lysander's friends. But by all accounts Lacratidas, who was then the presiding ephor, was concerned that if it was read the work might prove persuasive: so he restrained Agesilaus and said that there was no need to
disinter Lysander, but that they should bury the work with him, 230
since it was both criminal and persuasive in its presentation.

15. When after his death he was found to be a poor man, those who had wooed his daughters left off. The ephors fined them because they courted his daughters so long as they believed him to be wealthy, but once they discovered from his poverty that he was upright and honest they despised them.

NAMERTES

When he was despatched as envoy and a native of the country was congratulating him on having many friends, Namertes inquired if the latter had any means of putting a man with many friends to the test. Since he did not, but was eager to know of one, Namertes declared: 'Through misfortune.'

NICANDER

(Eighth-century Eurypontid king)

1. When someone mentioned that the Argives were slandering him, Nicander said: 'In that case they are being punished for slandering[41] good men.'

2. When someone asked why they have long hair and grow their beards, he said: 'Of all types of personal adornment, for a man this is the finest and least expensive.'

3. When one of the Athenians said: 'Nicander, you adhere very strongly to the principle of having no occupation,' he replied: 'You are correct; but our aim is that, unlike you, we shouldn't be concerned with every random pastime.'

PANTHOIDAS

(Spartiate officer of the early fourth century)

1. When Panthoidas was on an embassy to Asia and some people were showing him a great high wall, he said: 'By the gods, my friends, what splendid women's quarters!'

2. When the philosophers were engaging in much serious discussion in the Academy and Panthoidas was asked subsequently what impression their talk made on him, he replied: 'What else but serious? Yet there is no value in it unless you put it to use.'

PAUSANIAS SON OF CLEOMBROTUS

(Regent for his cousin, the Agiad boy king Pleistarchus, from 480. Removed and driven to death in the late 470s)

1. When the Delians[42] were maintaining their claim to the island against the Athenians and stating that under their law women

do not give birth on the island nor are corpses buried there, Pausanias son of Cleombrotus said: 'Then how could this be your fatherland, in which not one of you has either been born or will remain?'

2. When the exiles were urging him to lead his army against the Athenians and claiming that as his name was being called out at the Olympic Games they were the only ones who used to hiss him, he said: 'So what do you think those who used to hiss when their situation was favourable will do when it is unfavourable?'

3. When someone was asking why they made the poet Tyrtaeus a citizen,[43] he said: 'So that a foreigner should never be seen as our leader.'

4. To the man who was physically weak yet whose advice was to take all possible risks against the enemy by land and by sea, he said: 'So when giving us this advice to fight, are you willing to strip off yourself and show the sort of man you are?'

5. When amongst the spoils some people were amazed at the extravagance of the Persians' clothing, he said: 'Better for them to be men of great worth rather than to have possessions of great worth.'

6. After his victory over the Medes at Plataea[44] he gave orders that the Persian dinner which had been prepared beforehand should be served to his staff. Since it was incredibly expensive, he said: 'By the gods, with a spread like this what greedy characters the Persians were to chase after our barley-bread.'

PAUSANIAS SON OF PLEISTOANAX
(Agiad king, 408–395)

1. To the person who had asked why none of their ancient laws might be changed, Pausanias son of Pleistoanax said: 'Because the laws ought to control men, not men the laws.'

2. In Tegea, after he had gone into exile[45] and was praising the Spartans, someone said: 'So why didn't you stay at Sparta rather than go into exile?' He replied: 'Because even doctors don't

usually spend their time among fit people, but wherever there are sick ones.'

3. When someone was asking him how they could conquer the Thracians, he said: 'By making our doctor a general[46] and our general a doctor.'

231 4. When a doctor was examining him and said: 'You have nothing the matter with you,' he said: 'No. For after all, don't I employ you as my doctor?'

5. When one of his friends was criticizing him for disparaging a particular doctor even though he had never consulted him nor been done any harm by him, he said: 'My point is that, had I gone to consult him, I should not be alive now.'

6. When another doctor said to him: 'You have become an old man,' he said: 'Yes, because I didn't employ you as my doctor.'

7. He used to say that the best doctor is the one who doesn't let the sick rot but buries them very quickly.

PEDARITUS

(Spartan *harmost*, or governor, on Chios. Killed in action there in 411)

1. As someone was remarking that the enemy's numbers were substantial, Pedaritus said: 'Then we shall win greater fame since we shall inflict higher casualties.'

2. When he observed some effeminate person being nonetheless praised by the citizens for his fairness, he said: 'Men who are like women should not be praised nor should women who are like men, unless some necessity forces the woman.'

3. When not selected as one of the Three Hundred (which was rated as the outstanding distinction in the state) he withdrew with a bright smile. Yet when summoned back by the ephors and asked what was making him cheerful, he said: 'Because I congratulate the state on having three hundred citizens better than I.'

PLEISTARCHUS
(Agiad king, 480–458)

1. To the man who asked the reason why the royal lines do not derive their names from the first kings,[47] Pleistarchus son of Leonidas said: 'Because they wanted to exercise royal power to excess, whereas their successors in no sense did.'

2. When some advocate was making jokes, he said: 'My friend, as you keep cracking jokes, shouldn't you take care not to turn into a clown, in just the way that those who keep wrestling turn into wrestlers?'

3. He said to the man who was imitating a nightingale: 'My friend, I've found more pleasure in listening to the nightingale herself.'

4. On being informed by someone that a particular slanderer was praising him, he said: 'I wonder if somebody has told him that I'm dead, since he's incapable of speaking a good word about anyone alive.'

PLEISTOANAX
(Agiad king, 458–446/5 and 427/6–408. He was in exile for the intervening period)

When some Athenian politician was disparaging the Spartans as uneducated, Pleistoanax son of Pausanias said: 'Your point is correct, since we are the only Greeks who have learned nothing wicked from you Athenians.'

POLYDORUS
(Seventh-century Agiad king)

1. When someone was making constant threats against the enemy, Polydorus the son of Alcamenes said: 'Don't you realize that to a very great extent you are wasting your vindictiveness?'

2. As he was leading his army out against Messene, someone inquired if it was his intention to fight his brothers. 'No,' he

said, 'merely to proceed to that part of the country which is not divided into lots.'

3. After the pitched Battle of the Three Hundred,[48] when the Argives in full force had again suffered a defeat, the allies were urging Polydorus not to pass up the chance of assaulting the enemy wall and taking their city, which would be very easy to do with the men now dead and only the women left. So he said to them: 'While it's fine in my view to defeat one's opponents when fighting on equal terms, I do not consider it fair to want to capture their city after fighting over land boundaries. For I came to recover territory, not to seize a city.'

4. When asked why Spartiates boldly run risks in warfare, he said: 'Because they have learned to respect their leaders, not to fear them.'

POLYCRATIDAS

Polycratidas, as one of a group of envoys to the Great King's generals, was asked by them whether they were taking a private initiative, or had been sent by the state. His reply was: 'If we succeed, the latter; otherwise, the former.'

PHOEBIDAS[49]

When some people were saying prior to the peril of Leuctra that this day would prove who was brave, Phoebidas remarked that a day which was able to prove who was brave was indeed valuable.

SOÜS

(Early Eurypontid king)

232 There is a story that when Soüs was being besieged by the Cleitorians in a rugged waterless spot, he agreed to surrender them the territory which he had gained in the fighting, if all those with him might drink from the spring nearby, which the enemy were guarding. Once the oaths had been taken, he assembled his men and offered to confer the kingship of the area upon the one who refrained from drinking. Not one, however,

possessed such self-restraint, but they all drank. Soüs went down after everyone else, and with the enemy still there just splashed himself. Then he moved off, but retained control of the land because he had not drunk.

TELECLUS

(Eighth-century Agiad king)

1. Teleclus said to the man who told him that his father was slandering him: 'Unless he had a reason for speaking, he would not have spoken.'

2. When his brother mentioned that, even though they were from the same family, the citizens' behaviour towards himself was not the same as it was towards him, but was less courteous, he said: 'Yes, for you don't know how to suffer injustice, but I do.'

3. When asked the reason for their custom whereby the younger men get up and give their places to the older ones, he said: 'So that in showing such respect to men not related to them they may respect their parents all the more.'

4. When someone asked him how much property he owned, he said: 'No more than enough.'

CHARILLUS

(Eighth-century Eurypontid king, also called Charilaus)

1. When asked why Lycurgus made so few laws, Charillus said: 'Because men of few words need only a few laws too.'

2. When someone was asking why they let unmarried girls appear in public unveiled, but their wives veiled, he said: 'Because the girls need to find husbands, whereas the wives must stick to their own husbands.'

3. When one of the helots behaved rather insolently towards him, he said: 'Were I not angry, I would have killed you.'

4. When someone asked him which type of government he considered the best, he said: 'The one in which the largest

number of citizens are willing to compete with each other in excellence and without civil discord.'

5. When someone was inquiring why all the statues of the gods set up by them have weapons, he said: 'So that we may not blame the gods for cowardice just as we blame men, and so that our young men may not pray to unarmed gods.'

6. He said to the man who asked why they wear their hair long: 'This is the natural means of personal adornment, and it costs nothing.'

SAYINGS OF SPARTAN WOMEN

ARCHILEONIS

Some Amphipolitans came to Sparta and visited Archileonis, the mother of Brasidas, after her son's death.[1] She asked if her son had died nobly, in a manner worthy of Sparta. As they heaped praise on him and declared that in his exploits he was the best of all the Spartans, she said: 'Strangers, my son was indeed noble and brave, but Sparta has many better men than he.'

GORGO

(Daughter of King Cleomenes I, born about 506. Married her uncle, King Leonidas I)

1. When the Milesian Aristagoras was urging Cleomenes to make war against the Great King in support of the Ionians[2] and was promising him quantities of money, and also adding more to meet his objections, the king's daughter Gorgo said: 'Father, this miserable little foreigner will ruin you completely unless you drive him out of the house pretty quickly.'

2. Once when her father told her to give grain to some man as a means of payment and added: 'It's because he taught me how to make our wine really good,' she said: 'In that case, father, much more wine will be drunk and the drinkers will also be more fussy and will degenerate.'

3. After seeing Aristagoras having his shoes put on by one of his servants, she said: 'Father, the stranger has no hands.'

4. When a stranger in a finely embroidered robe was making advances to her, she rejected him with the words: 'Won't you get out of here? You can't even play a female role.'

5. When asked by a woman from Attica: 'Why are you Spartan women the only ones who can rule men?', she said: 'Because we are also the only ones who give birth to men.'

6. On her husband Leonidas' departure for Thermopylae, while urging him to show himself worthy of Sparta, she asked what she should do. He said: 'Marry a good man and bear good children.'

GYRTIAS[3]

1. Once when her grandson Acrotatus was brought home from some boys' combat badly battered and seemingly dead, and both her family and friends were sobbing, Gyrtias said: 'Won't you keep quiet? He's shown what kind of blood he has in him,' and she added that brave men should not be howled over but should be under medical care.

2. When a messenger came from Crete to report Acrotatus' death she said: 'Wasn't it inevitable that, when he proceeded against the enemy, either he would be killed by them or he would kill them? To hear that he died in a fashion worthy of me and the city and his ancestors is pleasanter than if he were immortal but a coward.'

DAMATRIA

After hearing that her son was a coward and unworthy of her, Damatria killed him when he made his appearance. This is the epigram about her:

> Damatrius who broke the laws was killed by his mother –
> She a Spartan lady, he a Spartan youth.

UNNAMED SPARTAN WOMEN

241 1. Another Spartan woman killed her son, who had deserted, as unworthy of his country, saying: 'He's not my offspring.' This is the epigram about her:

Away to the darkness, cowardly offspring, where out of hatred
Eurotas does not flow even for timorous deer.
Useless pup, worthless portion, away to Hell.
Away! This son unworthy of Sparta was not mine at all.

2. When another woman heard that her son had fallen in the battle-line, she said:

Let there be weeping for cowards; but you, child, without a tear
Do I bury: you are my son, and Sparta's too.

3. When some woman heard that her son had been saved and had escaped from the enemy, she wrote to him: 'You've been tainted by a bad reputation. Either wipe this out now or cease to exist.'

4. Another woman, when her sons fled from a battle and reached her, said: 'In making your escape, vile slaves, where is it you've come to? Or do you plan to creep back in here where you emerged from?' At this she pulled up her clothes and exposed her belly to them.

5. A woman, when she saw her son approaching, asked how their country was doing. When he said: 'All the men are dead,' she picked up a tile, threw it at him and killed him, saying: 'Then, did they send you to bring us the bad news?'

6. As someone was describing his brother's noble death to his mother, she said: 'Isn't it a disgrace, then, not to have gone on such a fine journey with him?'

7. A woman, after sending off her five sons to war, stood on the outskirts of the city to watch anxiously what the outcome of the battle might be. When someone appeared and she questioned him, he reported that all her sons had perished. She said: 'Yet this isn't what I asked you, vile slave, but rather how our country was doing.' When he said that it was winning, she remarked: 'Then I gladly accept the death of my sons too.'

8. As a woman was burying her son, a worthless old crone came

up to her and said: 'You poor woman, what a misfortune!' 'No, by the two gods, a piece of good fortune,' she replied, 'because I bore him so that he might die for Sparta, and that is what has happened, as I wished.'

9. When an Ionian woman was priding herself on one of the tapestries she had made (which was indeed of great value), a Spartan woman showed off her four most dutiful sons and said they were the kind of thing a noble and good woman ought to produce, and should boast of them and take pride in them.

10. When another woman heard that her son was behaving badly abroad, she wrote to him:[4] 'You've acquired a bad reputation. Either shake this off or cease to exist.'

11. In much the same way Chian exiles, too, came to Sparta and levelled many accusations against Pedaritus; his mother Teleutia sent for them, heard their charges, and having concluded that her son was in the wrong, sent him this message:[5] 'His mother to Pedaritus. Either behave better or stay there with no hope of a safe return to Sparta.'

12. Another woman, when her son was on trial for a crime, said: 'Son, release yourself either from the charge or from life.'

13. Another woman, as she was sending her lame son up the battle-line, said: 'Son, with each step you take bear courage in mind.'

14. Another woman, when her son arrived back from the battlefield wounded in the foot and in terrible pain, said: 'Son, if you bear courage in mind, you will have no pain and will be in good spirits too.'

15. A Spartan who had been wounded in battle and was unable to walk made his way on all fours, ashamed of being laughed at. But his mother said: 'Son, isn't it really much better to rejoice in your courage than to feel ashamed of being laughed at by idiots?'

16. Another woman, as she was handing her son his shield and

giving him some encouragement, said: 'Son, either with this or on this.'[6]

17. Another woman, handing over the shield to her son as he was going off on campaign, said: 'Your father always used to keep this safe for you. So you must either keep it safe too, or cease to exist.'

18. Another woman, in reply to her son who declared that the sword he had was a small one, said: 'Then extend it by a stride.'

19. When another woman heard that her son had died fighting 242
bravely in the battle-line, she said: 'Yes, you were mine.' But when she learned that her other son was still alive as a result of his cowardice, she said: 'No, you were not mine.'

20. Another woman, when she heard that her son had died in battle right at his place in the line, said: 'Bury him and let his brother fill his place.'

21. While taking part in a public procession another woman heard of her son's success in the battle-line but also of his death from many wounds. Her reaction was not to remove her garland but to say proudly to the women near her: 'Friends, how much finer it is to die victorious in the battle-line than to win at the Olympic Games and live.'

22. When a man was describing to his sister the noble death of her son, she said: 'While I'm happy for him, I'm equally sorry for you, since you've missed making the journey with such a valiant companion.'

23. Someone contacted a Spartan woman to ask if she would agree to let him seduce her. She said: 'When I was a child I learned to obey my father, and I did so; then when I became a woman I obeyed my husband; so if this man is making me a proper proposal, let him put it to my husband first.'

24. When asked what dowry she was giving the man marrying her, a poor girl said: 'My father's common sense.'

25. When a Spartan woman was asked if she had made advances to a man, she said: 'No, I didn't. But he made them to me.'

26. A girl who had been secretly deflowered and then brought on a miscarriage exercised such self-control – letting out not a single cry – that neither her father nor her neighbours besides were aware of her delivery. For the encounter of propriety with impropriety served to override her tremendous pain.

27.[7] A Spartan woman who was up for sale and was asked what skills she possessed, said: 'To be trustworthy.'

28. Another woman who had been taken prisoner and was being asked much the same question, said: 'To manage a household well.'

29. When a woman was asked by somebody whether she would be good if he were to buy her, she said: 'Yes, and even if you don't buy me.'

30. Another woman when on sale was asked by the auctioneer what skills she had and said: 'To be free.' When the man who bought her kept ordering her to perform certain services unfitting for a free woman, she declared: 'You'll be sorry that you didn't decide not to make a purchase like this!', and committed suicide.

APPENDIX

XENOPHON, *SPARTAN SOCIETY*

INTRODUCTION

In preparing his Lives of Spartans (*Lycurgus* in particular) Plutarch read many of the special studies of Sparta produced by Greek authors from the end of the fifth century onwards.[1] The title which such works were usually given in Greek – *Politeia* – has no suitable one-word equivalent in English. Though 'Constitution' is perhaps the nearest, and is commonly used, it fails to convey the much broader scope of *politeia*, which could be expected to embrace the entire social, as well as strictly constitutional, character of the *polis* or city-state. Such broader scope is certainly a feature of this sole *Politeia of the Spartans* to survive complete, which I have therefore preferred to render as *Spartan Society* rather than as the *Constitution of the Spartans*.

The work was preserved among the writings of Xenophon and seems to have found a considerable number of readers in antiquity, including Plutarch himself. However, even then the attribution to Xenophon was doubted, and it still remains in dispute, not least because plausible arguments can be made on either side. At first sight there does seem good cause to accept Xenophon as the author. The work clearly shows itself to be written by a non-Spartan who is concerned to convey his great enthusiasm for the state to other non-Spartans, while at the same time correcting what he believes to be certain common misconceptions about it. Xenophon can plausibly be seen in this role. An Athenian born no later than the early 420s into a well-to-do family, he became unsettled at home once democracy was restored not long after Athens' defeat in the Peloponnesian War (404 BC); a narrow oligarchy imposed by Sparta immediately following the surrender had not lasted. So he sought occupation abroad as a mercenary – first in the Persian empire,[2] and then in Sparta's campaigns against the Persians in Asia Minor. He formed a lasting friendship with the Spartan king Agesilaus, who came out as commander in 396. After serving with him both in Asia Minor and later in mainland Greece, Xenophon was rewarded with an estate near Olympia, and at the king's invitation sent his two sons to Sparta for their education. Even when forced to move in the aftermath of the great Theban defeat of the Spartans at Leuctra (371), Xenophon went to Corinth rather than back to Athens. It was there in old age that he wrote an admiring tribute to Agesilaus after the king's death in 360, and *A History of My Times*,[3] a highly partial account, almost invariably pro-Spartan, which reads more like memoirs than history. Thus Xenophon's career and sympathies would appear to make the attribution of *Spartan Society* to him a sound one; in addition considerable stylistic similarity to his other writings has been noted.

At the same time it may be claimed on the other side that nowhere else does Xenophon offer material of such poor quality. By any reasonable standard *Spartan Society* is often jejune in presentation and approach – attributing every single Spartan institution to Lycurgus, for example! Moreover the work furnishes only a very limited coverage of its subject. The last chapters in particular tend to dissolve into nothing better than a series of disjointed, scrappy notes. The reader's sense of confusion is heightened by the problem of whether Chapters 14 (the acknowledgement that the laws of Lycurgus are no longer obeyed) and 15 (on the relationship between kings and ephors) are correctly placed. While it is possible that *two* such unrelated sections were added as successive postscripts by the author, scribes later may equally have confused the order of their material, so that 15 was meant to follow on from 13 in a more or less logical way, and 14 *does* belong at the end (where it was placed, renumbered as '15', in the first edition of this volume).

Certainly Chapter 14 is most likely to be a postscript, which serves not least to show up the author as lacking personal knowledge of Sparta at the time he wrote his work. This could still fit Xenophon's case, if by chance he wrote (say) in the 390s on the basis of what Spartan comrades abroad told him, before he had ever been to Sparta himself. But against that the disillusionment of Chapter 14 hardly seems characteristic of Xenophon at any stage of his career. *Harmosts* are mentioned as still in post, which indicates that the chapter must have been written at the very latest in the 370s.[4] Yet, as we have seen, Xenophon's other writings show how his devotion to Sparta remained unshaken into the 350s.

While proof is lacking, my own inclination is therefore very much to doubt the attribution of *Spartan Society* to Xenophon, and instead to consider it the work of an unknown author who completed both the main text and the postscript within the years from 412 to 371 – the only period when Sparta had *harmosts* permanently stationed abroad. For the purposes of the present volume, however, the content of the work is more important than the identity of its author. It is particularly valuable for the light it sheds on the Spartan army. And there is no doubt that as one of the early works which idealized Sparta, it has had a notable influence from ancient times onwards.

NOTES

1. See Introduction, 'Lycurgus: Plutarch's Sources'.
2. His own account of this experience survives in *The Persian Expedition* (Penguin, 1967).
3. For both works, see further p. xxviii.
4. On the other hand it has been urged that there is no need to take this reference to *harmosts* as literally contemporary.

XENOPHON, *SPARTAN SOCIETY*

1. Now once it had struck me that Sparta, despite having one of the lowest populations, had nonetheless clearly become the most powerful and most famous state in Greece, I wondered how this had ever happened. But I stopped wondering once I had pondered the Spartiates' institutions, for they have achieved success by obeying the laws laid down for them by Lycurgus. I certainly admire him and consider him in the highest degree a wise man, since it was not by copying other states, but by deciding on an opposite course to the majority that he made his country outstandingly fortunate.

Putting first things first, think for instance of the production of children. Elsewhere girls who are prospective mothers and considered to be well brought up are fed the plainest practicable diet with as few extras as possible; certainly wine is not given to them at all, or only if watered down. Other Greeks require girls to be sedentary – like the majority of craftsmen – sitting still and working wool. But then how should girls brought up like this be expected to bear any strapping babies? In Lycurgus' view by contrast clothes could be produced quite adequately by slave women, whereas in his opinion the production of children was the most important duty of free women. So in the first place he required the female sex to take physical exercise just as much as males; next he arranged for women also, just like men, to have contests of speed and strength with one another, in the belief that when both parents are strong their children too are born sturdier.

Moreover, noticing that elsewhere men would have unlimited sex with their wives in the period immediately following marriage, he took the opposite approach to this too. For he made it a matter of disgrace that a man should be seen either when going into his wife's room, or when leaving it. For by having intercourse under these circumstances, their desire for one another was bound to be increased, and any children born would be much sturdier than if they had exhausted each other. Besides he would no longer allow each man to marry when he liked, but laid it down that they should marry when at their peak physically – his idea being that this too would help in the production of fine children. He observed, however, that where an old man happened to have a young wife, he tended to keep a very jealous watch on her. So he planned to prevent this too, by arranging that for the production of children the elderly husband should introduce to his wife any man whose physique and personality he admired. Further, should a man not wish to be married, but still be eager to have remarkable children, Lycurgus also made it lawful for him to have children by any fertile and well-bred woman who came to his attention, subject to her husband's consent. And he would approve many such arrangements. For the women want to have two households, while the men want to acquire for their sons brothers who would form part of the family and its influence, but would have no claim on the estate. For the production of children, then, he made these arrangements so different from those of others. The question of whether he did thereby endow Sparta with men whose size and strength are in any way superior, is for anyone who wishes to investigate for himself.

2. Now that I have explained about procreation I want to give a precise account of the education[1] of the two sexes as well. Elsewhere in Greece, of course, those who claim to give their sons the finest education, as soon as the children understand what is being said to them, immediately put them under the care of servants as tutors and at once despatch them to schools to learn reading and writing and music and the art of wrestling. Besides, they make their children's feet soft with shoes and their bodies delicate with changes of clothing. As for food, they certainly let them eat as much as their stomachs can hold. But

Lycurgus, in place of the private assignment of slave tutors to each boy, stipulated that a man from the group out of which the highest office-holders are appointed should take charge of them: he is called the Trainer-in-Chief.[2] Lycurgus gave this man authority both to assemble the boys and to punish them severely whenever any misbehaved while in his charge. He also gave him a squad of young adults equipped with whips to administer punishment when necessary. The result has been that respect and obedience in combination are found to a high degree at Sparta.

Rather than letting boys' feet grow soft in shoes, he told them emphatically to make them strong by not wearing shoes, in the belief that this practice should enable them to walk uphill with greater ease and come down in greater safety, while the boy who is accustomed to having no shoes on his feet should jump and bound and run faster than the one with shoes. And instead of their clothes serving to make them delicate, he required them to become used to a single garment all the year round, the idea being that thereby they would be better prepared for both cold and heat. As for food, he instructed the Eiren to furnish for the common meal just the right amount for them never to become sluggish through being too full, while also giving them a taste of what it is not to have enough. His view was that boys under this kind of regimen would be better able, when required, to work hard without eating, as well as to make the same rations last longer, when so ordered; they would be satisfied with a plain diet, would adapt better to accepting any type of food, and would be in a healthier condition. He also considered that a diet which produced slim bodies would do more to make them grow tall than one in which the food filled them out.

On the other hand, while he did not allow them to take what they required effortlessly, to prevent them suffering from hunger he did permit them to engage in some stealing in order to ward off starvation. I imagine everyone is aware that he did not let them get food by trickery because he was unable to provide for them. Clearly a prospective thief must keep awake at night, and by day must practise deception and lie in wait, as well as have spies ready if he is going to seize anything. So clearly it was

Lycurgus' wish that by training the boys in all these ways he would make them more resourceful at feeding themselves and better fighters. Someone might ask then, if he considered theft a good thing, why on earth did he inflict many lashes on the boy who was caught? My answer is, because – as in every other branch of instruction – people chastise anyone who does not respond satisfactorily. So the Spartans, too, punish those who are caught as being incompetent thieves. And after making it a matter of honour for them to snatch just as many cheeses as possible from Orthia, he commanded others to whip them, wishing to demonstrate thereby the point that a short period of pain may be compensated by the enjoyment of long-lasting prestige.[3] This proves that wherever speed is called for, the sluggard gains minimum advantage while also incurring maximum difficulty. With the intention that even in the absence of the Trainer-in-Chief the boys should always have someone in charge of them, he authorized any citizen who happened to be present at the time to give the boys whatever instructions he thought proper, and to punish any slip they might make. By this measure he gave the boys a greater sense of respect too, since there is nothing that either boys or men respect as much as those in charge of them. To ensure that someone should be in control of the boys even when no adult happened to be on the spot, he deputed the smartest of the Eirens to take command of each Squadron.[4] As a result the boys at Sparta are never without someone in charge of them.

It strikes me that a word should also be said about men's love for boys, since this too has some connection with their education. Now what happens elsewhere in Greece may be illustrated from Boeotia, where man and boy form a union and live together, or Elis where beautiful youths are won by favours; in contrast there are also places where would-be lovers are absolutely debarred from talking to boys. Lycurgus in fact took a position different from all of these. If out of admiration for a boy's personality a man of the right character himself should seek to befriend him in all innocence and keep his company, Lycurgus would approve that and consider it the finest training. On the other hand if someone was obviously chasing after a boy for his body, he regarded that as an absolute disgrace and laid it down that at Sparta lovers should refrain from molesting boys just as much as parents avoid having intercourse with their children or brothers with their sisters. It does not surprise me, however, that some people do not believe this, since in many cities the laws do not oppose lusting after boys.

This covers the method of education at Sparta as well as elsewhere in Greece. Which of the two turns out men who are more disciplined, more respectful and (when required) more self-controlled, is again something for anyone who wishes to investigate.

3. The time when boys develop into youths is the very moment when others remove them from tutors, remove them from schools and have nobody in charge of them any longer, but leave them independent. Here, too, Lycurgus took the opposite view. Because he appreciated that at this age youths become very self-willed and are particularly liable to cockiness – both of which produce very powerful cravings for pleasure – this was the age at which he loaded them with the greatest amount of work and contrived that they should be occupied for the maximum time. In fact his further prescription that anyone who avoided this work would gain no future honour prompted concern not just from public officials but also from the family of each of the youths, who did not want shirking on their part to result in a total loss of reputation in the community. Besides, in his wish to see a sense of respect strongly implanted in them, he gave orders that even in the streets they should keep both hands inside their cloaks, should proceed in silence, and should not let their gaze wander in any direction, but fix their eyes on the ground before them. In consequence it has become absolutely clear that by nature the male sex possesses greater strength than the female even in the matter of self-control. Certainly, compared with those youths you would sooner hear a cry from a stone statue or succeed in catching the eye of a bronze one: you would think the youths more bashful than the 'little girl' in the eye.[5] And whenever they attend the mess, the men are satisfied just to hear the youths' replies to any question put to

them. Such, then, was the amount of attention he devoted to youths.

4. However, it was for the young adults that he displayed by far the greatest concern, in the conviction that they would have the most influence for good on the state if they were of the right character. And from his observation that when people have a very strong innate spirit of competition their choruses are the ones most worth hearing, and their athletic contests the ones most worth watching, he came to think that if he could also urge the young adults to compete in excellence, then they would attain the height of manly gallantry. Let me explain how he used in fact to urge them.

From among them the ephors select three of those in their prime, men who are called *Hippagretae*. Each of these picks 100 men[6] with a clear explanation of why he is approving some and rejecting others. As a result those who do not achieve the honour are at war with both those who have dismissed them and those chosen instead of them, and the two groups are on the lookout for any negligent act which may contravene accepted standards of honour. This is also the type of competition most highly favoured by the gods and best suited to a citizen community – in which the conduct required of the brave man is spelled out and each of the two groups independently strives to ensure that it will always prove superior, while should any need arise they would as one protect the city with all their might. They must keep themselves physically fit too, since their rivalry actually makes them come to blows whenever they meet. However, all passers-by have the right to separate the combatants. Anyone who defies the man attempting to separate them is brought before the ephors by the Trainer-in-Chief. They levy a stiff fine in their desire to establish the principle that anger must never prevail over respect for the law.

As for those who have passed beyond the youngest grade of adulthood – the group from which the highest office-holders are in fact also appointed – other Greeks, after removing their obligation to keep up their physical strength, nonetheless require them to go on serving in the army. Lycurgus by contrast made hunting the noblest pastime for men of this age (unless some public duty prevented them), so that they too could stand up to the exertions of campaigning just as well as the youngest men.

5. This, then, pretty well completes my account of the training which Lycurgus prescribed by law for each age-group. Now I will attempt to explain the way of life that he laid down for all of them. Well then, when Lycurgus took the Spartans in hand, they were living in separate households like Greeks elsewhere. He concluded that this was the cause of a great amount of misbehaviour and so he promulgated his scheme for common messes on the reckoning that these would reduce to a minimum disobedience of orders. The rations he fixed in such a way that they should have neither too much nor too little food. In addition hunting expeditions produce much that was not part of the calculation, and there are occasions when rich individuals also supply wheat-bread for a change. Consequently there is never a shortage of food on the table until they leave the mess, yet neither is there a lavish spread. Moreover when it came to wine he stopped excessive drinking – which causes both physical and mental degeneration – and just let each man drink whenever he felt thirsty: in his view this would be the least harmful and most enjoyable way of drinking. Well now, with common messes of this type how would anybody ruin either himself or his household by greediness or alcoholism?

Besides, in other cities men of the same age generally congregate together, and the sense of respect in the group tends to be very limited. But at Sparta Lycurgus mixed ages together in the belief that in many ways it would be educational for the younger men to benefit from the experience of their elders. Indeed the local custom was for any noble act on the part of any citizen to be a subject of conversation in the messes, so that there was very limited opportunity for rowdyism and drunken behaviour, and equally for coarse actions or words.

Eating out certainly brings this benefit too, namely that to get home they have to walk, taking care not to trip and fall under the influence of wine, and aware that it is impossible to remain where they have been dining. They also have to do in the dark what they do by daylight; in fact men still liable to military service are not even allowed a torch. Now Lycurgus further noted that the same rations improve the complexion, physique and strength of hard workers, whereas they give lazy people a bloated, ugly and feeble appearance. He did not overlook this either, but bearing in mind that anybody who works cheerfully and spontaneously has a reasonably good-looking physique, he made it the duty of the oldest man in the gymnasium at any time to ensure that each man's workouts were not inadequately strenuous for his diet. And my view is that he was not mistaken in this either. For it would certainly not be easy for anyone to find men healthier or more physically adept than Spartiates, since they exercise their legs, arms and neck equally.

6. Lycurgus definitely held the opposite view to the majority in the following ways too. To begin with, in other cities each man is master of his own children, slaves and property. But Lycurgus, in his wish to arrange that citizens might enjoy a mutual benefit without injury to anyone, caused each man to be master of other people's children just as much as his own. When someone knows that fathers are to behave in this way, he is obliged to give orders to the children over whom he himself exercises control in the same fashion as he would like orders to be issued to his own as well. Should any boy ever disclose to his father that he has been beaten by another, then it is a disgrace if the father does not give his son a further beating. To such a degree do they trust each other not to give their children any dishonourable order.

He even authorized them to use other people's household servants too, if anybody needed them. He also authorized hunting dogs to be shared, so that men who need some ask to take them on their hunt, and the owner is pleased to send them if he is not at leisure himself. They have the same arrangement with horses too, so that if a person has fallen ill, or needs a carriage, or wants to reach somewhere fast, and happens to spot a horse anywhere, he takes it, and then duly returns it after use. The following practice besides, which is unparalleled elsewhere, was instituted by Lycurgus in cases where men have been kept out late by hunting and need food, but happen to have brought none with them. He arranged that those who did have a supply with them should leave some behind in the area, and that those who needed it could break the seals, take what they required and leave the rest sealed up again. Accordingly by sharing with each other in this way, even those who possess little can benefit from everything in the country whenever they are in any need.

7. There are also the following practices instituted by Lycurgus which are quite the opposite to those elsewhere in Greece. In the other states everyone naturally makes as much money as possible: some are farmers, others ship-owners or traders, while crafts support yet others. But at Sparta Lycurgus banned all free men from the pursuit of wealth, and prescribed that their sole concern should be with the things that make cities free. Indeed, why should anyone be seriously concerned to gain wealth there, where Lycurgus prescribed that provisions should be contributed on an equal basis and the way of life be uniform, thus doing away with a self-indulgent passion for money? Besides, there is no point in making money even for the sake of clothes, since it is physical vitality which gives these men a distinctive appearance, not lavish dress. There is no point either in amassing money to spend on fellow members of the mess, since Lycurgus prescribed that the person who helps his companions by undertaking physical labour is more reputable than the one who spends money – thus demonstrating that the former service comes from the heart, whereas the latter is a function of being rich.

In such ways as follows he also prevented moneymaking by illegal means. First he instituted currency of such a type that neither master nor servant could ever be unaware of a mere ten *minas* coming into a house: indeed this would require much space and a waggon for transport. Searches are made for gold and silver, and should any come to light anywhere, its possessor is fined. So what would be the point of being eager to make money when more trouble comes from having it than pleasure does from spending it?

8. Now we all know that at Sparta there is the strictest obedience to both the authorities and the laws. I think, however, that Lycurgus did not even attempt to establish this discipline until he had won the agreement of the most influential men in the state. I make this conjecture because in other states the more powerful people do not even want to give the impression of fearing the authorities, but instead consider that to be demeaning to free men. But at Sparta the most influential figures are in fact particularly submissive towards the authorities: they take pride in being humble as well as in responding at a run rather than by walking whenever they are summoned. For they believe that if they should take the lead in showing exceptional obedience, the rest also will follow – as has indeed been the case. It is also likely that these same figures collaborated in establishing the power of the ephorate[7] too, since they recognized that obedience is of the greatest benefit in a state, as in an army and a household. For the more power the office had, the more they thought it would also cow the citizens into submission. So the ephors have the power to fine anyone they wish, the right to secure payment on the spot, the right also to dismiss office-holders, and actually to imprison and put them on trial for their lives. With power of this degree they do not, as in other cities, always permit elected officials to exercise their authority just as they please for a full year; but in the style of tyrants and umpires at athletic competitions, if ever they detect any irregular behaviour on anyone's part, they at once punish it on the spot.

In order to make the citizens willing to obey the laws Lycurgus was responsible for many other admirable devices. One of the most admirable in my view is this: he issued his laws to the populace only after going to Delphi with the most powerful figures and asking the god[8] if it would be preferable and better for Sparta to obey the laws he personally had drawn up. Once the god responded that it would be better in every way, only then did he issue them, with the prescription that it would be not only unlawful but also impious to disobey laws ordained by the Pythian god.

9. Lycurgus merits admiration for this too, namely for bringing it about that the citizens considered an honourable death preferable to a life of disgrace. For in fact anybody would discover on investigation that casualties among them are lower than among men who prefer to retreat from danger. To be truthful, self-preservation in most instances is really associated more with bravery than with cowardice, since the former is in fact easier and more pleasant as well as having greater resources and strength. Clearly glory is the close companion of bravery: indeed everyone wants some alliance with brave men. Now it would be quite wrong to neglect how Lycurgus contrived this attitude. Well, clearly he offered the brave prosperity and the cowards adversity. For in other cities whenever someone displays cowardice, he merely gets the name of coward; yet the coward – if he wants to – goes out in public, and sits down, and takes exercise in the same place as the brave man. But at Sparta everyone would be ashamed to be associated with a coward in his mess or to have him as a wrestling partner. When sides are being picked for a ball game that sort of man is often left out with no position assigned, and in dances he is banished to the insulting places. Moreover in the streets he is required to give way, as well as to give up his seat even to younger men. The girls of his family he has to support at home, and must explain to them why they cannot get husbands. He must endure having a household with no wife, and at the same time has to pay a fine for this. He must not walk around with a cheerful face, nor must he imitate men of impeccable reputation: otherwise he must submit to being beaten by his betters. When disgrace of this kind is imposed on cowards I am certainly not at all surprised that death is preferred there to a life of such dishonour and ignominy.

10. Equally splendid in my opinion was Lycurgus' law that excellence be cultivated up to old age. For by establishing that election to the Gerousia[9] should occur near life's end, he ensured that they would continue to care about their moral excellence even in old age. He is to be admired also for the protection he offered to virtuous men in old age, for by making the Elders

supreme judges in capital cases he produced more respect for old age than for those at the peak of their strength. And it is certainly reasonable that of all mankind's competitions this one should prompt the greatest rivalry. For indeed athletic contests are honourable too, but they are merely trials of physique, whereas the competition for the Gerousia involves a test of the noble qualities of the spirit. Thus just as the spirit is superior to the body, to the same degree contests of spirit merit greater rivalry than those of physique.

How could one truly deny that the following measure by Lycurgus merits tremendous admiration? He recognized that where only enthusiasts show concern for virtue, their numbers are not sufficient to exalt their country: so at Sparta he made it compulsory for everyone to develop all the virtues as a public duty. Thus just as private individuals who cultivate excellence are superior to those who neglect it, so Sparta too is superior to all cities in this quality, because she alone makes the development of moral excellence a public duty. Isn't this splendid too, that where other cities inflict punishment in cases where one individual injures another, Lycurgus imposed even greater penalties if someone should openly neglect to be as good as possible? For his opinion evidently was that men who make slaves of others or commit some fraud or theft only wrong those they harm, whereas whole communities are betrayed by men who are unmanly cowards. Consequently it strikes me as appropriate that these were the ones on whom he imposed the heaviest penalties. He also made the exercise of all the good qualities of citizens an inescapable duty. Thus he gave an equal share in the state to all law-abiding citizens, without regard for physical or financial deficiencies. But Lycurgus made it clear that if anyone should shirk the effort required to keep his laws, then he would no longer be considered one of the Equals.[10]

Now it is plain that these laws are extremely ancient, since Lycurgus is said to have been a contemporary of the Heraclids. However, in spite of their age, even today other peoples find them very novel. And the most extraordinary thing of all is that despite the universal praise for such a code of behaviour, not a single city is willing to copy it.

11. Now these advantages they enjoy jointly in time of both peace and war. But if anyone wishes to understand how Lycurgus also caused their organization on campaign to be superior to that of others, he should pay attention to what follows.

First of all, the ephors announce to the cavalry and hoplites which age-groups are required for service, and then to the craftsmen too. Consequently even on campaign the Spartans are fully supplied with everything used by a city population. And orders are given for all the equipment required by the army generally to be supplied – some of it in waggons, and some on pack animals. As a result deficiencies are most unlikely to go undetected. Now as to their equipment for battle, he arranged that they should have a red cloak and a bronze shield, on the reckoning that the former presents the greatest contrast with any female dress, as well as the most warlike appearance; the latter certainly can be polished very quickly and is very slow to tarnish. He permitted those who had reached adulthood to wear their hair long too, in the belief that they would thereby look taller and have a nobler, more fearsome appearance.

Now he divided the men thus equipped into six *moras* of both cavalry and hoplites. Each hoplite *mora* has one *polemarch*, four *lochagi*, eight *pentecosters* and sixteen *enomotarchs*.[11] When the word is given, the *enomotiae* which make up these *moras* form up now in single file, now three abreast, now six.

The general view, that the Spartan battle formation is very complicated, is an assumption completely at variance with reality. For in the Spartan formation the men who stand in the front line are officers . . . and all the ranks co-operate by doing what is required of them.[12] It is so easy to grasp this formation that nobody who is capable of telling men apart should go wrong, since some have been assigned to lead and others to follow. Orders for deployment are given verbally by the *enomotarch* acting like a herald, so that the phalanxes[13] thin out or grow thicker as required. None of this is in any way difficult to grasp. All the same, what isn't at all easy to grasp, except for those trained under the laws of Lycurgus, is the tactic of continuing the fight with whoever is to hand after the line has been thrown into confusion.

Spartans also execute with complete smoothness manoeuvres regarded as very difficult by military instructors. For instance, whenever they are marching in column, naturally one *enomotia* follows behind another. If in this situation an enemy phalanx suddenly appears in front, the order is passed to each *enomotarch* to form a front to the left,[14] and this continues down the entire line until the counter-phalanx is in place. Now should the enemy appear from the rear when the Spartans are in this position, each line countermarches itself so that it is always the men of highest calibre who are facing the enemy. Even the fact that in these circumstances the commander is now on the left[15] is seen by them not as a drawback, but sometimes even as an advantage. For should any attempt be made to outflank them, such an encircling movement would catch them on their protected side,[16] not their exposed one. On the other hand if it happened to seem advantageous for some reason that the leader hold the right wing, they first turn the unit in file and reverse the phalanx to the point where the leader is on the right and the rearguard to his left. But on the other hand, should an enemy brigade appear to the right as they are marching in column, all they need to do is to turn each *lochus* like a trireme[17] with its prow facing the enemy, and thus the rear *lochus* again finds itself on the right. Of course an enemy approach on the left is not tolerated either. Instead they repulse it, or turn their *lochi* to face their foes, and thus the rear *lochus* is again positioned on the left.

12. I shall also explain Lycurgus' view of how a camp should be laid out. Given that the angles of a square are indefensible, he made his camps circular except where a secure hill or wall or river lay to the rear. Now in the daytime he posted sentries by the weapons facing inwards – men stationed to guard against their friends rather than their enemies. A watch for the enemy was kept by cavalry placed wherever they could spot anyone approaching from a great distance. For night-time he assigned Sciritae[18] to mount guard on the camp perimeter, and nowadays any mercenaries who happen to be present join them too. One should also be very clear that the practices of always walking

about with spear in hand and of keeping the slaves away from the weapons both have an identical purpose.[19] One should not be surprised that when they go off to relieve themselves they do not stray so far from either their comrades or their weapons as to cause each other distress. The point of these practices is certainly security. Moreover they change their camp-sites frequently, both to harm their enemies and to assist their friends.

All Spartans are also instructed by law to keep up their gymnastic training for the duration of campaigns, with the consequence that their sense of their own impressiveness is enhanced and they look superior to other men. No walking or running is to be done beyond the area occupied by the *mora*, so that nobody goes far from his weapons. After the exercises the first *polemarch* gives the order by herald to sit down – this is a kind of inspection – and then to have breakfast, and for the scouts to be relieved quickly. Then afterwards there is a period of leisure and relaxation before the evening exercises. Following these the order to prepare the main meal is given by herald, and then, after they have sung a hymn to those gods who have responded favourably to sacrifice, the order to sleep with weapons close to hand.

There is no need to be surprised at the length of my description, because anybody would discover that where military matters are concerned the Spartans have overlooked very little that demands attention.

13. Let me further describe the authority and prestige which Lycurgus bestowed upon a king on campaign. First, while on service a king and his entourage are maintained by the state. The *polemarchs* mess with him so as to be at his side at all times and to allow them to confer whenever necessary. Three other Equals are also members of the mess to take care of all the others' needs and ensure that they have no concerns to distract them from the business of war.

However, I should go back to how the king starts out with his army. Now first, while still at home, he sacrifices to Zeus the Leader and the associated gods. If the sacrifice then appears favourable, the Fire-bearer takes the fire from the altar and conveys it to the frontier of the country, where the king sacrifices again to Zeus and Athena. Only after both these divinities have reacted favourably does he cross the frontier of the country; and the fire from these sacrifices is conveyed onwards without ever being extinguished, while every type of victim goes with them. In every instance when he is making a sacrifice he begins the operation before daybreak, with the aim of being the first to win the god's favour. The sacrifice is attended by *polemarchs*, *lochagi*, *pentecosters*, mercenary commanders, superintendents of the baggage train, and such generals from particular cities' contingents as wish to come. Also present are two ephors, who do not involve themselves in any way unless the king calls them in, but observe each person's actions and ensure that they are correct in every case. Once the sacrifices have been completed, the king assembles everyone and announces what needs to be done. In short, if you witnessed this you would think that militarily others are amateurs, whereas Spartans alone are real masters of the craft of war.

Provided that no enemy appears, when a king is leading nobody goes in front of him except Sciritae and the cavalry on reconnaissance. However, at any time they think there will be a battle, the king takes the unit of the first *mora* and under his leadership it wheels right until they are placed between two *moras* and two *polemarchs*. The troops to be positioned behind these are marshalled by the eldest member of the king's entourage. This comprises all those Equals who mess with him, seers, doctors, pipers, the superintendents of the baggage train, and such 'volunteers'[20] as may be on the scene. As a result nothing which is required is lacking, since everything has been thought of in advance.

Lycurgus also made the following splendid, and in my view advantageous, arrangements for the actual armed combat. Once the enemy can see what is happening, a she-goat is sacrificed, and the law is that all the pipers present should play and every Spartan wear a garland; an order to polish weapons is also given. Young men may enter battle with their hair groomed . . . and with a joyful, distinguished appearance.[21] Words of encouragement are passed to the *enomotarchs* because each *enomotarch*, standing outside of his *enomotia*, cannot be heard over the whole of each one. It is the responsibility of the *polemarch* to see that this is carried out properly.

Now when it seems the correct moment to pitch camp, the king takes charge and indicates the right spot. It is also his function to despatch embassies to both friends and enemies. Everyone who wants to get some business done begins with the king. Now if the person has come seeking justice, the king directs him to the Hellanodicae;[22] if money, to the treasurers; if he has brought in spoils, then to the sellers of booty. With these arrangements the king is left with no other duty on campaign except to act as priest in the divine sphere and as general in the human one.

14.[23] Were anyone to ask whether I think that the laws of Lycurgus still remain in force unchanged even at the present time, by Zeus no, I would not have the confidence to make that claim today. For I am aware that in the past the Spartans chose to live together at home with modest means rather than to serve as *harmosts* in various cities and so be corrupted by flattery. I am also aware of how in the past they feared any disclosure that they had gold in their possession, though nowadays there are even some who glory in having acquired it. I know that in the past too, for this very reason, expulsions of foreigners used to occur and absence abroad was not permitted, so that citizens should not be infected by lax habits caught from foreigners. But I know that nowadays those who have the reputation of being leading citizens have proved keen to serve abroad as *harmosts* all their lives. At one time, too, they would have taken care to ensure that they deserved to occupy the leading position: but nowadays by contrast their main preoccupation is just to exercise authority rather than to be worthy of so doing. Thus in the past, for instance, the Greeks would come to Sparta and ask her to be their leader against those they felt were wronging them. But now many are calling upon each other to prevent a further period of Spartan rule.[24] It is certainly no wonder that these aspersions are being cast against them, since plainly they are obedient neither to heaven nor to the laws of Lycurgus.

15. I also want to explain the accord with the state which Lycurgus made for the kingship. For as an office it is unique in continuing to adhere to its original form, whereas one would find that other types of government have been altered and are still in the process of alteration even currently. Lycurgus laid it down that a king, by virtue of his divine descent, should perform all the public sacrifices on the city's behalf and should lead the army wherever the city despatches it. He also granted him the privilege of taking parts of the animals sacrificed, and he assigned him such selected land in many of the perioecic communities as would ensure that all his ordinary requirements should be met, yet would not make him excessively wealthy. Also, to make certain that the kings ate away from home he assigned them a state mess, and gave them the honour of double portions at meals, not for them to stuff twice as much, but so that they should have something to offer as a mark of respect to anyone of their choice. Moreover he permitted each king to select two fellow members for the mess as well, who – it may be noted – are also termed *Pythii*.[25] He further permitted a king to take a piglet from every sow's litter, so that he should never lack victims with which to consult the gods at any time the need arises. In addition a pool near his residence supplies plenty of water – an advantage in many ways, as those without it appreciate even more. And everyone rises from their place for a king, except ephors from their chairs of office. And there is a monthly exchange of oaths, ephors acting for the city, a king on his own behalf. The king's oath is to rule according to the city's established laws, while that of the city is to keep the king's position unshaken so long as he abides by his oath. These, then, are the prerogatives granted to a king at home during his lifetime – nothing much above the level of private citizens. For it was not Lycurgus' intention either that kings should acquire a tyrannical attitude or that citizens should come to envy their power. As to the honours shown a king after his death, the aim of the laws of Lycurgus here is to demonstrate that they have given special honour to Spartan kings not as humans but as heroes.[26]

Spartan Kings to 222 BC

For the sake of clarity and simplicity these lists do not indicate the many controversies which surround the order and dates of the early kings in different ancient traditions. From the fifth century onwards, the dates of each king's reign and his relationship to his predecessor are given.

Three generations were said to come between Heracles, founder of the family, and Aristodemus, father of Eurysthenes and Procles, the first kings.

Agiad Kings

Eurysthenes	
Agis I	
Echestratus	
Labotas	
Doryssus	
Agesilaus I	
Archelaus	8th century BC (contemporary with Charilaus/Charillus)
Teleclus	8th century
Alcamenes	8th century
Polydorus	7th century (contemporary with Theopompus)
Eurycrates	7th century
Anaxander	7th century
Eurycratidas	7th/6th century
Leon	6th century (contemporary with Agasicles)
Anaxandridas II	6th century
Cleomenes I (son)	*c.* 520–491
Leonidas I (brother)	491–480
Pleistarchus (son)	480–458

Pleistoanax (son of regent Pausanias)	458–446/5 and 427/6–408 (in exile for the intervening period)
Pausanias (son)	408–395
Agesipolis I (son)	395–380
Cleombrotus I (brother)	380–371
Agesipolis II (son)	371–370
Cleomenes II (brother)	370–309
Areus I (grandson)	309–265
Acrotatus (son)	265–*c.* 255
Areus II (son)	*c.* 255–*c.* 251
Leonidas II (grandson of Cleomenes II)	*c.* 251–242 and 241–235
Cleombrotus II (son-in-law)	242–241
Cleomenes III (son of Leonidas II)	235–222 (died 219)

Eurypontid Kings

Procles	
Soüs	
Eurypon	
Prytanis	
Eunomus	
Polydectes	(Lycurgus was his younger brother, according to Plutarch, *Lycurgus*, Ch. 1)
Charilaus/Charillus	8th century BC (contemporary with Archelaus)
Nicander	8th century
Theopompus	late 8th/early 7th centuries (contemporary with Polydorus)
Anaxandridas I	7th century
Archidamus I	7th century
Anaxilas	7th century
Leotychidas I	7th century
Hippocratidas	6th century
Agasicles	6th century (contemporary with Leon)
Ariston	6th century
Demaratus	late 6th century–491

Leotychidas II (distant cousin)	491–*c.* 469
Archidamus II (grandson)	*c.* 469–427
Agis II (son)	427–400
Agesilaus II (half-brother)	400–360
Archidamus III (son)	360–338
Agis III (son)	338–331
Eudamidas I (brother)	331–unknown date
Archidamus IV (son)	unknown date–294 or later
Eudamidas II (son)	after 294–244/3
Agis IV (son)	244/3–241
Eudamidas III (son)	241–227
Archidamus V (uncle)	227
Eucleidas (Agiad – brother of Cleomenes III)	227–222

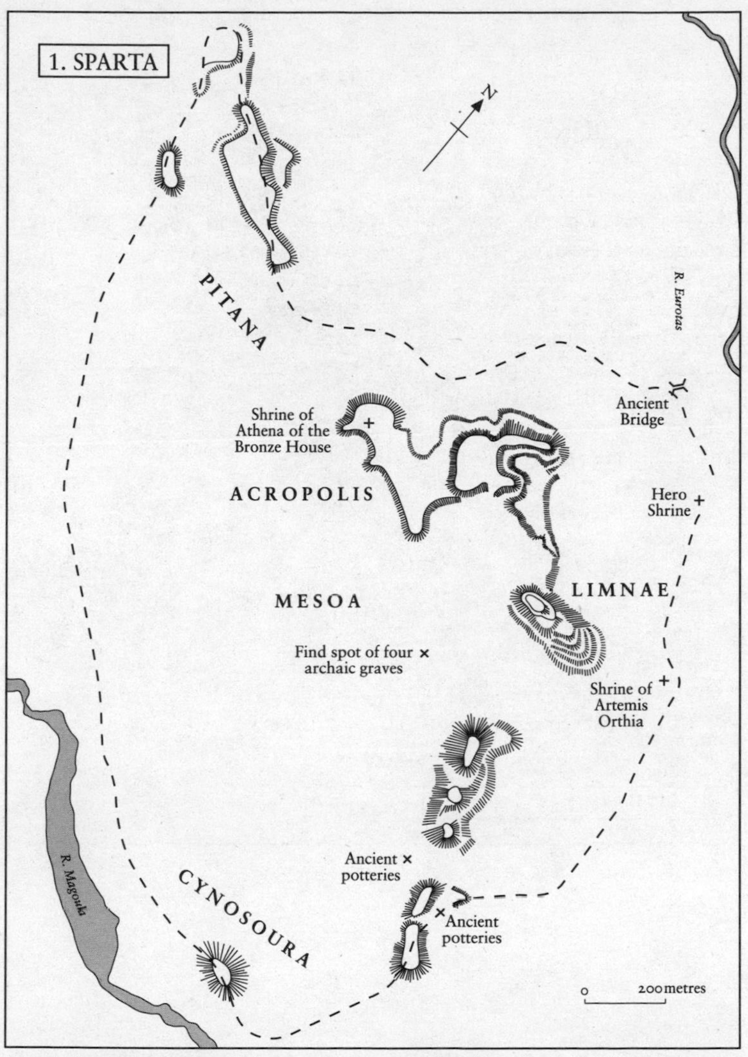

'The city has neither been consolidated nor does it possess lavish temples and buildings, but consists of village settlements of the antique Greek type.' This description by Thucydides (*The Peloponnesian War*, I.10) around 400 BC is borne out by such archaeological evidence as can be gained from an area where a modern town occupies much of the original site. Even the location of the *agora* is not known. There are references in ancient authors to suggest that the messes were situated to the south-east, along the 'Hyacinthian Way' which led to the shrine of Apollo at Amyclae about eight kilometres away. The dotted line represents the approximate course of the second-century encircling wall. The names of the four villages are marked in capitals (see further above, p. XIX)

THRACE
Perinthus
Abdera
Amphipolis
Arethusa
MACEDONIA
Samothrace
Thasos
Cyzicus
Olynthus
Aegospotami
Hellespont
PHRYGIA
Larissa
CHALCIDICE
Dodona
THESSALY
Pharsalus
LYDIA
Lesbos
Mt Narthacium
Thermopylae
Arginusae Is.
ACARNANIA
E.LOCRIS
Sardis
BOEOTIA
Chalcis
AEGEAN
SEA
W.LOCRIS
PHOCIS
Thebes
Aulis
IONIA
Geraestus
Ephesus
Athens
Priene
PELOPONNESE
Miletus
CARIA
Delos
Syros
Halicarnassus
Sparta
N
Caidus
Rhodes
Aigilia
Pergamia
0
50
100 km
CRETE
2. THE AEGEAN WORLD

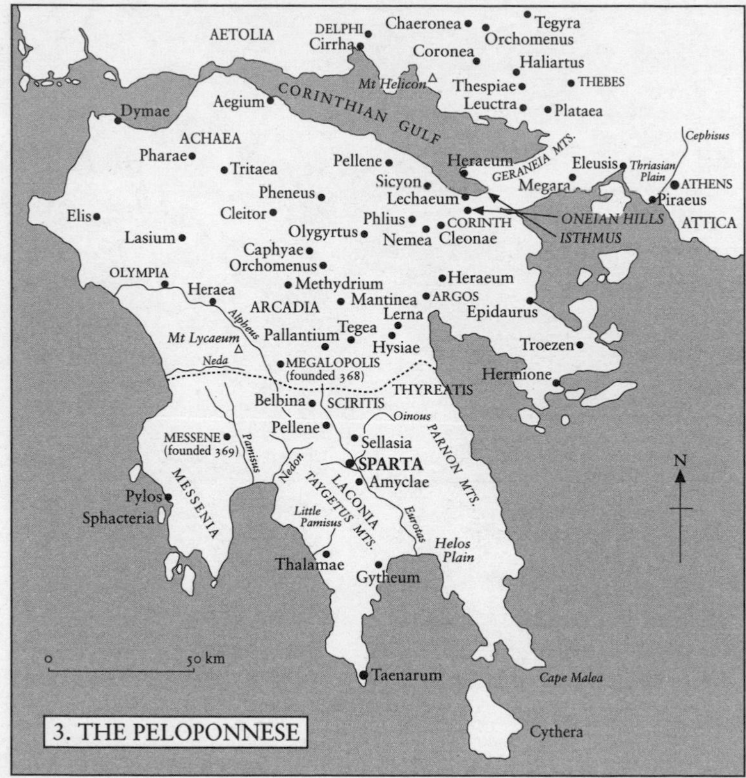

All the territory south of the dotted line was under Spartan control prior to the liberation of Messenia in 369 BC.

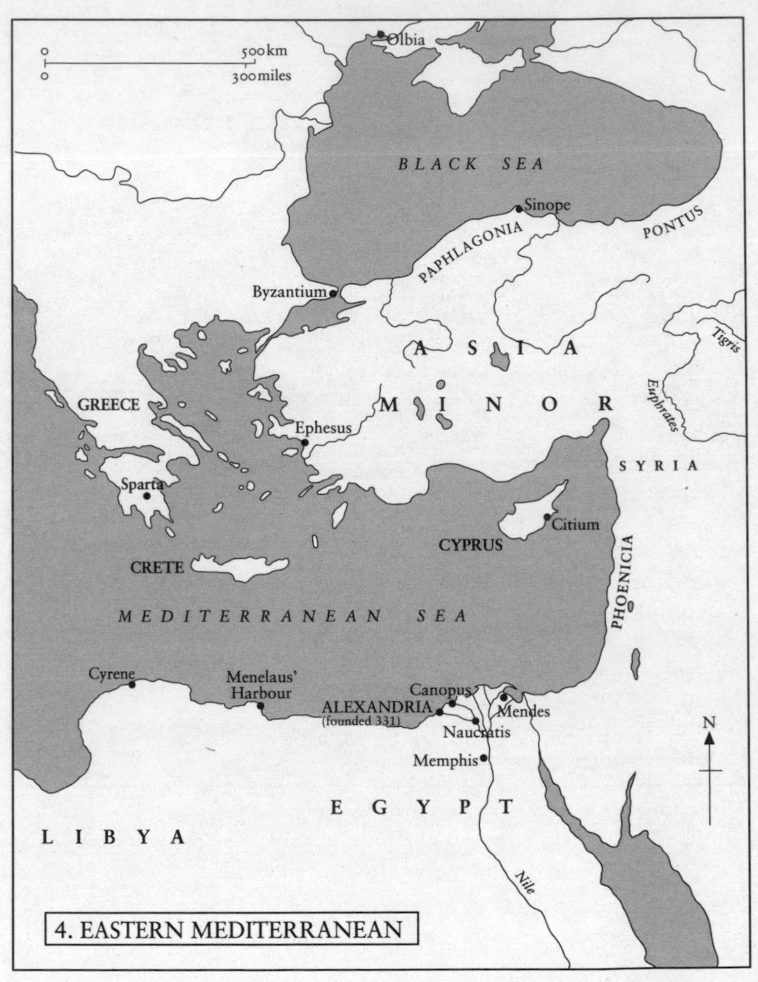

4. EASTERN MEDITERRANEAN

Glossary of Spartan Terms

Acropolis A Greek city's strong vantage point, citadel.

Agoge The distinctive Spartan system of upbringing and training.

Artemis See ORTHIA.

Bronze House Shrine of Sparta's patron deity Athena Poliachus ('holder of the city') It was situated on the low acropolis (see Map 1), and its walls were covered with bronze plates depicting mythical scenes. The site was excavated by British archaeologists early in the twentieth century.

Eiren A twenty-year-old who had proceeded at least two years beyond the class of boys (*paides*) in the *agoge* and was in command of his Troop (*agele*); he perhaps remained an Eiren to the end of his twenties. See *Lycurgus*, Ch. 17.

Elders Twenty-eight citizens aged sixty or over, elected for life to form (with the kings) Sparta's Gerousia.

Ephebes Youths in their late teens. See also Xenophon, *Spartan Society*, note 1.

Ephors Five magistrates elected annually from among all Spartiates (with no re-election possible). This board possessed sweeping powers – even over the kings – and took a leading role in the state's affairs.

Equals or Peers (*Homoioi*). Spartiates' term for themselves.

Gerousia Council of Elders: Sparta's supreme administrative, legislative and judicial body.

'Good Order' An approximation to the Greek *eunomia*, the condition of a stable state, well organized both socially and politically.

Gymnopaediae One of the principal annual festivals (literally that 'of the naked boys'; alternatively, perhaps, 'of the unarmed boys'). All Spartiates in good standing took part. It was said to have been founded in commemoration of Sparta's severe defeat by Argos at the battle of Hysiae, traditionally dated to 669.

Harmost Spartan appointed as military governor abroad.

Helots Local inhabitants of Laconia and Messenia, owned by the

Spartan state and required to work for its citizens in total subjection: they might on occasion be freed for military service.

Hoplites Heavily armed infantry who traditionally formed the principal troops of a classical Greek army.

Krypteia Organized, clandestine killing of random helots by youths of the Spartiate class.

Lesche A place where Spartiates gathered informally for conversation.

Mora Regiment: one of the six largest units of the Spartan army.

Orthia Later assimilated to Artemis (hence Artemis Orthia), goddess who had an important shrine at Sparta close to the west bank of the River Eurotas (see Map, p. 215). The character and purpose of the ritual are both obscure: see *Lycurgus*, Ch. 18, note 57.

Paidonomus 'boy-herdsman'. Senior Spartiate appointed as Trainer-in-Chief of the class of boys (*paides*) in the *agoge*.

Peltasts Lightly armed infantry (in contrast to hoplites).

Perioeci 'the dwellers round about'. Communities of free people occupying land in Laconia and Messenia granted them by the Spartan state in exchange for military service. See also Introduction, 'Lycurgus: Non-Lycurgan Institutions'.

Polemarchs At Sparta, the six senior army officers, immediately subordinate to whichever king was commander in the field; they also messed with him on campaign.

Rhetra A Spartan law. See also *Lycurgus*, note 16.

Satrap In the Persian and, later, Seleucid empires, the governor of a large region; in some instances tenure of the office became hereditary.

Skytale A Spartan device for sending secret messages. The text was written on a strip of leather wound round a staff, which the sender then retained. The recipient had a duplicate staff, and by correctly winding the strip round it could read the message. See Plutarch, *Lysander* (*The Rise and Fall of Athens*, rev. edn, Penguin, forthcoming), Ch. 19.

Spartiates Full Spartan citizens, who attained this status through a combination of birth, successful completion of the *agoge* and election to a mess. To remain such, they had to provide a stipulated minimum of produce for their mess and avoid demotion for cowardice or other anti-social behaviour. They referred to each other as Equals (see above).

Talent A large unit of weight, about 26 kg or 60 Greek *minas*, typically used for bullion or a mass of coins minted in a precious metal, silver in particular.

Three Hundred, also known as the *Hippeis*. The crack Spartan army unit of 300 men chosen and commanded by three *Hippagretae*. For its selection, see Xenophon, *Spartan Society*, Ch. 4.

Notes

For Spartan words and phrases, see the Glossary of Spartan Terms. All dates are BC.

LYCURGUS

1. *Olympic truce*: See further Ch. 23. According to legend, the earliest Olympic Games were ones in which gods took part. These lapsed, but were then revived by Iphitus of Elis – in 776 according to the reckoning made around the year 400 by his fellow Elean, the *sophist* (or teacher) Hippias. The sacred truce, whereby all Greeks were expected to suspend hostilities between each other for the duration of the games and a period both before and afterwards, was an essential feature of these and other panhellenic games (see *Cleomenes*, note 42).
2. *Aristotle the philosopher*: For the authors cited by Plutarch, see Introduction, 'Lycurgus: Plutarch's Sources'.
3. *name inscribed*: This cannot have been an authentic document, not least because the art of writing was only just reviving in Greece during the early eighth century.
4. *Homer's time*: The shadowy epic poet (*c.* ninth century) to whom the *Iliad* and *Odyssey* were attributed.
5. *Xenophon . . . Heraclids*: For Xenophon, see *Spartan Society*, Ch. 10. *Heraclids* are lists of kings were compiled from the fifth century, if not even earlier: the first surviving ones are those of Herodotus (*The Histories*, 7.204 and 8.131, Penguin, 2003). The further back they go, the less reliable historically they are likely to be. Heracles was the outstanding Greek hero and god, famous for his 'Labours' and other exploits.
6. *Simonides*: Of the late sixth/early fifth centuries.
7. *Spartiates . . . helots*: *Spartiates* are full citizens of Sparta. For

helots, see Introduction, 'Lycurgus: Non-Lycurgan Institutions' and Glossary of Spartan Terms.

8. *prodikoi*: Literally, defenders in legal proceedings.
9. *Creophylus'*: A legendary figure, variously made the follower, friend or even son-in-law of Homer.
10. *differentiating labourers*: Spartiates were distinguished by the fact that they were forbidden to practise any manual craft: see further Ch. 24 and *Agesilaus*, Ch. 26.
11. *Gymnosophists*: Literally 'naked sophists': Indian philosophers and teachers.
12. *Delphi . . . famous oracle*: *Delphi*: The most celebrated Greek oracle, located in the sanctuary of Pythian Apollo; thus his priestess was called the 'Pythia'. *famous oracle*: Quoted by Herodotus, *The Histories*, 1.65.
13. *agora*: Though commonly translated as 'market-place', in fact the *agora* in Greek communities had a wider function as the centre for most civic activities.
14. *Elders . . . Plato*: The twenty-eight Elders (*gerontes*, literally 'old men'), together with the two kings, comprised the Gerousia. Its powers are explained further in Ch. 6 and the method of election to it in Ch. 26. *Plato*: *The Laws*, 691e (Penguin, 2004).
15. *next perfect number after six*: The point is that 6 = 1 + 2 + 3, and 28 = 1 + 2 + 4 + 7 + 14.
16. *rhetra*: At the end of Ch. 13, Plutarch says that Lycurgus called his laws *rhetras* because they were divine oracles. But the word itself simply means a 'saying' (as opposed to a 'writing') and so could be used of any Spartan enactment.
17. *'After dedicating . . . power'*: Almost everything about the *rhetra* and its supplement which Plutarch proceeds to quote here – the former often termed the 'Great Rhetra' in modern discussions (see note 22) – has generated tremendous controversy. The manuscripts are defective and variant readings have been proposed for many words, especially in the last sentence of the Great Rhetra. All the same, there is general acceptance that a genuine archaic Spartan document in Doric Greek is being cited. Where Plutarch copied it from must remain unknown, although Aristotle's lost *Constitution* seems the most likely source.
18. *phylai . . . obai*: Very little more is known for certain about the organization of Spartiates into *phylai* (commonly translated 'tribes') and *obai*.
19. *Apollo*: Literally 'to *apellaze*' is to celebrate a festival of Apollo.

20. *Babyca and Cnacion . . .*: The 'present name' for Babyca has dropped out of Plutarch's text.
21. *theatres*: The size and design of Greek theatres made them obvious places to hold any large public meeting.
22. *rhetras*: In all likelihood the Great Rhetra embodies the resolution of a major crisis: the unique, and perhaps very novel, compromise achieved by it was to have a formative influence on the character of the Spartan state in the long term. The kings' sovereignty had presumably been under severe threat. Now this *rhetra* safeguarded their position, but at the cost of diminished authority. Thus the people, meeting in their assembly at regular intervals, gain the formal right to make the final decision on all matters of state. Political initiative, however, is skilfully reserved for the small Council of Elders (Gerousia) and the kings. They alone can lay business before the assembly (see further *Agis*, Ch. 11), and according to the supplement are even empowered to overrule any unacceptable decision by the assembly. Tyrtaeus, the Spartan poet of the mid seventh century, attributed this supplement at least to the action of the kings Polydorus and Theopompus, who probably reigned together at the beginning of the century. It is impossible to be sure how much earlier the Great Rhetra had been enacted – if, indeed, there was any interval at all. Plutarch's quotation probably derives from a longer poem by Tyrtaeus, which he called *Eunomia*.
23. *'inflated and fervent'*: *The Laws*, 692a.
24. *Theopompus*: Eurypontid king in the late eighth/early seventh centuries. For the ephorate – a magistracy which Plutarch significantly does *not* attribute to Lycurgus – see further Introduction, 'Lycurgus: Non-Lycurgan Institutions'. At the end of Ch. 29, Plutarch repeats his point that the institution of the ephorate strengthened the Lycurgan constitution.
25. *allocation of land*: According to legend there had been an agreed allocation of territories by lot at the time of the original occupation of Messenia, the Argolid and Laconia.
26. *9,000*: These totals have attracted suspicion in view of the coincidence that they just happen to be precisely double those proposed by Agis IV, king 244/3–241. By that period Spartan territory was roughly half what it had been in archaic times, because control of Messenia was lost after 369 (see *Agis*, Ch. 8).
27. *medimni of barley*: One *medimnus* is approximately 74 litres. Attempts to extrapolate from the figures here and in Ch. 12 the size and yield of a 'Lycurgan' lot are fascinating, but historically

unreliable. Note that barley was consumed, not wheat – as unappealing a choice to many in the ancient world as it would be today.

28. *property . . . divided between themselves*: It is entirely credible that at some early date there had been a redistribution of Spartan land – a demand commonly voiced in Greek states facing economic difficulties (Tyrtaeus alludes to such agitation at Sparta in his time). The details in Plutarch's account seem much less trustworthy, however. While it is true that the Spartiates did refer to themselves as *homoioi* (literally 'equals' or 'peers'), there can be no certainty that the respects in which they were thus 'equal' had ever extended to landholding. In historical times it is plain that their wealth (and thus landed property) varied widely: they did not each own just a single lot of equal productivity, as later idealists liked to believe.

The argument has been put that, *in addition* to whatever 'free market' property each Spartiate could afford, he did still hold an inalienable lot assigned to him by the state, until a *rhetra* proposed by the ephor Epitadeus early in the fourth century (see *Agis*, Ch. 5) allowed this lot too to be disposed of freely, and thus opened the way to concentration of landholding among a few owners. However, even this subtle attempt to reconcile differences in our evidence remains unsatisfactory. Inequality in landholding had developed long before the early fourth century, and was definitely not prompted by any *rhetra* of Epitadeus, which is most probably a fiction designed to offer a (lame) explanation of what had become a crisis. Moreover it is hard to credit that in a state with as limited an administrative structure as Sparta there had long existed a 'land bank' for the assignment and reclamation of state-owned lots of land.

29. *currency*: Since there was no coinage in early Greece, this measure is an obvious anachronism. Plutarch's statement is accurate to the extent that the Spartan state did not issue coinage until the early third century. Instead, the official currency long continued to be iron spits. In archaic times these had been widely used throughout Greece, though thereafter coins took their place – except in economically less developed areas, where values are found expressed in terms of 'spit *drachmas*' or other objects as late as the fourth and third centuries. Remains of spits have been uncovered in excavations at Laconian sanctuaries, though there is no knowing whether these had been used as money, cult objects or cooking utensils. Coins minted elsewhere in fact came into use

at Sparta too. For the value of a *mina*, compare *Cleomenes*, note 51.

30. *luxury atrophied*: Sweeping though the point may be, there is truth in it. While it can be shown that architecture and sculpture did continue to be appreciated at Sparta, without doubt many other art forms had gradually disappeared through lack of patronage by the end of the sixth century. Instead, wealthy Spartiates lavished their resources on such activities as breeding and racing horses, most notably abroad at the Olympic Games. See further *Agesilaus*, Ch. 20.
31. *Plutus*: God of wealth.
32. *andreia*: Literally 'men's places'. Instead of the official Spartan term *phiditia*, Plutarch subsequently uses the more common *syssitia* ('places to eat together'). For another instance of this practice, see note 52.
33. *barley-meal . . . meat*: All the provisions are local produce – the cheese being made from the milk of sheep or goats, not cows. Modern equivalents for the amounts cannot be offered with any certainty. However, the quantity of barley (a total of 12 *medimni*) over the year does seem modest by comparison with the 70 *medimni* which a Spartiate's lot was supposed to yield for himself alone, according to Ch. 8. *fish or meat*: A reflection of the fact that the ordinary diet of most ancient Greeks by no means always included either.
34. *King Agis . . . fined him*: Presumably the Eurypontid Agis II (king, 427–400) on his return from the battle of Mantinea in 418. Plutarch is probably more accurate when he repeats this story elsewhere and says that the fine was levied by the ephors.
35. *join a mess*: Although Plutarch is not concerned here to bring out its full significance, it is worth stressing that admission to full Spartiate status was contingent upon election to a mess, and that thereafter anyone who failed to furnish the required contributions forfeited his status. See in particular Aristotle, *The Politics*, 1271a (rev. edn, Penguin, 1992).
36. *hollow ballot*: Plutarch may well be thinking of the system in the Athenian courts where each juror was given two bronze ballots, one hollow and one solid – the former to vote for condemnation, the latter for acquittal.
37. *black broth*: Elsewhere Plutarch explains that this consisted of pork cooked in its own blood and seasoned with salt and vinegar.
38. *writing . . . prohibition*: It is clear from Ch. 6 that some *rhetras* might still attain written form. Presumably most did not; at least,

laws were not displayed publicly at Sparta as they were in Athens. However, one treaty with an ally does survive inscribed on stone.

39. *training*: The sense of the Greek term used here (*agoge*) cannot be conveyed neatly in English. It denotes a mixture of upbringing and training, and is used of the Spartan system in particular.
40. *education*: Plutarch's inconsistent attitude towards education in this section remains unexplained.
41. *Epaminondas . . . a meal*: *Epaminondas*: Famous Theban general who was responsible for Sparta's two great defeats at the battles of Leuctra (371) and Mantinea (362). See further *Agesilaus*, Ch. 27 onwards. *no treason in such a meal*: In other words, anybody content with such plain fare could have no wish to be extravagant and would thus prove incorruptible.
42. *Leotychidas*: Seventh-century Eurypontid king. Another version of this remark is attributed to Agesilaus (*Sayings of Spartans*, Agesilaus, no. 27).
43. *saw him wounded*: See *Agesilaus*, Ch. 26. The occasion of this incident is uncertain. Xenophon (*A History of My Times*, 5.4.58, Penguin, 1979) mentions that Agesilaus burst a blood vessel at Megara in 377, on his return from a campaign in which the Theban army reckoned itself to have performed well.
44. *Aristotle*: *The Politics*, 1269b.
45. *sheltered upbringing . . . of any kind*: Note the fragment of Heracleides Lembus, probably derived from Aristotle: 'The women in Sparta are deprived of make-up, and they are not permitted to have their hair long or to wear gold.'
46. *Gorgo*: See *Sayings of Spartan Women*.
47. *Plato*: *The Republic*, 458d (Penguin, 2003).
48. *Dercyllidas*: Of the late fifth and early fourth centuries.
49. *assigned . . . land*: Such alleged assignment of a lot by the tribe at a child's birth, when he had not even begun the process of gaining full Spartiate status (through completion of the *agoge* and election to a mess), only deepens the mystery of Spartan land tenure. See also note 28.
50. *Alcibiades*: Distinguished fifth-century leader; see further *Agesilaus*, Ch. 3 and note 7.
51. *Spartan girl*: But presumably not of citizen status.
52. *Troops*: Literally 'herds'. Plutarch uses the common Greek word *agele*, but inscriptions show that the official Spartan term was *boua* ('herd of cattle').
53. *Squadron*: The precise relationship of the Squadron (*ile*) to the Troop is unknown.

54. *Trainer-in-Chief*: Literally 'boy-herdsman' (*paidonomus*).
55. *boys' class*: The class of boys (*paides*) in the *agoge* included all those aged between seven and eighteen. For the subsequent classes, see the next paragraph and Xenophon, *Spartan Society*, Chs. 2–4 and note 1.
56. *ephebes*: The general Greek term for youths in their late teens. For the Spartan equivalent, *paidiskoi* (the class above the *paides*), see Xenophon, *Spartan Society*, Ch. 3.
57. *Artemis Orthia*: British archaeologists early in the twentieth century excavated a shrine of Orthia, later assimilated to Artemis (hence Artemis Orthia), set up close to the west bank of the River Eurotas before 700. Much remains obscure about the character and purpose of the ritual. Authors of the Roman period (like Plutarch) mention a contemporary ceremony where youths were lashed at the altar. But for the classical period we hear from Xenophon (*Spartan Society*, Ch. 2) of boys running a gauntlet of whips to steal cheeses from the altar. There is no knowing whether the former endurance test, or initiation rite, represents a crude partial revival of the latter, or whether the two are completely distinct.
58. *Agis retorted . . . our daggers'*: In *Sayings of Spartans* this remark is attributed to the Eurypontid Agis III, king 338–331.
59. *hand is not raised*: Notionally, therefore, games like boxing were banned. According to *Sayings of Spartans*, Lycurgus, no. 23, the aim was to prevent Spartiates acquiring the habit of crying off (by raising a hand) when in difficulties. In other words, any combat which a Spartiate entered was to be to the death.
60. *Hecataeus . . . Archidamidas'*: Neither figure can be identified with certainty. But the former may be Hecataeus of Abdera or Teos, and the latter the Eurypontid King Archidamus IV of the early third century.
61. *Demaratus*: Eurypontid king, late sixth century–491.
62. *Agis*: In *Sayings of Spartans*, Agis son of Archidamus, no. 10, this remark is appropriately attributed to Agis II.
63. *Pleistoanax*: Agiad king, 458–446/5 and 427/6–408. (He was in exile in the intervening period.)
64. *One Spartan*: Plutarch, *Agesilaus*, Ch. 21, attributes the remark specifically to Agesilaus.
65. *Ares*: God of war.
66. *tresantes*: The Spartan term for men who had shown cowardice in battle or had surrendered to the enemy. They were liable to a wide range of social and legal disabilities: most serious among

the latter was the partial loss of their citizen status. For details, see in particular *Agesilaus*, Ch. 30 and Xenophon, *Spartan Society*, Ch. 9.

67. *Terpander and Pindar*: *Terpander*: Musician and poet from Lesbos. He lived in Sparta in the mid seventh century. *Pindar*: Famous fifth-century lyric poet.
68. *the Spartan poet*: Alcman – in fact of uncertain origin, possibly a Laconian, possibly even an Asiatic non-Greek. He lived at Sparta in the second half of the seventh century.
69. *phalanx*: Battle formation of heavily armed soldiers standing several ranks deep.
70. *Castor's Air*: For Spartan devotion to the twin gods Castor and Pollux, see *Sayings of Spartans*, note 3.
71. *amount mentioned earlier*: See Ch. 8.
72. *refusal to work*: Early lawgivers were said to have made this an offence at Athens. It continued so in the fifth and fourth centuries, though precisely how the law was framed is unknown.
73. *statue of Laughter*: Note further in this connection *Cleomenes*, Ch. 9.
74. *Pedaritus*: Spartan military governor (*harmost*) on Chios; killed in action there in 411.
75. *Brasidas'*: Distinguished commander in the early years of the Peloponnesian War, killed in 422. See also note 93.
76. *red cloak*: Part of the Spartiate's battle dress. See Xenophon, *Spartan Society*, Ch. 11.
77. *died in labour*: The latter exception represents an attempt to make sense of what is otherwise a confused section of text. Given our knowledge of the Spartan ideals that men should fight for Sparta and women produce fine children, it seems highly plausible and is supported by the evidence of some inscriptions.
78. *abandon their grief*: It is notable that this restrained commemoration of the dead was abandoned in the case of any king, for whom elaborate ceremonies were held. See Xenophon, *Spartan Society*, Ch. 15 and Herodotus, *The Histories*, 6.58–9.
79. *Thucydides*: *The Peloponnesian War*, 2.39 (Penguin, 1972).
80. *Plato*: For his description of the *krypteia*, see *The Laws*, 633b.
81. *character was as follows*: The sketch by Plutarch here represents the fullest surviving account of this institution. Revolting though it may be, there seems no good reason to doubt the outline. However, we are still left with no clue as to the scale of the operations or their frequency (does 'periodically' denote some regular form of initiation for youths, for instance?).

82. *History of the Peloponnesian War*: 4.80. The context is the aftermath of the Athenian capture of Pylos and Sphacteria, where 292 Spartan troops, including about 120 Spartiates, had been taken prisoner, and the Spartan authorities were in a panic. This was their devious means of eliminating potential helot trouble-makers. Plutarch is no doubt writing from memory since, strictly, Thucydides has the helots themselves select the 2,000. Plutarch's implication that the *krypteia* eliminated them is his own conjecture.
83. *unmixed wine*: Normal Greek practice was to drink wine diluted with water.
84. *penetrated Laconia*: From 370 (following the Spartan defeat at Leuctra).
85. *Spendon the Spartan*: Otherwise unknown.
86. *freedom . . . slave*: We happen to know from a fragment elsewhere that this forceful phrasing must derive from Critias (see Introduction, 'Lycurgus: Plutarch's Sources').
87. *dire threat to the city*: There is no doubt that the severe earthquake of the mid 460s, which caused extensive damage to the city of Sparta and high casualties among its inhabitants, did prompt a great rebellion in which the Messenian helots were joined not only by some of the normally less troublesome Laconian ones, but also by two perioecic communities in Messenia. See Thucydides, *The Peloponnesian War*, 1.101–3, and Plutarch, *Cimon*, Chs. 16–17 (in *The Rise and Fall of Athens*, rev. edn, Penguin, forthcoming). It is less certain, however, whether Plutarch is right to suggest that after finally overcoming this rebellion the Spartans just became more brutal towards the helots. Instead they may have realized that there were also other, more diplomatic means of keeping this large, and by no means homogeneous, class in subjection. It is hardly remarkable that the Spartans themselves never drew attention to such alternative methods. But we may note the points that by the early fourth century thousands of ex-helots termed *neodamodeis* were loyally serving as free (though non-citizen) troops in Sparta's foreign campaigns, and that no further helot revolt is known until after Leuctra, despite a continuing fall in the number of Spartiates.

    Predictably enough, the tradition that helots received harsh treatment is reflected in a fragment of the lost *Messenian Affairs* written during the third century (and thus after the liberation of Messenia) by Myron of Priene:

They impose on the helots every kind of insulting work which leads to total degradation. For they made it a requirement that each should wear a dogskin cap and be dressed in leather as well as receive a fixed number of lashes annually – without reference to any offence – so that they should never forget to behave like slaves. Moreover, if the physical well-being of any surpassed the usual appearance of slaves, they prescribed a death sentence and also a penalty for owners who failed to curb those putting on weight.

88. *god*: Apollo at Delphi.
89. *Plato's description*: *Timaeus*, 37c (Penguin, 1971).
90. *Agis . . . Archidamus*: Agis II: Eurypontid king, 427–400. Archidamas II: *c.* 469–427.
91. *Lysander*: The outstanding commander of the late fifth and early fourth centuries, who played a crucial role in the achievement of Sparta's eventual victory over Athens in the Peloponnesian War. See further *Saying of Spartans* and Plutarch's Life in *The Rise and Fall of Athens.*
92. *undermining the laws*: Plutarch returns to this theme in *Agis*, Chs. 3 and 5.
93. *Gylippus and Brasidas*: Both achieved outstanding success during the Peloponnesian War. Gylippus reached Syracuse when it was on the point of surrendering to its Athenian besiegers and then retrieved the situation so completely as to destroy the enemy (414–413). At an earlier stage Brasidas, by his liberation of Athens' subject allies in Chalcidice, undermined her successes elsewhere (424–422).
94. *Lysander, Callicratidas and Agesilaus*: See *Sayings of Spartans* attributed to each.
95. *Stratonicus*: A fourth-century Athenian noted for his witticisms.
96. *Diogenes, Zeno*: Respectively, the founders of Cynicism in the fourth century and Stoicism in the early third.
97. *Euripides*: The fifth-century Athenian tragedian.
98. *Antiorus*: Plutarch says nothing of Lycurgus' wife.

AGESILAUS

1. *Archidamus . . . Agesilaus*: Archidamus II died in 427, after a reign of over forty years; he married twice. His second son Agesilaus II was born around 445, king 400–360.

2. *agoge*: See *Lycurgus*, note 39.
3. *Simonides*: See *Lycurgus*, note 6.
4. *Troops*: See *Lycurgus*, note 52.
5. *lover Lysander*: See *Lycurgus*, Chs. 17–18 and note 91.
6. *Archidamus was fined*: Presumably on the occasion of his second marriage.
7. *Agis' ... Alcibiades*: Agis II, son of Archidamus by his first marriage, succeeded his father in 427 and reigned until his death in 400. Alcibiades, the distinguished Athenian leader during the Peloponnesian War (see *Lycurgus*, Ch. 16), served as one of the three commanders of the forces sent to Sicily in 415, but when recalled to Athens shortly afterwards to stand trial for sacrilege he fled to Sparta. Plutarch offers a fuller account of his time at Sparta in *Alcibiades*, Chs. 23–4 (see *The Rise and Fall of Athens*, rev. edn, Penguin, forthcoming).
8. *Duris*: Ruler of Samos in the late fourth/early third centuries, and prolific writer of histories (all lost except for fragments), including one of his own island. Since Samos became Alcibiades' base not long after he fled from Sparta, he was a figure of special interest to Duris, who even claimed to be descended from him.
9. *naval victory over the Athenians*: At Aegospotami in 405: see *Sayings of Spartans*, Lysander, no. 5.
10. *illegitimacy disqualified Leotychidas*: For this episode, compare Xenophon, *A History of My Times* 3.3 (Penguin, 1979), and Plutarch, *Lysander*, Ch. 22 in *The Rise and Fall of Athens*.
11. *Heracles*: Claimed as the ancestor of all Spartan kings: see *Lycurgus*, Ch. 1.
12. *Poseidon ... earthquake*: God of the sea, earthquakes and horses. For his famous shrine at Taenarum, see *Agis*, Ch. 16, and *Cleomenes*, Ch. 22. Spartan territory was notoriously earthquake-prone: see *Lycurgus*, Ch. 28 and note 87.
13. *Lycurgus*: Chs. 5–7.
14. *ephors ... fined him*: By contrast, Xenophon (*Agesilaus* 6.8) claims that Agesilaus was never punished by his fellow citizens.
15. *philosophers ... stop*: Such views were articulated especially by Heraclitus around the beginning of the fifth century, and (somewhat later) by Empedocles.
16. *Sparta's lawgiver*: Lycurgus.
17. *'with fearsome words'*: A well-known episode cited in Homer, *Odyssey* 8.75–77 (Penguin, 2003).
18. *neodamodeis ... dispatched Agesilaus*: Helot volunteers who

were granted their freedom and recruited into the army: see *Lycurgus*, note 87. Agesilaus was sent in 396.

19. *Agamemnon . . . soothsayers*: In legend, Agamemnon, king of Mycenae and commander of the Greek expedition against Troy, sacrificed his daughter Iphigenia to Artemis at Aulis in order to gain a favourable wind for the fleet.
20. *Boeotarchs*: The eleven elected officials who led the league of cities in Boeotia (Thebes being the most prominent), and who particularly objected to Agesilaus promoting his expedition as a panhellenic initiative. This clash was to make Agesilaus an implacable enemy of Thebes.
21. *proceeded as follows*: For Plutarch's account of these events from Lysander's perspective, see *Lysander*, Chs. 23–4 (where Agesilaus *is* portrayed as envious and resentful).
22. *Pharnabazus'*: Persia's satrap of the region east and south of the Hellespont.
23. *death on campaign*: At Haliartus in 395.
24. *Tissaphernes*: Persia's satrap based at Sardis.
25. *Xenophon . . . in battle*: Xenophon's work *The Persian Expedition* (Penguin, 1967) records these exploits, which date to 401–399.
26. *Caria . . . Phrygia*: In other words, Agesilaus proceeded north towards the Hellespont, rather than southwards to Caria.
27. *sacrificial . . . lack lobes*: A bad omen.
28. *exempting . . . service*: See Homer, *Iliad*, 23.295 (Penguin, 2003).
29. *next season . . . territory*: In 395.
30. *Great King's*: Standard Greek term for the Persian king.
31. *a dispatch*: A *skytale*: see Glossary of Spartan Terms.
32. *Megabates . . . turned away*: Other versions of this story appear in *Sayings of Spartans*, Agesilaus, no. 15, and in Xenophon, *Agesilaus* 5.4–5. Although a kiss was a regular form of greeting among Persians, Agesilaus was evidently concerned that it might be misinterpreted by Greeks in this instance.
33. *you ran away*: Cowardice was, of course, a very damaging slur to level against any Spartiate: see Ch. 30.
34. *guest-friend*: This relationship (*xenia*) was a formal bond of trust, often hereditary, between men of equal or comparable social standing.
35. *war against the Athenians*: That is, during the latter years of the Peloponnesian War, which ended in 404.
36. *boy-athlete . . . trouble*: Xenophon (*A History of My Times*

4.1.40) sheds further light on this incident, which perhaps dates to the 380s. Evidently the boy's physique was considered too well developed to substantiate his claim that he was under eighteen and thus eligible to compete in the boys' race.

37. *Hidrieus the Carian* ... *Nicias*: The former is presumably the well-known member of Caria's ruling family, although he did not become satrap until after Agesilaus' death. Nothing is known about Nicias' identity or origin.
38. *Hieronymus the philosopher*: A Rhodian by origin, he taught at Athens during the third century. Only fragments of his many works survive. He no doubt used this story in a discussion of the moral dilemmas generated by conflicting duties.
39. *second year* ... *command*: In 394.
40. *sacred precincts by himself*: Agesilaus' purpose was to discount any allegation of dishonourable behaviour. The account of his practice in *Sayings of Spartans*, Agesilaus, no. 18, differs.
41. *Timotheus'*: Celebrated lyre-player and poet of the late fifth/early fourth centuries, from Miletus.
42. *Ecbatana and Susa*: The faraway Persian royal capitals in Media and Elam respectively.
43. *war in Greece*: In 395 an alliance headed by Corinth, Argos, Boeotia and Athens went on the offensive to curb Sparta's dominance.
44. *'Such* ... *cruelty'*: Line 764, spoken by Andromache, in Euripides' tragedy *The Trojan Women* (in *Electra and Other Plays*, Penguin, 1998).
45. *Demaratus the Corinthian*: A friend of Alexander the Great; his remark presumably dates to the 320s or thereabouts.
46. *Alexander* ... *Arcadia*: Alexander is regarded as Macedonian here, rather than Greek. All the battlefields mentioned (both specific and general) were the scene of fighting between the 390s and 360s.
47. *war at home*: The Romans invaded North Africa in 203 after Hannibal had been campaigning in Italy less and less successfully for fifteen years; this was the point at which he was recalled to Carthage. See Livy, *The War with Hannibal* 30.20 (Penguin, 1964).
48. *Antipater's battle*: In 331, Antipater, Alexander's viceroy in Greece, ended a Spartan rising led by Agis III, king 338–331, at a battle near Megalopolis. See *Sayings of Spartans*, Astycratidas.
49. *'leaving his task unfulfilled'*: Homer, *Iliad* 4.175.
50. *Erasistratus*: An Athenian politician of the late fifth century.
51. *Trochalians* ... *Xerxes*: *Trochalians*: Beyond what appears here, nothing further is known of these people or their location; there

is even doubt about the correct form of their name. *Xerxes*: The Persian king who invaded Greece by land in 480. See *Sayings of Spartans*, Leonidas son of Anaxandridas, no. 22.

52. *moras*: Regiments. See Xenophon, *Spartan Society*, Ch. 11.
53. *Peisander . . . Conon*: *Peisander*: The Spartiate in command of the fleet. *Conon*: An Athenian naval commander in the Persian service.
54. *a trophy erected long ago*: In 447. See also Ch. 32.
55. *established . . . had won*: When no clear winner emerged from a pitched battle, Greek custom awarded that distinction to whichever side held the field. Here the Thebans showed that they were in no position to contest the Spartans for it further.
56. *the god*: Apollo.
57. *Aristodemus*: According to tradition, a very early Spartan king. See *Lycurgus*, Ch. 1, and Spartan Kings to 222 BC.
58. *Epaminondas'*: See *Lycurgus*, note 41.
59. *Cynisca . . . Olympic Games*: In fact she won at the games of 396 – the first female owner ever to do so – and again at the next games in 392. A poem inscribed on stone at Olympia in honour of her success survives (see Pausanias, *Guide to Greece*, vol. 2 (Penguin, 1984), p. 286).
60. *bring them up in Sparta*: Twin sons of Xenophon evidently did receive at least part of their education at Sparta.
61. *Lysander's death . . . assembly*: In 395. Plutarch, *Lysander*, Chs. 24–6 gives an account of Agesilaus' schemes; note also *Sayings of Spartans*, Lysander, no. 14. Nothing more is known of Cleon.
62. *father had been banished*: Strictly speaking, King Pausanias fled after being sentenced to death for failing to avenge Lysander's defeat and death at Haliartus (see Ch. 8 and *Agis*, Ch. 3).
63. *Lycurgus*: Chs. 17–18.
64. *the Long Walls*: They joined Corinth to its port at Lechaeum.
65. *while Teleutias . . . when Agesilaus appeared*: These events date to 391, and Agesilaus appeared the following year. The bracketed words are supplied to fill a gap in the manuscripts.
66. *contest . . . competed*: See *Lycurgus*, Ch. 14.
67. *nightingale's song*: In *Lycurgus*, Ch. 20, Plutarch records the remark as an anonymous illustration of pithy Spartan humour.
68. *During his time on Corinthian territory*: In 390.
69. *Iphicrates*: A talented Athenian commander. At least 250 men on the Spartan side were killed, although how many of these were Spartiates is unknown.

70. *Next*: In 389.
71. *land all sown*: For a community to lose its staple food supply for the next year was catastrophic.
72. *negotiate with Tiribazus*: Tissaphernes' successor as satrap at Sardis. The agreement reached (in 386) is often termed the 'King's Peace'.
73. *'medizing' . . . 'laconizing'*: In other words, the Spartans were not taking the Persian side, but the Persians the Spartan.
74. *Boeotia become independent*: Thebes dominated the league of Boeotian cities: see Chs. 6 and 28.
75. *Phoebidas . . . Cadmeia*: In 382 the Spartan commander Phoebidas was leading an army northwards to campaign in Thrace; when offered the opportunity by Archias and Leontiadas, two pro-Spartan leaders at Thebes, he seized the city's acropolis or citadel, the Cadmeia.
76. *liberated their city*: In 379. This important episode is narrated at length by Plutarch, *Pelopidas*, Chs. 7–13 (*The Age of Alexander*, rev. edn, Penguin, forthcoming), and is also the subject of his dialogue *On Socrates' Personal Deity* (in *Essays*, Penguin, 1992, pp. 308–58).
77. *polemarchs in name*: Chief magistrates (the same title is used at Sparta, but for a different post: see Glossary of Spartan Terms).
78. *Agesipolis was dead*: He succumbed to fever in 380.
79. *military service*: A Spartiate was liable for military service between the ages of twenty and sixty. Only on reaching the latter age did he become eligible for election as an Elder (see *Lycurgus*, Ch. 26).
80. *Phlius*: A strategically placed city in the northern Peloponnese, whose recent record as a member of Sparta's alliance had been a loyal one. It was ruled by a democracy, however, and Agesilaus was persuaded to install a group of exiled oligarchs instead.
81. *seizing the Piraeus*: Sphodrias attacked the port of Athens, 7 km from the city, in 378.
82. *Cleonymus . . . Archidamus*: Cleonymus was probably a little under twenty, and Archidamus in his early twenties.
83. *his children*: We only hear of three: a son, Archidamus, and two daughters whose names Plutarch was proud to have discovered (Ch. 19).
84. *rhetras*: Spartan laws: see *Lycurgus*, note 16 and Ch. 13, where Antalcidas' remark is also quoted.
85. *manual craft*: See *Lycurgus*, Chs. 4 and 24.

86. *back from Thebes*: In 377, after campaigning in Boeotia for a second successive year.
87. *Tegyra . . . a settlement*: In 375 and 371, respectively.
88. *Laconia . . . independent*: Agesilaus was implying that Thebes' domination of its Boeotian allies should be brought to an end. Epaminondas in turn raised the even more shocking prospect of the perioecic communities in Laconia being released from Spartan control; as a result, Sparta would no longer be able to rely on their military support.
89. *Prothous the Laconian*: Nothing more is known of him or his status.
90. *in front of the king*: A place of honour: see *Lycurgus*, Ch. 22.
91. *Xenophon*: *Conversations of Socrates* 1.1 (Penguin, 1990).
92. *proud, cheerful mood*: These attitudes are repeatedly reflected in *Sayings of Spartan Women*.
93. *tresantes*: See *Lycurgus*, Ch. 21 and note 66.
94. *invaded Arcadia*: In 370.
95. *abandoned the rest. At this time*: It is important to remember that there was no city-wall to give protection; see Map, p. 215. It was the winter of 370/69.
96. *temple of Artemis*: Said to be somewhere north of the acropolis in the Pitana quarter; see Map, p. 215.
97. *happy life . . . state*: Compare *Lycurgus*, Chs. 30–31.
98. *tyrant . . . 'Tearless Battle'*: Dionysius I of Syracuse. In 368.
99. *Thucydides*: *The Peloponnesian War* 5.64–75 (Penguin, 1972); the battle occurred in 418.
100. *city of Messene*: In 370/69. See Introduction, 'Agesilaus: Historical Introduction'.
101. *The occasion . . . help*: In 362.
102. *beyond his years*: Agesilaus would have been over eighty, an exceptional age by ancient standards.
103. *the Egyptian Tachos*: Pharaoh of Egypt, which had broken free of Persian rule about forty years before Agesilaus served there in 360. Strictly speaking, Tachos was now going on the offensive against the Great King rather than 'rebelling'.
104. *worldwide reputation*: Compare Theopompus' assessment cited in Ch. 10.
105. *freedom of the Greeks*: In Asia Minor.
106. *papyrus*: A marsh plant of the Nile delta that was put to many uses, in particular the production of the classical world's equivalent of paper.

107. *they believe will advance Sparta*: This is the viewpoint articulated by Agesilaus in Ch. 23.
108. *war at home*: No doubt he had in mind continued efforts to regain Messenia.
109. *230 talents*: Compare the 1,000 talents which Agesilaus brought back from Asia Minor (Ch. 19).
110. *died, aged eighty-four*: In the winter of 360/59.
111. *kings' bodies were brought home*: Note in this connection Xenophon, *Spartan Society*, Ch. 15.
112. *This Agis was the fifth in descent from Agesilaus*: See Plutarch's Life of him. To be really precise, Agis was a fifth-generation descendant of Agesilaus, but the sixth king after him in the Eurypontid line.

AGIS

1. *Sophocles'*: The fifth-century Athenian tragedian, in a lost play.
2. *Phocion . . . Antipater*: *Phocion*: An Athenian (402–318) noted for his long service as general; Plutarch's Life of him appears in *The Age of Alexander* (rev. edn, Penguin, forthcoming). *Antipater*: Macedonian viceroy of Greece during Alexander the Great's absence in Persia.
3. *Tiberius and Gaius Gracchus*: Roman senators of the late second century, noted for their wide-ranging legislative proposals. See their Lives in Plutarch, *Rome in Crisis* (rev. edn, Penguin, forthcoming).
4. *Megalopolis*: Agis' death at this battle ended his anti-Macedonian rising (see Introduction, 'Agis and Cleomenes: Historical Introduction'.
5. *succeeded by . . . the Agis*: For the succession of Spartan kings, see Spartan Kings to 222 BC.
6. *exile . . . at Tegea*: See *Agesilaus*, Ch. 20.
7. *death*: Around 255.
8. *Leonidas . . . Seleucus*: Nothing more is known of Leonidas' earlier career, beyond the allegations in Chs. 10 and 11. The Seleucid empire was one of the great 'successor kingdoms' carved out at the end of the fourth century following Alexander the Great's death. Its centre was in Syria; individual regions were governed by satraps. The king served by Leonidas is most likely to have been Seleucus II, great-grandson of the Macedonian founder of the dynasty.

9. *Athenian hegemony*: In 404, with the conclusion of the Peloponnesian War.
10. *to his son*: This is completely wishful thinking, since Spartiate numbers fell at an alarming rate from the early fifth century onwards. Moreover, there is no sign that equality of landholdings between Spartiates had ever existed during historical times, and the *rhetra* of Epitadeus is probably fiction. At the end of the chapter Plutarch is wrong to imagine that each Spartiate still held a 'lot' of land. See further *Lycurgus*, Ch. 8 and note 28.
11. *Lysander elected an ephor*: The chronology is uncertain. Possibly Agis became king in late 244 or early 243, and Lysander was elected an ephor for 243/2.
12. *messes of 400 and 200*: Note the departure from the traditionally small, intimate size of mess (compare *Lycurgus*, Ch. 12).
13. *ancestors*: According to tradition, Lycurgus assigned equal landholdings to all Spartiates: see Ch. 9 and *Lycurgus*, Ch. 8.
14. *discussed the matter with the citizens*: Only informal consideration was possible, since no valid decision could be taken unless the business was duly proposed by the Gerousia. See further Ch. 11 and *Lycurgus*, Ch. 6.
15. *oracle ... Thalamae*: Thalamae lies not far south of the Little Pamisus river which marked the border between Messenia and Laconia (see Map 3). Though nothing is known of the origin of the oracle or the development of its links with Sparta, it was already functioning by the fifth century. Those wishing to consult it slept in the sanctuary, and the goddess's response came to them in a dream: see further *Cleomenes*, Ch. 7.
16. *Terpander, Thales and Pherecydes*: *Terpander*: See *Lycurgus*, note 67. *Thales*: See *Lycurgus*, Ch. 4. *Pherecydes*: Sixth-century thinker and writer about religion and the natural world, born on Syros.
17. *Ecprepes*: Fifth-century ephor.
18. *Timotheus*: See *Agesilaus*, note 41.
19. *preliminary approval*: See Ch. 9 and note 14, and *Lycurgus*, Ch. 6.
20. *majority of one*: If the Gerousia comprised just the two kings and twenty-eight Elders, and all voted on the issue, this result is impossible. But it seems that the five ephors were also involved (see especially Chs. 8 and 12), so that the vote could have been 17–18. It is not clear whether the ephors had normally participated in meetings of the Gerousia in earlier periods, except when it sat as a court.

21. *convicted by the omen*: Even though this practice is otherwise unattested, and its use here sounds suspiciously convenient, it may genuinely have been ancient. A persuasive case has been made for its use in the deposition of the Eurypontid king Demaratus in 491.
22. *newly installed ephors*: For 242/1.
23. *opposition . . . unlawful*: Such a power is not known to have been invoked before, and gives every impression of having been fabricated for the occasion. On the development of the ephorate, see further Introduction, 'Lycurgus: Non-Lycurgan Institutions'.
24. *appointed others*: Appointment of ephors by kings (here and in Ch. 18), as opposed to their election in the assembly, was, of course, irregular.
25. *wrote to the ephors*: Traditionally Sparta had been an implacable opponent of Macedon, and she is not said to have displayed any interest in allying with the Achaean League since its revival from 280 onwards. Thus the date and circumstances of the alliance to which Aratus appealed here are a puzzle. Agis' part in arranging it, if any, is unknown. It must have lapsed after his death.
26. *Agesilaus . . . Lysander . . . Leonidas*: For each of these commanders, see the *Sayings* attributed to them, and the *Life of Agesilaus*.
27. *Baton of Sinope*: An orator and prolific historical writer, possibly contemporary with these events. This is the only citation of him anywhere in Plutarch's works, and no further light can be shed on it. Sinope was a Greek city on the southern shore of the Black Sea.
28. *dismissed his forces*: Aratus' reasons of deciding against a battle are unknown. But in part he may have been wary of offering Agis and his Spartans the opportunity to display their new prowess. Aratus later routed the Aetolian invaders at Pellene, north-west of Sicyon.
29. *further term as ephor*: This was unconstitutional.
30. *shrine of Poseidon*: At Taenarum, on the far south-western tip of Laconia. The shrine was especially famous for the asylum it offered to runaway helots.
31. *put on trial*: This aside is consistent with the fact that the Gerousia heard capital cases. The demand made near the end of the chapter for trial 'in front of the citizens' was highly irregular.
32. *Cleombrotus . . . Theopompus . . . Aristomenes*: Cleombrotus was defeated and killed by the Thebans at Leuctra in 371 (see *Agesilaus*, Ch. 28). Plutarch phrases his point with care! King

Leonidas' death at Thermopylae in 480 need not count because his opponents were Persians. Certainly in the century and more after Leuctra a succession of kings did die in battle – Archidamus III, Agis III, Areus I and Acrotatus (see Ch. 3) – although again their enemies were not always Greeks. *Theopompus*: See *Lycurgus*, note 24. *Aristomenes*: See Introduction, 'Plutarch and Sparta'.

CLEOMENES

1. *newborn infant*: This was Eudamidas III (less probably Eurydamidas), who succeeded to the Agiad throne on his father's execution in 241, though of course in a purely formal capacity: no regent is known to have been appointed for him. It was his death which offered Cleomenes the opportunity of inviting back Agis' brother Archidamus V to occupy the Agiad throne: see Ch. 5. Pausanias (see Introduction, 'Lycurgus: Plutarch's Sources'), claims that Eudamidas was poisoned by Cleomenes (2.9.1). Not least because other points in his account of Cleomenes' career are demonstrably inaccurate, the claim should be viewed with considerable scepticism.
2. *Sphaerus from Olbia*: See Introduction, 'Lycurgus: Plutarch's Sources'. Olbia was a Greek city on the northern shore of the Black Sea.
3. *Leonidas ... Tyrtaeus'*: Respectively, the Agiad king, 491–480; and see *Lycurgus*, Ch. 6.
4. *by then*: About 235.
5. *system of education*: The *agoge*: see *Lycurgus*, note 39.
6. *Aratus ... and inexperienced*: The Eleans were allied to the Aetolians. While Sparta's earlier alliance with the Achaeans had lapsed, the main impetus for hostilities against her came not from Aratus but from Lydiadas and Aristomachus, former tyrants of Megalopolis and Argos respectively, who had relinquished their positions and joined their cities to the Achaeans – the former in 235 (see Ch. 6), the latter in 229/8. In 229 a Spartan force led by Cleomenes had taken over the Arcadian cities of Tegea, Mantinea, Orchomenus and Caphyae, possibly at their own request; they had previously been remote allies of the Aetolians. If Aratus' 'testing' of the Spartans really did go back to the death of Leonidas and the accession of Cleomenes, we are ignorant of how it proceeded until 229.
7. *Caphyae ... again*: Following Cleomenes' seizure of the shrine

near Belbina, the Achaeans formally declared war on Sparta late in 229 or early in 228. Aratus' capture of Caphyae must occur before May 228, when his term as general ends. He is succeeded by Aristomachus.

8. *Aratus . . . moved off*: Methydrium was an Arcadian town belonging to Megalopolis. Pallantium lies just west of Tegea. The figure for the Achaean force here sounds inflated. Aratus' caution may reflect a reluctance to see the Achaean breach with Sparta deepen further, as well as a concern not to upset Ptolemy III, who was a friend and supporter of both the Achaeans and Sparta.
9. *advance . . . this rout*: These events occurred in the first half of 227, when Aratus was re-elected general of the Achaeans from May. Mount Lycaeum is in Arcadia.
10. *other royal house*: It was the death of Agis' son, the boy Agiad king Eudamidas III (see note 1), which offered Cleomenes the opportunity to invite back Archidamus.
11. *forced Cleomenes' hand*: Polybius (*The Rise of the Roman Empire*, 5.37, Penguin, 1979) states flatly that Cleomenes ordered Archidamus' execution. According to him, Cleomenes' chief intermediary in the negotiations which led to Archidamus' return was Nicagoras, on whom see further Ch. 35.
12. *town walls*: More operations of 227. Leuctra was a fort about ten kilometres south of Megalopolis.
13. *Tarentines and Cretans*: Names given to troops of mercenaries – light cavalry and archers respectively – who did not necessarily come from Tarentum or Crete.
14. *sanctuary of Pasiphaë*: See *Agis*, Ch. 9 and note 15.
15. *captured Heraea . . . long marches*: This campaign and the subsequent coup both occurred late in 227. Heraea was a city in the west of Arcadia, near the frontier with Elis. Asea, or Alea, are possible emendations of a name garbled in the manuscripts, but Plutarch is probably referring to somewhere in the vicinity of Orchomenus, to which Aratus had laid siege after his capture of Mantinea (Ch. 5). Orchomenus in fact fell to him early in 226. Cleomenes' stepfather Megistonous was among those taken prisoner; he was later ransomed.
16. *mothakes*: The significance of the term is not altogether clear. As here, it certainly denotes men who had passed through the *agoge* alongside those of unblemished Spartiate birth, and it may also be a general term for all such men. However, even after a successful passage, not all were eligible to become full Spartiates, though some *mothakes* did. This should indicate that they were born of

Spartiate parents – who in all probability had come to be degraded.

17. *been well said*: By the early epic poet Stasinus of Cyprus.
18. *'I respect . . . their leaders'*: Respectively, Helen addressing Priam in Homer, *Iliad*, 3.172 (Penguin, 2003) and *Iliad*, 4.431.
19. *developed a magistracy*: See further *Lycurgus*, Ch. 7 and Introduction, 'Lycurgus: Non-Lycurgan Institutions'.
20. *king . . . goes to them*: Compare *Sayings of Spartans*, under Anaxilas.
21. *King Charillus*: See *Lycurgus*, Chs. 3 and 5, where he is called Charilaus.
22. *Aetolians and Illyrians*: See Chs. 18 and 27.
23. *a sarissa . . . arm-strap*: The change to Macedonian styles of equipment and fighting as late as the 220s shows how conservative Sparta had been in this regard – perhaps partly due to lack of means. But in fact the Boeotians had not made the same change until the mid third century, and the Achaeans were only to do so well after Sparta. The Greek heavy infantryman wore a large shield on his left arm and carried a spear in his right. His counterpart in the Macedonian army was armed with a *sarissa*, a massive tapered pike up to 6.5 metres in length, which had to be gripped with both hands. While he did still carry a shield, it needed to be small enough not to obstruct his manipulation of the *sarissa*, and in battle was evidently either held in position on the left forearm by means of a loop, or was just slung over the shoulder and ignored.
24. *invaded . . . Megalopolis*: In 226.
25. *minas*: For the value of this amount, compare Ch. 23 and note 51, and *Lycurgus*, Ch. 9.
26. *two cotylae*: Just over half a litre.
27. *abandoned the area*: The account of Cleomenes' operations in 226 is resumed. Hyperbatas was general of the Achaeans from May of that year. Pharae was one of the oldest members of the League. Cleomenes was now determined to shake the League to its foundations, and at the same time impress the Eleans (with their considerable military strength) to abandon the Aetolians and ally with Sparta.
28. *Dymae*: Another founder member of the Achaean League. Little is known of the Hecatombaeum, which was a shrine near the town.
29. *Lasium*: This (rather than Langon) is the most likely reading of another uncertain name: it was a fort on the border between Achaea and Elis.

30. *relinquishing his own authority*: Aratus declined to stand for the generalship of 225/4. His motive may have been not so much dismay at the League's difficulties (as Plutarch suggests), but a wish to leave himself free to pursue approaches to Antigonus III of Macedon.
31. *leadership be handed to him*: Achaean negotiations with Cleomenes had begun during the winter of 226/5. The 'leadership' which he might gain was an honorary office (previously voted to Ptolemy III in 243), not a permanent active generalship (which the League's constitution did not allow for).
32. *thirty-three years*: Since his career only began with his liberation of Sicyon in 251, the claim that by 225/4 he had occupied the leading position for thirty-three years remains a puzzle.
33. *filled the Peloponnese with Macedonians*: Aratus is in fact known to have authorized approaches to Macedon as far back as the winter of 227/6. Though well aware of how controversial this policy was, his main concern was to preserve the Achaean League (and his own influence within it) rather than accept outright subjugation to Sparta, possibly to be accompanied by revolutionary social measures. Though by no means all League members agreed, he calculated that a distant Macedonian overlord would prove preferable to Cleomenes. He also knew that the League's disintegration had prompted Ptolemy III to cease supporting it and to subsidize Sparta instead.
34. *liberated Acrocorinth*: The fortress on top of the mountain which rises sheer to the south of Corinth, a vital strongpoint for domination of the Peloponnese. Aratus liberated it from the Macedonians in 243.
35. *free . . . from Macedonians*: With Aratus' assistance the Athenians negotiated the departure of the Macedonian garrison from their port of Piraeus in 229.
36. *right into its women's quarters*: Aratus' daughter-in-law was later seduced by the Macedonian king Philip V.
37. *Sicyonians and Tritaeans*: Sicyon was Aratus' own city; Tritaea is cited as a typical, ordinary member state.
38. *Achaeans had arrived*: Summer 225.
39. *outside the city*: Probably beyond the south-east gate.
40. *Aegium*: The usual meeting-place of the League assembly.
41. *Penteleium*: A fortress close to Pheneus.
42. *Nemean Games*: A panhellenic festival similar in character to the Olympic Games, held in alternate years. This celebration was in

July 225. Note that Cleomenes broke the usual sacred truce (compare *Lycurgus*, Ch. 1 and note 1).

43. *near the Aspis*: At Argos there were two hills fortified as citadels – the Larisa on the western edge of the city and the smaller Aspis on the north-eastern edge. However, not least because the theatre is closer to the Larisa, it has been argued that it is really this citadel which Plutarch means to refer to here and in Ch. 21.

44. *Pyrrhus*: King of Epirus, who died thus in 272. See Plutarch, *Pyrrhus*, Chs. 31–4 (in *The Age of Alexander*, rev. edn, Penguin, forthcoming).

45. *Solon*: Famous for his reforms at Athens in the early sixth century. Plutarch's Life of him appears in *The Rise and Fall of Athens* (rev. edn, Penguin, forthcoming).

46. *this was the occasion*: Both the date and the occasion are uncertain, but it may be 241 after the death of Agis and the abandonment of his reforms – reflecting how Sparta was once again militarily weak. Many of the slaves captured must have belonged to *perioeci*; even so, the figure of 50,000 sounds exaggerated.

47. *Corinth*: The total of five cities mentioned here and in the previous paragraph as coming over to Cleomenes from the Achaeans all did so during the summer of 225: these gains drove a wedge through League territory. In addition to blockading Acrocorinth, Cleomenes made Aratus virtually a prisoner in his own city for three months. By then he must have been aware that negotiations between Antigonus and Achaean envoys were at an advanced stage, and this accounts for his desperation to achieve an accommodation with Aratus. However, when the League assembly met in the spring of 224, Aratus did gain assent to the Macedonian terms, as Plutarch records, though by then Antigonus was in any case moving south with his army.

48. *the rebellion*: This revolt – a decisive turning-point for Cleomenes – cannot be dated securely, but is most likely to have occurred in the latter months of 224.

49. *the second watch of the night*: Around midnight.

50. *Once Antigonus*: The events in this chapter occurred in 223.

51. *talents*: From the figures, we can deduce that there were as many as 6,000 helots sufficiently wealthy and eager to take up Cleomenes' offer. One Attic *mina* weighed about 430 grams (of silver, in this instance), and sixty *minas* made up a *talent*.

52. '*White Shields*': His crack troops.

53. *Rhoeteium . . . Helissous*: The names are again uncertain: Zoitium and Helicous are also possibilities.
54. *was in the city*: Though Plutarch does not mention it, this successful assault on Megalopolis in fact followed an abortive one three months earlier.
55. *separate account of him*: *Life of Philopoemen*, Ch. 5 (in *The Rise of Rome*, rev. edn, Penguin, forthcoming).
56. *council at Aegium*: Autumn 223.
57. *winter quarters*: These were mostly in Macedon itself.
58. *invaded . . . Argos*: Spring 222.
59. *Heraeum*: The famous sanctuary of Hera, about eight kilometres north of the city of Argos.
60. *Demades*: Athenian politician active in the second half of the fourth century. The exact wording of his remark is uncertain, but the point is presumably that any expedition must be adequately prepared.
61. *Archidamus of old*: Eurypontid king, *c.* 469–427. The Peloponnesian War began in 431.
62. *an engagement*: Polybius, *The Rise of the Roman Empire*, 2.63, cites Phylarchus for the point that just ten days before the battle Cleomenes learned of Ptolemy's decision to withdraw subsidies and to urge peace with Antigonus.
63. *ready for battle*: This was fought at Sellasia, about fourteen kilometres north of Sparta, in mid 222. Plutarch wrote another description of the battle in his *Life of Philopoemen*, Ch. 6.
64. *krypteia*: See *Lycurgus*, Ch. 28.
65. *stades*: One *stade* is a little under 200 metres.
66. *Gytheum*: Sparta's port, forty-five kilometres to the south.
67. *restored both her laws and her constitution*: The scope of this 'restoration' remains obscure. Antigonus certainly reversed Cleomenes' political changes: the ephorate was restored, while the kingship was left vacant. Whether he also cancelled the social and economic reforms is disputed.
68. *victory . . . barbarians*: Antigonus defeated the Illyrians late in 222, and probably died early the following year.
69. *Cyrene*: A major city under Egyptian control, close to the coast in present-day Libya.
70. *Ptolemy's*: The reign of Ptolemy III (nicknamed *Euergetes* or 'Benefactor') dated back to 246. He was ruler of another of the Macedonian 'successor kingdoms' carved out following the death of Alexander the Great (compare *Agis*, note 8, for the Seleucids); Egypt, with its capital Alexandria, was its centre.

71. *the king*: Ptolemy IV Philopator (aged just over twenty) succeeded his father Ptolemy III Euergetes in February 221 after the latter had been murdered at the instigation of his senior adviser Sosibius.
72. *Apis*: The bull which was the object of an official cult at Memphis in Egypt. When the sacred bull died it was mummified and entombed, and a successor chosen.
73. *Continued . . . fighting*: Homer, *Iliad*, 1.491–2.
74. *Nicagoras*: See note 11.
75. *Cybele*: The great mother-goddess of Anatolia, popular in the Greek world from the fifth century. A state of ecstasy was characteristic of her worship.
76. *Canopus*: Twenty-five kilometres east of Alexandria, and linked to it by canal. The city was the site of a temple of Sarapis, as well as being a popular resort. It gave its name to one of the three principal mouths of the River Nile.
77. *king . . . sixteen years*: Thus if his accession is correctly dated to 235, his death occurred in 219.

SAYINGS OF SPARTANS

1. *"whate'er . . . a nod of the head"*: A reference to Homer, *Iliad*, 1.527 (Penguin, 2003).
2. *in line to become king*: There must be confusion here, since Agesilaus only became king following the death of his elder half-brother Agis II and a dispute over the succession. Thus he had passed through the *agoge* in the normal way: exceptionally this was *not* required of an heir apparent. See *Agesilaus*, Chs. 1–3.
3. *two gods*: The divine twins, Castor and Pollux. In myth they were the sons of the king of Lacedaemon, Tyndareus, and his successors as joint kings. Thus the twins had a special link with the royal houses and in general were greatly revered at Sparta.
4. *Thasians'*: The correct proper name has been garbled irrecoverably in the manuscripts. *Agesilaus*, Ch. 36, relates no. 24 here in the context of Agesilaus' service in Egypt as a mercenary commander (360).
5. *cowards . . . distinguished*: Presumably the eager advance of the brave will contrast with the nervous shuffling of the cowards.
6. *recalled him*: In 394.
7. *letter*: The Greek text uses the Doric dialect throughout for the sake of 'authenticity'.

8. *moras*: Regiments. See Xenophon, *Spartan Society*, Ch. 11.
9. *Xenophon*: For the Athenian Xenophon, see further in general Introduction to Appendix; for his participation in the battle (in 394), see *Agesilaus*, Ch. 18.
10. *loss of status*: See *Lycurgus*, Ch. 21. The battle occurred in 371.
11. *battle near Mantinea*: According to Xenophon (*A History of My Times*, 7.5.10, Penguin, 1979), Agesilaus was not present, but remained at Sparta. Plutarch, in *Agesilaus*, Ch. 35, gives him no part in the battle either.
12. *call from . . . Egyptians*: In 360. See further *Agesilaus*, Chs. 36–40.
13. *demolished Olynthus in a few days*: Since this occurred in 348, the reference must be anachronistic. Confusion with Agesipolis' brother and successor, Cleomenes, seems the most likely explanation.
14. *Philip . . . inaccessible to them*: The fact that Philip's rule (over Macedon) dates from 359 to 336 indicates confusion over the attribution of these remarks. They are more likely to have been made by Agis the Younger.
15. *Demades*: An Athenian politician. See *Cleomenes*, note 60.
16. *Agis the last Spartan king*: Presumably 'the last Spartan king *of that name*' is meant.
17. *'They take many days . . . open'*: Anaxandridas' explanations are consistent with fragments of what is probably Theophrastus' lost *Laws* of the fourth century, in which recommendations are made that cases should be 'heard for a number of days, as at Sparta', and that 'when some (judges) have heard and questioned (a defendant), even if he is acquitted he ought to be made subject to examination again in some sanctioned manner, as at Sparta'. The Agiad king Pausanias was made to suffer in just this way: after being narrowly acquitted of undue leniency towards the democrats at Athens in 403, he was charged with the same offence again in 395.
18. *kings . . . 'overseers'*: For the relationship of kings and ephors, see further *Cleomenes*, Ch. 10.
19. *wounded . . . Thebans*: See *Lycurgus*, note 43.
20. *Dionysius . . . disreputable to me'*: Another example of anachronism, since Dionysius only seized power in 405. The same story is told of Lysander (no. 1).
21. *battle of Chaeronea*: This defeat of the Athenians and Thebans in 338 secured Macedonian domination of Greece. Archidamus was in fact in southern Italy at the time, where he met his death in battle against the Messapii at Mandorium (Plutarch, *Agis*,

Ch. 3) – on the very same day as the battle of Chaeronea, in one version of the story.

22. *battle against the Arcadians*: The so-called 'Tearless Battle' of 368. See *Agesilaus*, Ch. 33.
23. *Peloponnesian War . . . amounts'*: Anachronism. Since the Peloponnesian War dates to 431–404, the remark is more plausibly attributed to Archidamus, son of Zeuxidamus (see *Cleomenes*, Ch. 27).
24. *'While a sheep . . . object'*: Another anachronism. This saying should be attributed to Agis the Younger, who led the abortive revolt against Macedon mentioned in the next saying.
25. ANAXIBIUS: This saying has probably slipped to this position through confusion over the name; the manuscripts read 'Bias' or 'Bios'. For the same story told by Xenophon of a commander named thus, see *A History of My Times*, 4.8.37–8 (about 390).
26. *he wrote*: In Doric dialect.
27. *Dercyllidas . . . to us'*: For the appeal of King Areus' exiled uncle Cleonymus, which led to Pyrrhus' invasion in 272, see Plutarch, *Pyrrhus*, Ch. 26 (in *The Age of Alexander* (rev. edn, Penguin, forthcoming)). This remark is made there by Mandrocleidas. Its attribution to Dercyllidas here suggests some confusion with the distinguished general of the late fifth and early fourth centuries (see *Lycurgus*, Ch. 15).
28. *King's parasite*: A man maintained by the Great King as jester and flatterer.
29. *Xenocrates*: Philosopher, head of Plato's Academy, 339–314.
30. *all exiles except Thebans*: 324. Thebans were made an exception because of their city's resistance to Macedonian domination, which had resulted in its destruction by Alexander in 335.
31. *Thermopylae*: The battle here against Xerxes occurred in 480.
32. *Hesiod*: From Boeotia, active *c.* 700. Farming is the topic of his *Works and Days* (in *Hesiod and Theognis*, Penguin, 1973).
33. *envoys from Samos . . . Polycrates*: The occasion is possibly anachronistic since Polycrates was assassinated by the Persians in about 522. Alternatively, some confusion may have arisen with the incident in no. 16.
34. *previous defeat . . . substituting one syllable*: The occasion is obscure. Sparta defeated Argos in the mid sixth century, and again (under Cleomenes) in about 494. *substituting one syllable*: That is, in English, 're*trieve*' for 're*peat*'. In Greek, where the change happens to be more awkward, 'adding two syllables' is required.

35. *Maeandrius . . . fled to Sparta*: About 516.
36. *Demaratus'*: Leotychidas' distant cousin: his deposition in 491 gave Leotychidas the kingship.
37. *a dispatch*: A *skytale*. See Glossary of Spartan Terms.
38. *hand is not raised . . . difficulties'*: Compare *Lycurgus*, note 59.
39. *sent as envoy*: About 401, *if* there was any such visit in fact.
40. *Aegospotami*: 405.
41. *punished for slandering*: The point is that Nicander was ravaging Argos at the time.
42. *Delians*: Inhabitants of the small Aegean island of Delos, sacred to the god Apollo, who had a shrine there.
43. *Tyrtaeus a citizen*: According to some stories he was not Spartan by origin, but from Athens or another city.
44. *Plataea*: 479.
45. *into exile*: Pausanias was deposed mainly for the inadequacy of his generalship against the Thebans in 395.
46. *doctor a general*: The point must be that treatment by him would kill off the enemy.
47. *the first kings*: The Agiads were named after the second king of their line (Agis), and the Eurypontids after the third of theirs (Eurypon). See *Lycurgus*, Ch. 2.
48. *Battle of the Three Hundred*: There seems to be confusion here with the mid-*sixth*-century battle where, according to Herodotus (*The Histories*, 1.82, Penguin, 2003), after a fight between 300 men on each side, only two Argives and one Spartan remained alive. Subsequent argument over which side should be considered victorious led to a further battle, which Sparta won.
49. *PHOEBIDAS*: The name seems either a mistake or anachronistic, since the only known Phoebidas was killed in 378, seven years before the battle of Leuctra. See *Agesilaus*, Chs. 23–4.

SAYINGS OF SPARTAN WOMEN

1. *Brasidas . . . death*: 422.
2. *war . . . support of the Ionians*: 500.
3. *GYRTIAS*: Perhaps best identified as mother of the Agiad king, Areus I. Although he had campaigned in Crete, his son Acrotatus was actually killed in battle near Megalopolis (*Agis*, Ch. 3).
4. *wrote to him*: In Doric dialect.
5. *this message*: In Doric dialect. For Pedaritus, see *Sayings of Spartans*.

6. *either with this or on this'*: Most naturally taken as instructions for his return – either alive and victorious carrying his shield, or lying dead upon it after a fight to the finish. In fact most Spartans killed abroad were buried on the spot: compare no. 20 and *Agesilaus*, Ch. 40.
7. 27: This saying and the following ones all relate to the sale of Spartan women as slaves.

XENOPHON, *SPARTAN SOCIETY*

1. *account of the education*: This chapter and the two following in fact set out the three main stages of training for males of the Spartiate class: that of the boys (*paides*), aged 7 to 18, in Ch. 2; the youths (*paidiskoi*, equivalent to *ephebes* elsewhere in Greece), aged 18–19, in Ch. 3; and the young adults (*hebontes*), aged 20 to 29, in Ch. 4.
2. *Trainer-in-Chief*: Compare Plutarch, *Lycurgus*, Ch. 17 and note 54.
3. *cheesas . . . prestige*: Compare Plutarch, *Lycurgus*, note 57.
4. *Squadron*: See *Lycurgus*, note 53.
5. *bashful than the 'little girl' in the eye*: A play on the double meaning of *parthenos* – (bashful) little girl and pupil (of the eye). In English the latter word derives from the Latin *pupilla*, which has exactly the same double meaning as the Greek *parthenos*.
6. *Hippagretae . . . picks 100 men*: The men thus chosen composed the crack army unit termed the 'Three Hundred' or *Hippeis*. For the selection process compare Plutarch, *Lycurgus*, Ch. 25. It is open to question whether the *Hippagretae* in fact chose more than replacements for men no longer available to serve.
7. *ephorate*: For this annually elected board of five magistrates, see Introduction, 'Lycurgus: Non-Lycurgan Institutions'.
8. *the god*: Pythian Apollo. Compare Plutarch, *Lycurgus*, note 12.
9. *Gerousia*: On this council, see further Plutarch, *Lycurgus*, Chs. 5 and 26.
10. *Equals*: *Homoioi* in Greek – the term by which the full citizens, the Spartiates, referred to themselves.
11. *mora . . . enomotarchs*: The six *polemarchs* were the senior army officers, immediately subordinate to the king as commander. It is hard to elucidate the remarks made about the various other officers, since the size and precise relationship to one another of the units mentioned both here and later are obscure; in all

likelihood, too, there were changes in the army's organization over the centuries. For concise, balanced discussion of these military matters, see N. Sekunda, *The Spartan Army* (1998), especially pp. 13–18.

12. *required of them*: The text is corrupted irrecoverably at this point.
13. *phalanxes*: The battle formations of heavy infantry.
14. *front to the left*: The arrangement must be for the leading *enomotia* to halt, and then for each following one to move up level with it and left of the *enomotia* ahead.
15. *commander . . . the left*: It was normal for a commander to be on the right.
16. *protected side*: That is, the hoplite's left arm, protected by his shield: his right arm, in which he held a weapon, was exposed.
17. *trireme*: The classical Greek warship with three banks of oars (as the name indicates). In battle the main objective was to ram enemy ships with the prow.
18. *Sciritae*: A distinct corps of men named after Sciritis, the rough hill-country on the northern edge of Laconia.
19. *the practices . . . identical purpose*: Precautions of the type mentioned by Xenophon are also reflected in a fragment of Critias' lost *Constitution of the Spartans* (see Introduction, 'Lycurgus: Plutarch's Sources'):

> Out of mistrust for these helots a Spartiate at home removes the handle from his shield. On campaign the frequent need for quick action makes it impossible for him to do this; instead he always carries his spear about with him, in the conviction that this way he will get the better of a helot who might attempt a rising with just a shield. They have devised locks too, which they believe have the strength to withstand a helot plot.

20. *'Volunteers'*: Never mentioned elsewhere; their role and status remain unknown.
21. *groomed . . . appearance*: Whether or not some words have dropped out here is a matter of debate.
22. *Hellanodicae*: Nothing further is known of these judicial officers.
23. *14*: For the placement of Chs. 14 and 15, see Introduction to Appendix.
24. *But now . . . Spartan rule*: This looks a tempting clue from which to date the postscript, but it remains too vague.
25. *Pythii*: When required they went as official envoys to the oracle of

the 'Pythian' god Apollo at Delphi. See Herodotus, *The Histories*, 6.57 (Penguin, 2003).

26. *special honour . . . heroes*: For the elaborate ceremonies on the death of a king, see Herodotus, *The Histories*, 6.58–9.

Index

The listing of proper names and technical terms is reasonably complete, but the coverage of topics has inevitably had to be selective.